# PHILOSOPHICAL ESSAYS IN PRAGMATIC NATURALISM

# PHILOSOPHICAL ESSAYS IN PRAGMATIC NATURALISM

## PAUL KURTZ

**PROMETHEUS BOOKS**
**BUFFALO, NEW YORK**

Essay Index

Published 1990 by Prometheus Books
700 East Amherst Street, Buffalo, New York 14215

Copyright © 1990 by Paul Kurtz
All Rights Reserved

Library of Congress Cataloging-in-Publication Data

Kurtz, Paul 1925–
     Philosophical essays in pragmatic naturalism / Paul Kurtz.
          p.     cm.
     Includes bibliographical references.
     ISBN 0-87975-592-X
     1. Naturalism. 2. Pragmatism. I. Title.
B945.K87P45     1990
1456—dc20                                                    89-49060
                                                                  CIP

Printed on acid-free paper in the United States of America

# Contents

Preface                                                                    7

### PART I: PRAGMATIC NATURALISM

1. Pragmatic Naturalism in American Philosophy                            11
2. Pragmatic Naturalism and First Principles                              43
3. Neo-Behaviorism and the Behavioral Sciences                            61
4. Coduction: A Logic of Explanation in the
      Behavioral and Social Sciences                                  83
5. Meta-Metaphysics, the Categories and Naturalism                        97

### PART II: NATURALISTIC ETHICS

6. Naturalistic Ethics and the Open Question                             123
7. Human Nature, Homeostasis, and Value                                  141
8. Does Ethics Have Any Metaphysical Presuppositions?                    165
9. Rule-Making                                                           179
10. Need Reduction and Normal Value                                      191
11. Has Ethical Naturalism Been Refuted?                                 207
12. Moral Faith and Ethical Skepticism Reconsidered                      223

### PART III: NATURALISM VS. PHENOMENOLOGY AND EXISTENTIALISM

13. Phenomenology and Naturalism                                         241
14. Existentialism, Kierkegaard, and Naturalism                          249

270455    5

# Preface

Naturalism, broadly conceived as a philosophical movement, wishes to use the methods of science, evidence, and reason to understand nature and the place of the human species within it. Science is not interpreted as an esoteric method of inquiry, but is continuous with standards of critical intelligence used in common, ordinary life. Pragmatic naturalism attempts to relate knowledge to human purposes and interests within contexts of inquiry; it also seeks to evaluate claims to knowledge by their observable effects in practice. The naturalistic outlook is skeptical of the postulation of a transcendental realm beyond nature, or of the claim that nature can be understood without using the methods of reason and evidence.

Naturalism thus provides a contrast with other philosophical movements in the contemporary world. It is the preeminently unique philosophical position that seeks to draw on the sciences and technology, not only to understand nature but to resolve human and social problems. It considers the great challenge of the post-modern world to be the expansion of the methods of scientific inquiry to other fields of human endeavor, such as ethics, politics, and religion, and the transformation of our knowledge and behavior in terms of these methods. As such, it reflects the impact of modern science and technology on contemporary human civilization, and it seeks to draw the implications of these for our cosmic outlook on nature.

Naturalism in ethics is the thesis that similar empirical and rational methods of inquiry can be used to test claims to ethical truth and to resolve human problems. Although values cannot be deduced from facts in any simplistic way, the facts of the case are relevant to our decisions and choices; at the very least, our ethical values and moral principles may be modified in the light of our knowledge of nature in general, human nature in particular, the means at our disposal, the causal conditions, and the consequences of our actions.

These are the central arguments underlying the essays in this volume, which were written and published over a period of thirty-five years. They originally appeared as papers in philosophical journals, magazines, or books, generally not accessible to the public.

In my earlier years, I was chiefly interested in examining pragmatic naturalism as based in the philosophy of science or, as I sometimes call it, "empirical metaphysics." I was also keenly interested in meta-theories concerning naturalistic ethics, and especially in responding to critics of naturalism, such as emotive theorists, ordinary language philosophers, phenomenologists, and existentialists. Many essays in this volume focus on these theoretical issues, which were dominant in the literature at the time.

In recent years, I have concentrated primarily on normative ethics and eupraxophy (i.e., good practice and wisdom) and I have written a great deal about secular humanism and concrete issues in ethics. The papers in this volume, however, do not by and large deal with humanistic themes. Secular humanism nevertheless presupposes a cosmic outlook about the universe and the place of humankind in the scheme of things, and it is committed to scientific methods of inquiry. Similarly, "naturalistic ethics" is a term used in philosophy to designate a meta-epistemological theory of decision making and value. The kind of humanism that I have espoused also presupposes a naturalistic theory of ethics.

I should point out that these papers were written in different contexts and for a variety of purposes and that I may no longer agree with all of the concepts developed. In some cases I have amended or corrected certain passages. Although there may be some overlap in discussing various topics, there is, I trust, a common thread running thoughout. In any case, they should be considered as philosophical excursions into the presuppositions of both pragmatic naturalism and secular humanism.

# Part I

# Pragmatic Naturalism

# 1.
# Pragmatic Naturalism in American Philosophy

## I. INTRODUCTION

At this late date, it might be considered redundant to restate the naturalistic philosophy. For some critics naturalism, like an earlier philosophical idealism, is rapidly becoming a remembrance of things past. Surely naturalism had been a considerable force in American philosophy, and its influence still continues strong, though admittedly much less than before. Lest analytic critics exult in naturalism's demise, let it be reminded that many histories of analytic philosophy are now being written, which may be a symptom of its own impending burial, and which only points out the fate that all philosophical movements seem to share: they are at the mercy of the winds of

Originally published as "Naturalism in American Philosophy," in *Philosophy and the Civilizing Arts: Essays Presented to Herbert W. Schneider*, edited by Craig Walton and John P. Anton (Athens, Ohio: Ohio University Press, 1974), pp. 178–212. Reprinted by permission of the publisher.

fashion. In any case, it is often easier after a movement has reached its prime to summarize it than during its early heyday; thus it may be useful to view naturalism in America in historical sweep. I submit that it presents a philosophical outlook of the nature of the universe, and the place of the human species within it, and of the foundations of ethical value that still are viable today—especially when compared with alternative philosophical conceptions.

In a sense, naturalism is the heir, and perhaps the climax of what has been labeled, "The Golden Age of American Philosophy." Regretfully, even at this late date, all too little clarification has been offered of the definition of the term "naturalism." Perhaps the failure to find a precise definition of "naturalism" is the fate also suffered by most philosophical schools and tendencies, which are generally too broad to be given a specific platform, and which may count in one way or another many adherents and writers who are difficult to categorize. Most philosophers are notoriously individualistic and no sooner is a tradition announced than dissent arises and a new one is heralded in its place.

This is the case with naturalism, which has had a long career in the general history of philosophy. There are many varieties of "naturalism" and many meanings which have been attributed to the term. Broadly conceived, naturalism has two primary sources in philosophy: materialism in metaphysics and empiricism or experimentalism in epistemology. Thus the materialists, Democritus, Leucippus, Epicurus, Lucretius, Hobbes, D'Holbach, LaMettrie, and Marx provide historical antecedents to twentieth-century naturalism. But naturalism also draws upon the empiricism and skepticism of Carneades, Ockham, Bacon, Locke, Hume, Mill, Russell, Popper, and Ayer. There are no doubt difficulties with this classification; for example, some materialists are rationalists and some empiricists are phenomenalists. Moreover, there are several distinguished philosophers who might not fit into the above tradition, yet have been labeled as precursors of naturalism. I am thinking here, for example, of Aristotle and Spinoza, of the Carvaka movement in Indian philosophy, and Lao Tzu in Chinese thought.

What is common to naturalistic philosophy is its commitment to science. Indeed, naturalism might be defined in its more general sense as *the philosophical generalization of the methods and conclusions of the sciences.* Insofar as America is preeminently a scientific-technological society and will most likely continue to be so, it may very well be that naturalism still provides the most appropriate philosophy for the future. But to say that naturalism is intimately related to science says both too much and not enough, for there are several other important characteristics which naturalism manifests.

Naturalism has been an especially prominent movement, as I have said, in America in the twentieth century, though here again its delimitation is difficult. Undoubtedly its main sources are two strong philosophical tendencies at the beginning of this century: pragmatism and realism, and the subsequent importation of logical positivism in the thirties. Materialism, Marxism, and humanism in twentieth-century American thought also has been closely aligned with naturalism. Among the important American naturalists have been George Santayana, F. J. E. Woodbridge, Morris R. Cohen, W. P. Montague, Ralph B. Perry, Durant Drake, Roy W. Sellars, and C. I. Lewis. Undoubtedly the most important naturalistic philosopher in America is John Dewey; and like him there are a large number of writers infuenced by the pragmatic tradition: Willard V. O. Quine, Ernest Nagel, Sidney Hook, Richard Rorty, John H. Randall, Jr., Abraham Edel, Morton G. White, Justus Buchler, and Abraham Kaplan, among others.

Naturalism in America has had to contend since the Second World War with analytic philosophy, existentialism, and phenomenology, and there have been some attempts by naturalists to modify naturalism somewhat and to incorporate features of these alternative philosophies into its point of view. Although there is danger in blithely throwing all distinctions to the wind, features of existentialism, and phenomenology, and especially of analytic philosophy can be said to be naturalistic.

Naturalism thus cuts across many traditional philosophical demarcations, so much so that it perhaps would be wise to concentrate upon only one variety of naturalism—*pragmatic or experimental naturalism,* which those influenced by Dewey especially have advocated in the United States. At least these are the philosophers most likely to label themselves as "naturalistic." I will begin by stating what I take to be the dominant characteristics of naturalism—as will be seen the rationale for including so many diverse philosophical movements under the heading "naturalism," as I have done, is that they have in some way shared many or most of these principles. But

13

I then wish to concentrate upon what is clearly the central epistemological principle, naturalism's commitment to the methods of science, and to show how the naturalists have attempted to apply this principle to human behavior, morality, politics, art, and religion. Throughout, I shall be concerned solely with contemporary naturalism.

## II. DOES NATURALISM HAVE A METAPHYSICS?

In interpreting the naturalists one must bear in mind the key point— that naturalism is committed to science in the broadest sense of that term. This is sometimes interpreted as the principle of continuity of inquiry. It means that all phenomena can in principle be described and explained in terms of natural causes and events, or at least there are no *a priori* reasons against their being so described and explained. Does this methodological principle entail a metaphysical view of the universe? Many naturalists have denied this, insisting that naturalism is a method, not a comprehensive account of the universe or of reality and that it is relatively neutral in its ontological commitment, thus allowing for a number of diverse metaphysical positions. Nevertheless, some naturalists have admitted that their methodology does presuppose or imply certain root categories, or a view of certain "generic traits" of nature and of human transactions. If scientific method is the fundamental principle of inquiry and if this involves a commitment to the explanation of things in terms of natural causes and processes, then everything that we can encounter, experience, or talk about must be considered to be "natural" and in some sense a part of "nature." Accordingly, any attempt to bifurcate nature into two realms, "appearances" versus "reality," the "phenomenal" versus the "supernatural," is for the naturalist based upon antecedent definitions which exclude as "non-natural" and prior to inquiry certain aspects of the world.

Naturalism as so construed is dubious of transcendental metaphysical systems which claim that there is an "unknowable ground of being," a "divine essence," a "mystic presence," or a "theistic cause" over and beyond man's capacity to experience or understand. In modern and contemporary philosophy, a massive critique has been leveled by naturalists against the traditional transcendentalist views of the universe. This critique has been three-fold. It has maintained, first, that the traditional metaphysical views of the universe are based on prescientific or nonscientific grounds and that they come into conflict with rapidly developing scientific discoveries; second, that the claims for the existence of a theistic source or ground of being have not been conclusively "demonstrated" or verified and have failed to satisfy adequate methodological conditions; and third, and most devastatingly, that most of the terms, concepts, assertions, and propositions alleged about God are devoid of cognitive significance and incapable of confirmation or disconfirmation.

For the naturalists a key methodological criterion is that all assertions about the universe which are descriptive and informative in content and function must be confirmable directly or indirectly by the methods of science. Insofar as transcendental theories violate this principle, they are open to criticism.

Viewing the world as interpreted by the principles of science naturalists maintain that in some sense material processes and events or mass and energy are present in all things which we can describe or explain. In other words, material causes and events are basic to the universe, and all things which we can assert to exist, have in some sense material components or constituents. This suggests that the concepts and hypotheses of the natural sciences have a kind of priority in our accounts of the world and that to ignore the physical basis of things is to behave ostrich-like in the face of a whole range of tested hypotheses and observations in these sciences. However, while naturalism shares with materialism an appreciation for the physical-chemical basis of processes and events, it does not consider that an account of these processes and events simply in terms of their material or efficient cause is always sufficient. Naturalism is accordingly nonreductive, recognizing the manifold variety, diversity, and multiplicity of things. Thus unlike traditional reductive materialism, which claims that nothing but material particles exist, or that only a reductive explanation suffices, present-day naturalism recognizes, indeed insists, that the plurality and richness of nature be admitted and that there are many kinds of events, properties, and qualities which we encounter in the world. In methodological terms, this means that sciences other than physics and chemistry (the biological and the behavioral sciences) are important in characterizing natural processes and events. It also suggests a contextualism;

for if natural properties manifest diversity, then the characterization of things must take into account the various ways that things are observed to function in different contexts. Closely related to this view is the recognition that processes could only be understood in dynamic terms by reference to their historical origins, and an appreciation for the importance of evolutionary and developmental concepts. The universe appears to science not as a fixed scheme of eternal essences or of static structures, but one of dynamic processes and events in continuous change and flux.

The above is a brief account of the world as viewed by the naturalist. It is a naturalism which focuses on material events and processes, pluralism, contextualism, and historical evolution. But naturalism can also be interpreted in *methodological* terms as a philosophy which prescribes a set of regulative principles for dealing with the world. In this sense, naturalism attempts to be as neutral as possible in its metaphysics and is first and foremost a program of inquiry. Does this methodological program exclude *any* reference to the nature of man? Many naturalists would concede that their approach, at a minimum, *does* entail a "theory of human experience."

## III. THEORY OF HUMAN EXPERIENCE

Naturalism's "theory of experience" is indeed central to its entire philosophical position. It is sometimes said that even though naturalism prescribes a methodology and has a theory of experience, it lacks an "epistemology." Even if an "epistemology" can be attributed to naturalism, it is unlike other epistemologies; for the "theory of experience" of naturalism is not subjectivistic; nor does it focus upon inner "mentalistic" processes; rather it deals with perception, cognition, and other psychological processes as forms of behavior. If all processes are to be explained in scientific terms, then this applies to humans as well; for the human species does not have a privileged position in the executive order of events, but is part of "nature."

This twentieth-century naturalistic conception of human experience may be traced most directly to Darwinism and the radical reinterpretation of the human species that it entailed. Man was no longer a fallen creature from divine grace, but rather an animal like other animals; a product of evolution from simpler forms of life. Man's biological characteristics thus were not to be attributed to any special act of divine creation or teleological purpose, but were rather a product of many factors: chance mutation, natural selection, differential reproduction, and the transmission of genetic characteristics. Of causal significance in the evolution of the human species are the processes of its adjustment and accommodation to nature. All biological functions, such as respiration, digestion, and locomotion, have adaptive or survival value. But the same considerations apply to the so-called higher functions of perception, cognition, motivation, and valuation.

The most important consequence to the naturalistic philosophy of human nature and of the biologizing of human functions was the new interpretation of "consciousness" and other "mentalistic" properties of *homo sapiens*. William James, in the article "Does Consciousness Exist?"[1] did not deny the existence of "consciousness"; he simply asserted that it was a function, not a substance. But the significance of Darwinism can be nowhere more patently seen than in the writings of Dewey. If man is a product of natural evolution, like all other animals, and if he can in principle be interpreted by a scientific methodology, then this will have far-reaching implications for many or most of the traditional problems of philosophy and epistemology, and especially to the conception of experience, knowledge, idea, concept, belief, meaning, and truth. In a famous article, "Charles Darwin and His Influence on Science," Dewey made clear the impact that Darwin had on pragmatic naturalism, when he said that the publication of *The Origin of Species* "precipitated a crisis" and "introduced a mode of thinking that in the end was bound to transform the logic of knowledge and hence the treatment of morals, politics, and religion."[2] For Dewey the destruction of dualisms between man and nature or mind and body is the inevitable result: all knowledge is to be considered as instrumental to the human being, a means by which he may resolve practical problems. C. I. Lewis, in his work *An Analysis of Knowledge and Valuation,* maintains a similar view when he states that "cognitively guided behavior is merely the farthest reach of adaptive response."[3]

Many naturalists thus have wished to avoid any commitment to a narrowly conceived epistemology; for much of traditional epistemological inquiry is based upon purely formalistic logical analysis independent of experimental inquiry. In spite of their disclaimers, however, the naturalists have presupposed a general theory of experience which, if not an epistemology in name, comes very close to it in function. Instead of a theory based on prescientific speculation, they have insisted, along with most behaviorists, that the starting point is always the behavioral action of the human organism, as viewed by the sciences. Thus man is properly conceived as an interacting field, not as split from his environing field. The term *transaction* best expresses the point. All human functions are organic functions related to a field which includes objects and goals. This is clearly the case for processes of digestion and respiration which could not proceed separately from physical-chemical and biological causes, but it is also the case for sensation, thinking, and other "psychic" functions, which historically were excluded from such treatment.

The point is that all "conscious" and intellectual processes are continuous with other biological processes and are to be considered as having natural causes and effects in the world. Conscious functions are not the inner spiritual or non-natural qualities of a human soul but merely instances of biological behavior. Perception and thinking are related to certain goals and purposes of the organism and stimuli in the environment. Thus for Lewis "the principle function of empirical knowledge is that of an instrument enabling transition . . . from the actual present to a future which is desired."[4] Ideas are related to action and beliefs are implicit dispositional tendencies or plans of action, on the basis of which we are prepared to act. "Knowledge," for this view, has a biological and psychological basis, but it also has, as G. H. Mead pointed out, a social fulfillment. For man not only has an enlarged cortex, which is an essential precondition for the emergence of intellectuality, but he is a social being interacting with others and communicating his wants, interests, and needs. It is only with the development of symbolic language in the communication process that advanced abstract conceptual thinking is made possible. And it is largely within the social process that such belief and knowledge develop.

## IV.  LANGUAGE AND "MEANING"

The study of language and of "meaning" is at the center of twentieth-century philosophy. Pragmatic naturalism, like logical positivism and philosophical analysis, has taken as fundamental the problem of the meaning of our concepts, terms, and symbols; though language is related to experience and behavior.

Peirce's original formulation of pragmatism was as a criterion for the clarification of our ideas: "Consider what effects, that might conceivably have practical bearings, we conceive the object of our conceptions to have. Then, our conception of these effects is the whole of our conception of the object."[5] Peirce did not intend this criterion to be of universal applicability to all concepts. He limited it to abstract intellectual concepts, and he intended a rigorous experimental test. The meaning of abstract ideas can be clarified by reference to their consequences in practice. What it means to say that "salt is soluble" is only that if salt were placed under certain test conditions, it would most likely dissolve. James later extended Peirce's original criterion, and especially the notion of "useful" consequences, to include moral and aesthetic consequences, much to the objections of other pragmatists. It is clear that the pragmatic criterion is too broad and imprecise to serve as a general theory of meaning and that the confusion of truth with utility was an unfortunate result. Language is far more subtle than the early pragmatic criterion allowed.

But Peirce had made a telling point, one that all subsequent pragmatic naturalists have accepted, and this I think remains in spite of limitations of the criterion itself; namely, that concepts, and the terms and symbols which express them, are related to human *praxis* or conduct, and that they take on meaning and significance in relation to their effects upon such conduct. Language is not descriptive of the Logos, nor is it to be construed simply as an abstraction from or reflection of "reality." It is adjectival and adverbial, an instrument of human desire and purpose, with functions and uses in human experience.

Language is biopsychological in function in that it serves as a sign in terms of which organisms may draw inferences. Ideas expressed in the form of beliefs are implicit dispositional tendencies and plans of action; they are vehicles by which humans can interact within a natural and social environment. Language is thus a tool with jobs to perform. It is normative in that it presupposes grammatical and logical prescriptive rules, and it fulfills and satisfies our purposes and needs.

Language is social because it is used by a group of human beings in the process of communication. There is a trinitarian conception of language; for the linguistic situation includes interpreters, interpretees, and interpretants; that is, a linguistic context involves (1) individuals who use linguistic symbols or phrases, (2) symbols which function as dispositional proxies, and (3) ranges of reactions ("meanings") aroused in people who respond to the symbols. Pragmatic naturalism shares with analytic philosophy and Wittgenstein the view that (a) linguistic symbols, terms, and sentences have *many* uses and jobs to perform (the descriptive model is *not* the sole model), and that (b) their uses can only be discovered by reference to the concrete *contexts* in which they function.

Naturalism goes beyond analytic philosophy on one key point, and that is in the definition of the language context. For the naturalist, the analyst unduly tends to restrict the context of language to linguistic elements; whereas for him the context is eventually *behavioral,* for language is continuous with biosocial processes. Naturalism today is dubious of the formalist notion of "meaning," for this may suggest a kind of inverted Platonism. Language is best conceived in its broad sense as verbal or sign-behavior.

Although naturalism, like ordinary language philosophy, begins with common sense, it does not take ordinary language as beyond criticism or modification. Indeed, the pragmatic theory of language suggests that new uses for terms and concepts can be introduced into the language stock. If the scientific use of language is any guide, then we can stretch old terms, stipulate and introduce new terms, and reconstruct language, providing that we can justify our doing so as fruitful to the process of inquiry.

The analytic-synthetic distinction has raised a good deal of controversy in recent years. I do not know that there is any one naturalistic position here. Some naturalists (such as Lewis) have accepted the positivistic view that analytic statements, though necessarily true, are empty and tautological, saying nothing about the factual world, and that synthetic statements are descriptive and tested by empirical observation. Pragmatic analysts (such as Willard V. O. Quine and M. G. White) have considered the analytic-synthetic dualism as untenable, and have held that there are many borderline cases which are neither strictly analytic nor synthetic, but a combination of both. The criticism here especially applies to "analyticity" or "being synonymous with" in natural languages and the distinction between "essential" and "accidental predication." For all naturalists the analytic and synthetic distinction, even if accepted, is based upon our purposes and determined by the conventional rules that we have adopted; it is not grounded on any alleged realistic foundation.

The naturalistic conception of logic is especially critical of formalism in logic. Logic is not construed in traditional Aristotelian or Thomistic terms as part of the nature of Being; nor in terms of the Hegelian view that the laws of thought are equivalent to the laws of Being. Many naturalists have sought to do logic without traditional ontology. Logic is conceived as a generalization from human inquiry, a statement of the most general propositions involved in effective thinking. The rules of logic—deductive, inductive, and the logic of practice—are *instruments,* tested by their demonstrated utility in investigation. Thus logic is not simply a formal discipline, but in its wider sense refers to the assumptions and methods employed in the search for reliable knowledge. Logical principles have the character of intellectual tools, even though they may in part be analytic and necessary; and these tools are the result of a slow process of evolution in which the habits of inference that are most adaptive remain as part of the stock of logical principles and distinctions.

# V. SCIENTIFIC METHODOLOGY

Pragmatic naturalists who are willing to talk about "epistemology" generally take as their main concern methodology, i.e., the analysis of the criteria and standards for formulating beliefs and testing hypotheses. C. I. Lewis, for example, claims that his task in *An Analysis of Knowledge and Valuation* is not the "phenomenological construction of the real, but to discover by analysis the criteria of validity in knowledge."[6] An examination of the naturalistic position in methodology illustrates the importance of the methods of science, for as we have said, pragmatic naturalism may be defined as a philosophy committed to the use of scientific methodology in the testing of knowledge. Thus Ernest Nagel defines the scope of his influential book *The Structure of Science* as "primarily an examination of logical patterns exhibited in the organization of scientific knowledge as well as of the logical methods whose use . . . is the most enduring feature of modern science." The book accordingly ignores many of the issues of traditional epistemology, such as the epistemology of sense perception.[7]

Although the naturalists focus upon scientific methodology, their conception of science is much different from that which has usually been offered or defined in philosophy. This conception, however, is continuous with the theory of experience and language discussed above. Science, for the naturalist, is primarily a way of behaving, a mode of acting or inquiring, and not a fixed body of knowledge. It is by viewing the process of scientific inquiry, and not simply the product, that we are best able to grasp its significance. The method of science is not something esoteric or mysterious; it is not a black art available only to a few specialists initiated into its cult. Rather, scientific inquiry is continuous with the procedures and standards that we employ in ordinary life. Scientific thinking, though more sophisticated, is merely an extension of what the plain man uses in resolving everyday problems. According to Sidney Hook, there are effective working procedures on the level of practical life which everyone recognizes, and must recognize to some extent, if he is to live and function in the world, even at a minimal level.[8] There are ways of using means to achieve our ends; there are canons of rationality, intelligibility, consistency, and practical tests of trial-and-error observation and experiment which are exhibited in behavior and involved in the arts and crafts. Scientific inquiry is nothing more than the refinement and elaboration of these commonly recognized procedures. It is acting responsibly and dispassionately, with care and caution in verifying judgments and testing beliefs. Scientific method is the method of ordinary intelligence at work in the most difficult and complex areas of inquiry.

The nature of the criteria and standards of scientific methodology has been vigorously debated in modern times, with the dispute between rationalists and empiricists commanding the center of interest. From the vantage point of the contemporary world, we now see that this dispute has in a sense been resolved and that the scientific method incorporates the contributions of both. If we ask, what are the criteria for adequacy of knowledge, we find, first, an empirical-experimental *criterion of verification:* if a hypothesis, proposition, or belief is warranted, then it should be experimentally verified directly or indirectly by reference to a range of empirical observations. This point is fundamental to naturalism: that concepts without perceptual or observational rules of application to the concrete world are empty. Second, there is also a *consistency criterion:* if a hypothesis, proposition, or belief is warranted, then it should be logically consistent with all other beliefs held; if not, either the belief in question or other beliefs with which it is inconsistent must be eventually replaced. This internal deductive test of noncontradiction applies to all propositions which are part of a system of propositions.

However, modern scientific methodology is more complex than this, and there are other characteristics which an objective methodology should satisfy. Thus we say with Peirce that human beliefs are to be considered as *fallible* in the sense that they are always corrigible and open to revision. In other words, beliefs are not certain or absolute, but only *probable,* since they are based upon a range of evidence. Moreover, the grounds for the acceptance of scientific hypotheses must be *publicly repeatable* or *replicable,* and based upon the tested judgments of a community of inquirers, who are committed to the canons of scientific objectivity. This fallibilism and probabilism of knowledge applies to the scientific method itself, which is *self-corrective* in the sense that its rules, techniques, and procedures are open to possible revision and modification in the light of future practice and considerations of fruitfulness. One feature that the naturalistic theory of inquiry emphasizes and which has been previously overlooked is the view that hypotheses have an *instrumental* function, and are to be judged by their consequences.

Some have argued that this instrumental test of hypotheses refers to their ability to resolve existential problems of practice. Dewey's theory of inquiry holds that theories are related to practice and that all beliefs are a function of the situations in which they occur. A hypothesis is accepted if it helps to resolve an indeterminate or problematic situation, overcome the difficulty, and enable blocked action to continue.[9] It is generally argued that Dewey had overstated his case, for there are many contexts of inquiry in which no genuine practical problem is encountered as initiating inquiry. Instrumentalism thus must be extended to apply to problems which are primarily intellectual in character. Hypotheses in this sense are warranted in basic research as distinct from applied research if they overcome intellectual doubt in a community of inquirers.

For the naturalist it is the task of science to formulate hypotheses which function as instruments to fulfill our purposes and goals.

The basic goal of science is the development of causal explanations and descriptions stated in hypothetical "if, then" form, on the basis of which a range of data can be ordered, accounted for, and predicted. Ernest Nagel, in *The Structure of Science,* has made explicit the role of explanation in science and the importance of the covering law or regularity model. According to Nagel:

> It is the desire for explanations which are at once systematic and controllable by factual evidence that generates science; and it is the organization and classification of knowledge on the basis of explanatory principles that is the distinctive goal of the sciences. More specifically, the sciences seek to discover and to formulate in general terms the conditions under which events of various sorts occur, the statements of such determining conditions being the explanations of the corresponding happenings.[10]

Naturalists have attempted to avoid the use of the term "truth," and prefer to talk instead of "warranted," "adequate" or "tested" hypotheses. For knowledge, and especially scientific knowledge, is not simply descriptive; it does not provide a simple one-to-one correspondence between a hypothesis or theory and the external world; rather hypotheses are functions of inquiry. Hypotheses are convenient if they fulfill their roles effectively within the process of inquiry. This methodological view of scientific inquiry does not deny or preclude realism. Indeed, although some pragmatists have refused to be drawn into the realist-phenomenalist controversy, it is clear that naturalists are in general sympathetic to realism (as Peirce noted) in the sense that there is a world independent of our wishes and fancies, and that the verification of our hypotheses only makes sense if we grant that they are related to an external world. Thus the context of inquiry and the transactions of human beings are not subjective but have an objective foundation in nature.

# VI. BEHAVIORISM AND NEO-BEHAVIORISM

Naturalism, as we have seen, is thoroughly committed to the extension of the scientific method to all areas of nature; but it is the application of this principle to the study of the human species which is at once the most distinctive and most influential characteristic of the naturalistic approach. And it is the principle that all events and processes, including human events and processes, can be explained by reference to natural causes and events that has contributed in no small way to the development in America of the behavioral sciences. Although not all naturalists accept all aspects of the behavioristic program, naturalism has been closely identified with its development, from James and Dewey to the present. Naturalism shares with other contemporary philosophical movements—logical positivism, philosophical analysis, and even with Marxism to some extent—the desire to create a behavioral science based on *praxis.*

There are, however, various types of behaviorism; and, although naturalists would consider themselves sympathetic to some forms, they would not wish to be identified with all of them. In the early part of this century, Watson ad Pavlov introduced mechanistic or reductive behaviorism within psychology. They attacked the reification of "mind" or "consciousness," wished to exclude subjective introspection as untenable, and to concentrate upon physicalist and mechanistic explanations. This view was later modified by functional behaviorism, as advanced by C. L. Hull, E. C. Tolman, and the pragmatists; the reductive model was held to be too narrow; and purposive or goal-directed explanations were to be admitted.

Since the Second World War a veritable explosion has occurred in the sciences which investigate man, and behaviorism is no longer restricted to psychology. Thus there are a great number of behavioral sciences which investigate man, from political science, sociology, anthropology, economics, education, and jurisprudence to cybernetics, information or communication theory, game and decision-making theory. I prefer to use the term "neo-behaviorism" here rather than behaviorism to characterize this new departure, and I think that most present-day naturalists are neo-behaviorists rather than simply behaviorists.

Most neo-behaviorists do not conceive of their inquiry as providing a general theory of man, aside perhaps from the minimal statements as discussed above under the naturalistic theory of experience: they are dubious of the postulation of any subjective "consciousness," "mind," or "self" separate and distinct from the body, and they wish to focus instead on the field of observable transactions. Unlike earlier behaviorists, they wish to avoid premature metaphysical speculation about the nature of man. Neo-behaviorism, they insist, should be interpreted primarily as introducing a set of regulative principles which recommend *how* we should go about studying human beings. The neo-behaviorists are interested in proposing prescriptive rules for investigating man, not in offering general accounts of his "essential traits," "nature" or "being." Thus neo-behaviorism is best construed as a strategy of research or a methodological program.

What does the neo-behavioral program involve? Unfortunately no precise platform has been worked out which would be acceptable to all of its proponents. What is clear is that neo-behaviorism cannot be identified simply with the Pavlovian-Watsonian program of physicalist reductionism; nor is neo-behaviorism today to be identified with any one school in psychology, such as the SR conditioned-response learning theory. The restricted definition of behaviorism which a B. F. Skinner in psychology might employ would hardly be acceptable to a neo-behaviorist in political science, sociology, or economics. Virtually all neo-behaviorists, including even the most extreme physicalist behaviorists of earlier days, are now willing to deal with psychological areas which were formerly considered *verboten,* such as perception, thinking, and motivation, and they recognize the importance of introspective reports as psychological data to be explained. Some of the recent advocates of neo-behaviorism are also receptive to the use of functional, holistic, intentional, and motivational explanations. Many do not believe that a reduction of the many sciences of man to a single physical science is at this stage of research possible or even desirable. The term "coduction" best describes the existence within the social and behavioral sciences of many kinds of explanation drawn from many levels of inquiry.[11]

Some philosophical critics have interpreted behaviorism as "logical behaviorism," that is, as a theory of meaning in which every statement or definition of a psychological fact is equivalent to or must be translated into some statement of a physical fact. Others have interpreted behaviorism as an operationalist theory of definition whereby all definitions admitted into behavioral science must be framed in terms of a set of operations to be performed. But these interpretations of neo-behaviorism are also far too restrictive and would exclude a great number of inquirers who would wish to be considered as participating in the neo-behavioral program. It is clear that for the neo-behaviorist only a looser theory of meaning and definition is possible. He does not insist that all sentences in behavioral science be directly stated in physicalist or operational terms, but simply that they be related to other sentences which are, thus allowing for the admission of intervening variables and hypothetical constructs. Logical behaviorism and operationalism are wedded to early versions of logical positivism and pragmatism, both of which have been superseded.

We have said what the neo-behaviorist program is not, may we say more directly what it is? What is crucial to neo-behaviorism and naturalism is simply the insistence that all hypotheses introduced in science must be *experimentally confirmable* and these verifications must be *intersubjectively or publicly repeatable* by the community of inquirers.

While neo-behaviorists stress the role of experimental verification as essential to all scientific inquiry, this in no way precludes the use of mathematical models and theoretical systems, which all but the most extreme empiricists concede to be essential to any developed science. Many behavioral scientists today are reluctant to build high-level theoretical deductive systems, which they frequently consider to smack of premature philosophical speculation or intuitive guess-work. They prefer to concentrate upon the data and upon detailed experimental observation and statistical correlation. Most take as their immediate goal the development of hypotheses of the middle range, i.e., hypotheses amenable to some theoretical generality, yet closely related to concrete empirical contexts or particular facts. Yet behavioral science like natural and biological science has as its eventual goal the development of a set of mutually related hypotheses of wider deductive and theoretical significance. In the last analysis, however, neo-behaviorists insist that all statements that are considered warranted must be experimentally confirmed by reference to publicly observable changes.

Many philosophical critics have questioned the entire naturalist-behavioristic program and have argued that a science of man is *in principle* not logically possible, and that intuitive *verstehen,* phenomenological description, or other methods must be employed. There are various forms to this critique. Thus one hears the following: that motives, intentions, and decisions are essential to characterize man, that teleological explanation and not causal explanation should be used, that historical method must be used, that man is "free," or that he possess a "mind" independent of causal explanation. I wish to respond briefly to each of these charges.

Neo-behaviorism surely would not wish to deny the first claim that motive explanations have an appropriate use in the social sciences and psychology. We could perhaps not very well understand many kinds of historical, political, and economic events unless we knew the plans and purposes of the human agents involved; nor could we operate fully in many psychological or psychiatric contexts without interpreting the motives and intentions of human beings (even though these motives may be "unconscious," as in psychoanalysis.) The question however is whether motives and intentions are capable of behavioristic treatment. The answer I think is in the affirmative. Motives and intentions can be interpreted as "intervening variables"; they can be put in operational and experimental form as "tendencies to act." Moreover, one can show that motive explanations are not logically different from causal explanations; for they involve dispositional statements. These are like hypothetical or conditional statements in that they satisfy the logical form of covering law explanations, i.e., given certain dispositions (motives) within the organism, then he will tend to behave in certain predictable ways. We must add however, that although motive explanations may have a use in the sciences of man, they are surely not the only kind of explanations that are employed.

Similarly, it is sometimes argued that in biological, psychological, and sociological contexts teleonomic,[12] functional, and holistic explanations are necessary; for they point to the purposive maintenance of the system as a whole. Clearly, teleonomic explanations which are purged of teleological overtones are used fruitfully in social and biological sciences along with others. But it can again be argued that these explanations indicate the conditions necessary for the maintenance of an organic system or social organization, and that in this sense they are an important aspect of causal explanation.

The claim of historicists that the sciences of man must be "historical" in a special way, for man has a past, not a nature, or the claim that human history is "unique" and incapable of generalization overlooks the argument that the historical method is an essential ingredient of the social sciences, and that historical inquiry is continuous with and dependent upon them. A great deal of discussion has been expended recently on the nature of history and whether it is a science. Naturalism and behaviorism share with positivism the covering law thesis (Popper-Hempel) that historical events in principle are explainable by reference to statements of general conditions or causal laws. Far from opposing the scientific treatment of man, historical inquiry is dependent upon the sciences for the derivation of many of its key causal generalizations and explanations.

There is another traditional objection to science based upon the argument from "freedom of the will," though recently this argument has been restated in different forms. There is, for example, the existentialist's view that man has no "nature" or "essence," only an "existence" as a subject. Man, it is said, is "free" to create his own nature; he is the sum and substance of his plans and projects. This view, however, neglects the large body of causal hypotheses that we have from the behavioral sciences, which enable us to explain much human behavior. Or there is the objection that man is a decision-maker, and that his choice can be "contra-causal," i.e., that an individual "could have acted otherwise" if he so wished. Few would deny that in many cases a man could have acted otherwise, *if* the circumstances and conditions under which he acted were somewhat different. It is difficult if not impossible to know, however, whether an individual could have acted otherwise, if all the conditions were *exactly* the same. The argument from contra-causality thus seems incapable of verification; it is nonfalsifiable and hence appears to be grounded in supposition. Another objection has been introduced to show the logical impossibility of a complete science—this is sometimes called the "self-fulfilling" and "suicidal prophecy" arguments. Science, it has been said, predicts that given the occurrence of a range of initial conditions, specific kinds of effects should follow. But in regard to human behavior, serious complications enter into our calculations, for our knowledge of a prediction, itself may influence the data. It may tend to either confirm what might have otherwise been false ("the self-fulfilling prophecy") or to disconfirm what might have otherwise been true ("the suicidal prophecy"). This kind of objection, I think, is the most serious that has been raised, but it can be answered perhaps in this way: for our initial theories to be adequate they must include as one of their conditions the role that knowledge of the causal hypotheses will itself play in future outcomes. Furthermore, prediction in science does not involve "prophecy" of the future, so much as it involves confirmation of an explanation.

All of these objections, however, are based upon a still more fundamental notion that is questionable, the notion that causal explanations involve hard determinism, compulsion, or constraint between condition and effect. A science of human behavior does not entail strict determinism; only the principle of determinableness, i.e., that there are no *a priori* reasons for preventing us from inquiring into behavior, and of determining applicable causal explanations. Most naturalists and behaviorists today are weak determinists; they interpret "cause" not as a necessary constraining force, but rather as a statement of a hypothesis: given certain antecedent conditions, certain observed effects will most likely follow. Weak determinism need not deny the existence of decision making in human life. It claims, however, that the fact that human beings make decisions that follow from their own motives, character, and personality does not in turn invalidate the possibility of causal explanation. On the contrary, one can argue that moral choice and responsibility, far from presupposing contra-causal freedom, would seem to require some regularity and order in human character and conduct, else punishment would be without foundation—one does not punish a man who acts without motive or cause. The punishing of offenders under this interpretation is still meaningful, for punishment operates as one of the regulative conditions of social behavior.

There is still another classic objection to the scientific treatment of man, which we have already touched upon, and that is the view that man possesses a "self," mind, or "consciousness" entirely independent of his bodily processes or the context in which he interacts, and that this psychic entity is not amenable to objective treatment. The "mind-body dualism" or "ghost-in-the-machine doctrine" (as it has been called by Ryle[13]) has had, as we have seen, rough sledding in the behavioral sciences, for to postulate a separate "mind" for the behaviorist has little experimental warrant and is of little explanatory value in concete contexts of inquiry. Moreover, the claim that the inner "subject" can only be known by a special "introspective," "intuitive," or "empathetic" *verstehen* raises the questions of what is meant by "knowledge," and how one can determine whether assertions about the "inner life" are adequate or inadequate. The behaviorist does not deny the existence of conscious awareness, or the life of feeling suffering, joy, desire, or imagination; he merely asks that statements about phenomenological data be verified and tested by publicly observable correlations. Poetic insight may originate or suggest hypotheses, but it can never be held to confirm them.

Thus in answer to this range of objections, the naturalist does not maintain that a science of man is necessary or even that it is easy to achieve. There are profound experimental and practical difficulties in isolating and controlling the data under observation. The naturalist is simply denying that the alleged *a priori* arguments against a science of man have been conclusively demonstrated; for those who would seek to limit such a behavioral science generally do so from an untested theory of human nature that has been assumed beforehand. Nor can the naturalist *prove* the case for science. The question for him is still an open one. I reiterate that behaviorism should be construed primarily as a methodological program. Its basic justification as a program is that of convenience: given the great advances in the biological and natural sciences, there is some warrant to expect that application of similar rigorous methods of inquiry to the study of man will yield fruitful results. But to say this is not to argue in a vacuum, for the behavioral sciences have *already* achieved considerable success. Indeed, the growing body of behavioral research is both impressive and promising. There can be no more adequate justification for the behavioral sciences than their actual consequences. The test of the method is its pragmatic results: does it provide us with effective instruments which enable us to describe and explain how and why man behaves the way he does to test these explanations, and to apply this knowledge to human affairs? One has to beware of repeating the errors of the past: the history of philosophy is littered with dead metaphysical principles which have been adduced to demonstrate the alleged impossibility of the extension of the methods of the sciences to new areas of research.

## VII. NATURALISTIC ETHICS AND VALUE

There is perhaps no area in which the naturalistic thesis has provoked more controversy than in the area of ethics and value. And this has involved a dispute not only with nonnaturalists but with other naturalists as well.

Naturalism in ethics and value has both a broad and a specialized interpretation. In its broad sense, all naturalists seem agreed that values are relative to human experience, and that any attempt to support or derive values from a transcendental source is mistaken. Nature is indifferent to man; she expresses no value preferences or moral purposes apart from the values and purposes of living organisms. Human values are in the last analysis *human.*

Pragmatic naturalists accept this basic humanistic thesis, but they go beyond it by also maintaining the more specialized thesis that value judgments are in principle at least amenable to objective empirical and scientific treatment. It is this latter claim that has engendered the widest dissent, particularly from positivistic and analytic philosophers. G. E. Moore charged that the naturalists committed the "naturalistic fallacy" when they attempted to provide an empirical definition for value terms; and this was later supported by the emotivist attack on objectivistic ethics.

What many often fail to see is that Moore's critique applies, if it applies at all, not only to naturalistic theories, but to all ethical theories, including the metaphysical accounts of the "good." According to Moore, "good" was indefinable because it was a "simple nonnatural quality"; and any and all theories of the good failed. Accordingly, Moore's critique is not the naturalist's burden alone to bear, and it applies likewise to transcendental and nonnaturalistic theories. Similar considerations apply to the emotivist critique, which was offered by the positivists, who may otherwise be considered to be naturalists. The emotivists maintained that value judgments are expressive and imperative in function, and that any attempt to define value terms involves "persuasive definitions." But this critique, too, was intended to apply to any and all ethical definitions and theories, and not simply to naturalistic theories.

I think that a good case can be made for the view that the Moorean-emotivist critique of naturalism was an attack upon a straw man—possibly a crude kind of nineteenth-century scientism—but that it did not undermine the main thesis of pragmatic naturalism. I am here thinking of the kind of naturalistic position advanced by John Dewey, C. I. Lewis, Ralph B. Perry, Stephen Pepper, Abraham Edel, and others. In the first place, twentieth-century ethical naturalism, in America at least, has attempted to avoid many of the old issues by concentrating upon questions of value and valuation, rather than upon ethics or moral philosophy. "Value" has a wider denotation than "good" or "right"; and it refers to preferential behavior *in general*. Moral values are only one species of the broader class of values. In the second place, the basic problem of value theory for the naturalist is not that of definition. It is true that some naturalists, such as Perry, were concerned with providing scientific definitions of value (for example, that "value is the object of any interest"[14]); and no doubt the emotivists' charge of "persuasive definition" does apply in some sense. But the central issue for the naturalist has always concerned the question of the validation or verification of value judgments, valuations, and appraisals.

Lewis has stated clearly the key thesis: that valuations are "a form of empirical knowledge," and that they are in principle capable, to some extent at least, of empirical or factual verification.[15] The naturalist has simply maintained that valuation judgments concerning the preferences of human beings and their social norms grow out of concrete situations and are capable of modification by reference to the range of facts within such situations. For Dewey valuation judgments are hypotheses to be tested by reference to the conditions under which they arise, the means available, and the consequences of actions.

This naturalistic thesis on value is in many ways quite similar to the Aristotelian doctrine of the mean of the *Nichomachean Ethics*: what should be done is always a function of particular circumstances and is relative to the time, place, agent or agents involved. But the naturalist has attempted to go one step beyond Aristotle by claiming that there is a means-end continuum and that a deeper scientific knowledge of the conditions under which we act and of the alternative techniques available will enable us to evaluate plans and appraise ends.[16] Valuation judgments, including moral rules and principles, may be treated as hypotheses open to revision and modification in the light of new knowledge and altered circumstances. The naturalist is an objective relativist, in the sense that although he believes valuation judgments are relative to human experience, he does not think that this implies subjective caprice or the lack of all standards. Rather, there are some canons of objectivity, he claims, that are available to the rational man. Linguistic-analytic philosophy has approached naturalism on this point, and there has been a "reunion" in philosophy.[17] Many ordinary language Oxford philosophers maintain that the emotive theory had misinterpreted what we do in everyday life; there is a "logic of decision" which we can discover embedded in the stock of moral terms and judgments; there are standards and criteria of choice.

One point of confusion about naturalism on the part of its critics concerns the question as to whether valuation judgments can be resolved *simply* in factual terms alone, and whether these "facts" are neutral or "value free," i.e., whether normative judgments are deducible or derivable from nonnormative premises. Misconception about what the naturalistic thesis *is* on this key issue is so prevalent that perhaps no one should be blamed but the naturalists themselves for not clearly explicating their position. Yet a careful inspection of the writings of the naturalist will show, I think, that naturalists have always *insisted* that part of what is given within the situation are the existing interests, prizings, likings, values, and norms that men have, and that any normative judgment is always in terms of this "valuational base." Thus, valuation judgments are not antiseptic or devoid of value in content, but are intimately related to the *de facto* value experiences that human beings actually have. The very subject matter that our valuation judgments are about is the immediate experience of value, of enjoyment, liking, or need that people possess. But, say the naturalists, these value experiences are always open to modification in the light of a considered inquiry into the full factual situation, and they become *de jure* only after such inquiry. In any case, the primary need in ethics and value, according to the naturalists, is to develop "a science of valuation" in terms of which our judgments of value are facilitated and reconstructed.

One can argue on purely logical grounds about the adequacy or inadequacy of naturalistic methodology in valuation and social policy. But we should not overlook the remarkable and in many ways startling development that has occurred in the behavioral sciences in the past two decades, a development which can be traced in no small way to the influence of writers such as Dewey. I am thinking here of the new sciences or techniques of decision making, operations research, game theory, etc., which have been attempting to develop scientific strategies of choice, and with considerable success, or of the policy sciences and applied sciences which provide important prescriptive rules for resolving problems of human conduct. To deny that there can be a "science of valuation," at least up to a point, is to overlook a whole body of tested valuation judgments which we already possess.

Most naturalists have also maintained that problems of value choice do not concern simply the isolated individual, but apply to social contexts and institutions. Thus pragmatic naturalists, perhaps more than most philosophers in the contemporary scene, have had a deep and abiding interest in social and political questions. Indeed, for the pragmatic naturalist, an essential function of the philosopher is his role in helping to resolve the problems of men in society. And here he has maintained that the same methodological approach that applies to valuation judgments in ethics also applies to the solution of social problems. John Dewey and Sidney Hook have written at length on the use of pragmatic or scientific intelligence and the need to develop an objective method for dealing with social issues. Under this interpretation, political and social policies and ideals should be treated as hypotheses and tested experimentally by their consequences in action. There are no absolute or universal ideological formulas which we can impose upon social life; rather our principles, rules, and laws grow out of, should be related to, and modified in the light of, the expressed needs and interests of human beings. Pragmatic naturalism as such has had a profound impact upon American life. For example, the movement known as progressive education in no small way can be traced to the writings of the pragmatic naturalists. Similarly, for the development of liberal democratic ideas in legal jurisprudence and political theory—liberalism under their influence has become not so much a fixed platform as a method of approach. But in being interested in the role of their theories in society pragmatic philosophers have only been acting upon their principle that theories must be related to their consequences in practice.

# VIII. AESTHETIC AND RELIGIOUS EXPERIENCE

One complaint often heard against science and *a fortiori* scientific naturalism is that although naturalism claims to be concerned with experience as a basis for scientific knowledge, it fails to appreciate or do full justice to other dimensions of human experience, primarily aesthetic or religious experience. This charge had been hurled against historical materialism, which had been accused of ignoring and denigrating other qualities of human experiences; it has also been leveled against naturalism—but unjustly, I think. For naturalism, as distinct from reductive materialism, makes the special point that aesthetic, religious, and moral qualities can only be dismissed at a great price, and that any philosophy of experience, such as naturalism claims to be, must recognize the significance that these qualities play in human life. Far from excluding them from consideration, naturalism emphasizes and focuses on them: Santayana talks at great length about the "realm of spirit"[18]; and indeed, one of the most important collected volumes on naturalistic philosophy is entitled *Naturalism and the Human Spirit,*[19] so as to emphasize the fact that naturalism does not ignore the "human spirit." It is important to point out however that "human spirit" is herein being used metaphorically and that it does not represent any nonnatural or subjectivistic entity.

The naturalists do not deny that aesthetic and religious experiences have been central to human life; in a sense they provide content to a rich and full life. The real issue for the naturalists however is how you interpret these experiences. Dewey constantly talks about the immediate experiences that we have, undergo, suffer, enjoy: but he denies that the term "knowledge" should be applied to this range of awareness in any special way. For it is one thing to have a raw, brute, and unrefined immediate experience, it is another thing to interpret, relate, organize, or deduce from this experience "concepts," to claim that they apply to the world, and to act upon them. Most naturalists have withheld the term "knowledge" from the immediately sensuous given and they have insisted that knowledge must be qualified so as to involve interpretation, reflection, manipulation, and prediction. "Knowledge by acquaintance" is often applied to that which is directly given, but unless the given is analyzed and related to previous experience, it hardly can be called "knowledge."

Aesthetic experience, for the naturalist, involves heightened sensitivity, appreciation, and expression of feeling. It is not appropriate to say that such experiences are "true" in any but a metaphorical way unless we can restate and assert what it is that is contained in the aesthetic experience. Aesthetic symbols, a novel or a painting, for example, may denote and describe qualities of objects in the world, and this no doubt enhances their aesthetic effect. But a work of art is not true *per se,* and any claims that are made about the world on the basis of an aesthetic experience, however eloquent and moving that experience may be, must be submitted to independent tests of public confirmation. The primary function of art is to express and stimulate feeling and mood, not to communicate special or esoteric truths. Art may, as incidental to its aesthetic function, render and dramatize certain truths. But if we are to accept the "message" or "theme" of the work, then we must be able to state, define, and verify its claim. To allow the contrary is to open the flood gates to subjective feeling and romantic irrationalism and to overwhelm cognition as a basis for knowledge and belief.

Similarly, the naturalist does *not* deny the existence of reverence, awe, piety, or of mystical ecstasy, nor does he deny that the experiences can be prized or cherished by individuals who undergo them. The key epistemological issue, however, concerns what these experiences point to and what they assert, if anything, about the universe. It is one thing to *have* an experience, it is another to endow the universe with qualities in its name. And here we must proceed with care and caution, lest we read into nature any and all human experiences—love and hate, hope and fear, desire and aversion. The naturalist is unwilling to consider mystic claims as self-confirming unless they can be independently checked or publicly confirmed, no more than he would allow that the fact that people have dreams and hallucinations suffice that they are true. If a cognitive claim is to be drawn from such private experiences, then the naturalist insists that the same responsible criteria and canons of adequacy used in other areas must apply to it as well. Naturalists tend to be humanists, for they believe that religious experiences are natural and that they can be explained by reference to natural processes and causes. A great deal of attention has been paid to religious language: naturalistic humanism would interpret its symbols and sentences primarily as moral and expressive in function. These do not designate or describe any alleged transcendental state of affairs, but rather recommend a way of life and an attitude of response. And they express our "ultimate concerns" and the basic ideals by which we live.

## IX. FIRST PRINCIPLES

One last objection to naturalism must here be discussed, for it is the most frequent argument that is heard against it, and that is, that if scientific naturalism is not primarily a metaphysical theory of reality, but a methodological program of inquiry, then is not its basic epistemological criterion based upon a subjective value judgment? How can the naturalist justify, confirm, or vindicate his commitment to scientific method, other than by an act or leap of faith, and why is not the supernaturalist or transcendentalist entitled to his leap or act of faith in the same sense? If all first principles are matters of choice, why choose one rather than another?

This oft-heard criticism of scientific naturalism is most puzzling, and an analysis of it will reveal its speciousness. Are we to argue that *all* first principles are alike, since all are unarguable and indefinable? For example, are we willing to argue that the first principles of the Druid Cult or the Buddhist, the Fascist, the Communist, and poet, the charlatan, the scientist, and the theologian are all on the same level and one is as good as the next, but merely a question of taste or caprice? Surely not, responds the naturalist, for although first principles cannot be deductively demonstrated or inductively verified, without begging the question, this still does not mean that some principles are not more reasonable than others and that a range of evidence does not apply to some more than others. One test of a first principle is whether it carries with it a whole set of additional unsupported truth claims about the universe. The naturalist would be dubious of the transcendentalist's first principles precisely because they seem to presuppose further assumptions about the nature of the world, whereas the naturalist's commitment to scientific method does so only to a minimal degree. Another test of first principles is their consequences. Granted a rule of behavior, we may ask what follows. And here the pragmatist points to the profoundly dramatic results that have ensued upon the application of scientific method to the world and to human affairs. "Mysteries" concerning "depths unspoken" and problems which seemed beyond the ken of any human understanding *have been* resolved as science has proceeded step by step to push the frontiers of knowledge. But the claim here being adduced is not simply that scientific method is justified because it has provided us with powerful explanatory theories of wide generality and tested precision, but that scientific method also provides us with tools in terms of which we can modify and control nature. Indeed, no matter what our other first principles and values may be, we need to come to terms with the intractable world of events which resist our desires and fancies, our ideals and dreams; and we need adequate means to fulfill our ends. There is a world and there are the brute limitations of facticity, and only a methodological tool which is grounded in nature and tested by its effectiveness can enable us to cope with the encountered world.

Perhaps the strongest support of the use of scientific methods and of the standards of empirical verification and logical consistency in establishing our judgments and hypotheses is this: that science is continuous with ordinary life and that its methods are a product of historical evolution, the hard and difficult task by means of which civilized man has learned to turn nature to his purposes. Science is simply a more refined extension of the principles which we already employ in ordinary life and which the plain man uses to carry on the basic arts and crafts of social living. The first principles of naturalism are thus generic, as far as I can determine, to all humans and all cultures. For men are faced with common tasks and problems of living, functioning, and of responding to the challenges from the environment. Experience and intellect are the instruments of survival, and adjustment, and they are the common possessions of humankind in general, transcending the limitations of custom and culture. Is it thus unreasonable to demand of naturalism that it justify the effective principles and criteria that we as human beings already use in ordinary affairs? Naturalism does not invent its principles out of thin air: it derives them from a reflection upon root human experiences and upon the assumptions and presuppositions that guide critical intelligence and action.

The real problem for the naturalist is not to justify the methods of critical intelligence in general—we could not live without them—so much as to justify their extension to other areas of experience, to human behavior, morality, politics, and religion. Naturalism does not wish to exclude human conduct, value, and social ideals from critical scientific treatment. Nor does it wish to exclude the "unknowable" by definition, as is sometimes claimed; it only asks that any claims about it be submitted to the same responsible critical standards that we use in ordinary life.

Naturalism considers all aspects of human experience to be a part of nature and hence available to scientific explanation and treatment. Yet, to borrow a phrase from Sartre, man expresses "bad faith" when he denies his natural roots, flees from the full use of his intelligence, or refuses to accept responsibility for his own destiny. In the last analysis, for the naturalist and humanist it is man himself who is ultimately responsible for what he is; and it is the height of irresponsibility for him to renounce his capacity for critical intelligence and to look outside himself for blame or support. Naturalism's first principle is its commitment to and confidence in responsible and intelligent inquiry—whether in ordinary life, the arts and crafts, morals, religion, science, or philosophy. The application of this principle is a serious matter, and whether or not it is used fully may help to determine whether or not humankind will persist in a state of self-deception, or whether it will continue to develop and progress.

But is it "naive optimism" to place so much reliance upon the use of scientific intelligence by human beings? Surely there are some things which are within our power as human beings, but there are some things which are not. There are some problems that are difficult, if not impossible, to resolve, and even for those problems which have solutions, some solutions are only in terms of the lesser of many evils. The naturalist who is honest will recognize that there is no guarantee in life of complete success or of the avoidance of failure, but that both are part of the drama of human existence.

The naturalist is not unmindful of the tragic character of the human condition and the ever present possibilities of failure and betrayal, error and inadequacy; but at the same time he does not suppress the positive potentialities of human experience for achievement and adventure, discovery and fulfillment. He recognizes the limitations and frailties of men *and* the promises and capacities; and he has the "courage to be" in the face of the dual character of the human condition.

Pragmatic naturalism today asserts that if humankind is to persist in the face of adversity and conflict, it must continue to express the best that is within it; and that its scientific reason (which many have thought most akin to the "divine"), if not perfect, at least is among the most effective instruments that it possesses. To renounce the use of this power or to deny its extension and applicability to other aspects of experience is for the naturalist morally irresponsible. And it is an irresponsibility that contemporary man can no longer afford to commit. For the complex problems and great crises of contemporary life are such that if man responds to them with anything less than the full use of his intelligence, then he is possibly betraying the last hope that he may have to continue to survive on this planet, at least in the form that he has heretofore known.

# NOTES

1. From *The Journal of Philosophy, Psychology and Scientific Method*, 1 (1904).
2. From *The Popular Science Monthly*, 65 (July 1909).
3. C. I. Lewis, *An Analysis of Knowledge and Valuation*, (LaSalle, Ill.: Open Court Publishing Co., 1946), p. 12.
4. Ibid., p. 4.
5. From *Dictionary of Philosophy and Psychology*, ed. James Baldwin (New York: Macmillan, 1902), Vol. 2, p. 322.
6. Lewis, *An Analysis of Knowledge and Valuation*, p. 23.
7. Ernest Nagel, *The Structure of Science: Problems in the Logic of Scientific Explanation* (New York: Harcourt Brace & World, 1961), p. viii.

8. Sidney Hook, *The Quest for Being and Other Studies in Naturalism and Humanism* (New York: St. Martin's Press, 1961), esp. Part 3.

9. Dewey defined "inquiry" as "the controlled or directed transformation of an indeterminate situation into one that is so determinate in its constituent distinctions and relations as to cover the elements of the original situation into a unified whole." John Dewey, *Logic: The Theory of Inquiry* (New York: Henry Holt, 1938), p. 104–105.)

10. Nagel, *The Structures of Science,* p. 4.

11. See Paul Kurtz, *Decision and the Condition of Man* (Seattle: University of Washington Press, 1965), chapter 5 for a discussion of this principle.

12. Teleological explanations without metaphysical overtones.

13. Gilbert Ryle, *The Concept of Mind* (London: Hutchinson, 1949).

14. Ralph Barton Perry, *General Theory of Value* (New York: Longmans, Green, 1926).

15. Lewis, *An Analysis of Knowledge and Valuation,* Part III. Lewis, however, unlike other naturalists, exempts ethical judgments of right and obligation from this classification.

16. See especially John Dewey, *Theory of Valuation,* International Encyclopedia of Unified Sciences, Vol. II, No. 4 (Chicago: University of Chicago Press, 1939). See also Abraham Edel, *Ethical Judgment: The Use of Science in Ethics* (Glencoe, Ill.: The Free Press, 1955); *Science and the Structure of Ethics* (Chicago: University of Chicago Press, 1961).

17. See Morton G. White, *Toward Reunion in Philosophy* (Cambridge: Harvard University Press, 1956).

18. George Santayana, *Realm of Being: The Realm of Spirit* (New York: Scribners, 1940).

19. Yervant H. Krikorian, ed., *Naturalism and the Human Spirit* (New York: Columbia University Press, 1944).

# 2.

# Pragmatic Naturalism and First Principles

I

As a former student and lifelong colleague of Sidney Hook, I have been especially influenced by his form of naturalism. Hook is heir to two philosophical traditions in American thought: naturalism and pragmatism. To accentuate their similarity and wed their common themes he has defined his point of view as "pragmatic naturalism." Many things have been attributed to pragmatism and to naturalism. If, according to Arthur Lovjeoy, there are thirteen varieties of pragmatism, naturalism has perhaps had an equal number of interpretations.

Hook's conception of pragmatic naturalism differs in emphasis from at least one other prevailing conception of naturalism: Although sympathetic to a naturalistic world view, his is more a methodological naturalism committed to a scientific method of inquiry than a metaphysical naturalism committed to a doctrine of irreducible categories or generic traits of nature or being.

Metaphysical naturalism is concerned with establishing the fol-

From *Sidney Hook and the Contemporary World,* edited by Paul Kurtz. Copyright © 1968 by The John Day Company, Inc., New York.

lowing two claims about the universe: First, all processes and events in nature have natural causes and are basically material in character, and second, since man is part of nature, there is no dualism between mind and body. Sidney Hook accepts both of these claims. Consequently, his naturalism is decidedly antisupernaturalistic and nontranscendental. Even though Hook considers naturalism to be "the systematization of what is involved in the scientific method of inquiry,"[1] he does not wish it to be dependent upon a specific metaphysical view of the universe or man, or to be limited by the particular sciences of any one age. Thus, for example, the mechanistic reductionism of an earlier Newtonian naturalistic metaphysics has been correctly modified and replaced in his view by a pluralistic, contextualistic, and evolutionary view of nature.

Hook's pragmatic naturalism is grounded primarily in a key epistemological and methodological principle: the centrality of the scientific method in achieving and testing knowledge. According to Hook, naturalism is that philosophy which subscribes to the view that the "scientific method is the only reliable way of reaching truth about man, society, and nature."[2]

This thoroughgoing commitment to science is at once the most distinctive aspect of pragmatic naturalism and, according to its critics, its most tenuous premise. I wish to examine the scope of this commitment, how it may be justified, and how it compares with an ordinary language view of "knowledge." Hook's naturalism was forged in a previous generation when there were different issues to be clarified and different battles to be won. Today some regard the defense of scientific method by the scientific naturalist, or his ally, the logical positivist, as outdated and antiquarian. Is this commitment to science a relic of a bygone philosophical era, which had its faith in "scientism," or is it important in the light of contemporary philosophical inquiry? I submit that the basic point of Hook's pragmatic naturalism is still significant. Consequently, in what follows, I shall state Hook's argument, defend and extend it, and point out some of its problems as well as some of its virtues.

## II

Hook's concept of science as being continuous with commonsense knowledge is very important in this post-Wittgensteinian philosophical period. Science is not an esoteric art or technique accessible only to a limited number of initiated high priests of technology who draw on a special kind of experience unavailable to ordinary human beings. Rather, it is a method of inquiry basically similar to the pattern of inquiry found in daily life. Like Dewey, Hook insists that science is an extension of and continuous with common sense. There are certain practical working rules which the ordinary man uses as he conducts the business of living. Science is simply the refinement of the canons of rationality and intelligibility already exhibited by the techniques of behavior involved in the arts and crafts of men. The plain man uses his intelligence to ford a stream, extinguish a fire, use a chisel, or construct a house: he attempts to adapt means to end in the most effective way.

Hook's pragmatism is clear: Thinking is related to our motives and purposes; it is intentional or teleonomic in character. Insofar as it aids us in selecting means to fulfill our ends, it is instrumental and functional. Thinking thus is related to behavior, action, praxis. Further, the most adequate and effective way of reaching the truth about the nature of things is the method already implicit in normal behavior wherein men attempt to function in accordance with intelligent principles and rules. It is that method which "comes to full fruition in the methods of science"[3] and involves the formulation of hypotheses in relation to specific problems or contexts and the testing of them by means of evidence. According to Hook, the basic pattern of inquiry which we use, *if* we want to acquire new knowledge, is the pattern of hypothetical-deductive-experimental observation: we "recognize the problem, state the hypothesis, draw the inferences, perform the experiment, and make the observation."[4]

A fact that is rarely appreciated is that the pragmatic naturalist makes no real distinction between "knowing how" and "knowing that." All cases of knowing that are held to be cases of knowing how; and knowing how is the general model of inquiry for both science and ordinary life. The pragmatists have taken the applied, practical, or technological sciences as the model for all scientific theory, since they are related to practice and to the solution of concrete problems encountered in experience. The uses of thinking and science in relation to purposes are essential: to know how to do something, to have a skill or téchné (e.g., to play the flute, repair a car, build a missile), best illustrates the basic pattern of inquiry, which involves means-ends deliberation.

In addition to this basic pattern of inquiry, Hook maintains that a plurality of scientific methods is used from field to field. Physics is not the model which all modes of inquiry follow. Actually there is no scientific method *überhaupt,* but only scientific methods and procedures. Thus the hypothetical-deductive-experimental method is utilized in the different sciences in different ways, depending upon the specific subject matters. Yet he maintains that in spite of some diversity and plurality there is a basic and underlying pattern of inquiry, which all reasonable or rational men will use, and there are canons of intelligibility and of critical intelligence which we all understand and accept. In agreement with both Russell and Dewey, Hook insists that in the last analysis "all knowledge that men have is scientific knowledge."[5]

## III

Wittgensteinians frequently maintain that it is not the task of philosophy to present us with simple definitions of "knowledge" or "truth." The term "know" has several uses, and any attempt to subsume them under a single formula or model is allegedly mistaken. According to this view, instead of providing an ideal definition of "knowledge" we should undertake a detailed analysis of cases in which people actually use the word "knowledge." That is, we should inspect the rules of use that the word "know" follows in ordinary language.[6]

Is there one meaning of the term "knowledge" in general, or is it always to be used distributively? Do the same limitations which apply to the theory of meaning also apply to a theory of truth? In other words, if we now recognize that it was a mistake to introduce the principle of verifiability as a universal criterion of meaning, or to take the descriptive model as the sole model, thereby ignoring other important uses of ordinary language, does a similar mistake occur in taking "scientific knowledge" as the general model of "truth," and are there not other senses of "know" equally valid and useful?

As we have seen, Hook agrees to some extent with this general line of argument. He claims that our conception of knowledge is continuous with ordinary experience and language. Science is an activity "whose propositions are constructions of, or inferences from, the data or ordinary experience and describable in language either continuous with ordinary language or constructed from terms which are ultimately so derived."[7] But he goes beyond this when he asserts that "all knowledge is scientific knowledge." This statement, according to Hook, reflects and summarizes a historical fact about certain bodies of knowledge that have been developed. But he adds that at the same time it is not a mere summary of historical fact or usage, but a *proposal* that we use the term "knowledge" in such a way "that all other claims to knowledge of the world shall be initially assessed as to validity in the light of criteria drawn from common sense and from scientific knowledge universally agreed to be highly reliable."[8] In other words, to maintain that all knowledge is scientific involves a *decision* and a *definition,* though Hook insists that to so define knowledge in terms of science is neither arbitrary nor capricious.

Hook's analysis of knowledge is based upon an analysis of ordinary language and experience, the arts and crafts of men and the sciences, wherein he claims to find a basic continuity of method and patterns of inquiry. However, unlike the later Wittgenstein, Hook goes beyond a descriptive analysis of how we use "knowledge" in ordinary language, and he *prescribes* or recommends how we should use it. What is at stake is his proposed methodological rule. The rub is that although we may be "objective" in certain areas where we use our critical scientific intelligence, in other areas we are deficient and do not employ critical intelligence. Thus the pragmatic naturalist is interested in advocating the extension of this basic pattern of scientific inquiry to all fields in which we seek knowledge— to the social sciences, morality, politics, and religion. All men recognize that there are wide deviations from the norm in these areas, and that persuasive, emotive, intuitive, and subjective methods intrude. The pragmatic naturalist thus clearly proposes that we extend or modify our uses of the term "knowledge." Following the typical use of "knowledge" in science and technology, we should use this as a model in all the other areas of human life wherein science is not presently employed.

# IV

Two questions immediately arise. First, is Hook correct when he argues that there is one basic pattern of inquiry and one reliable method of knowing, i.e., the scientific? Second, how would he justify the scientific method and its extension to other fields? Most philosophers who have faced the "riddle of induction" have noted difficulties in attempting to justify it. The pragmatic naturalist is faced with an even greater problem. For he is making a wider claim, and he is not simply attempting to justify present inductive procedures, but their extension to other fields of inquiry.

In response to the first question—Is there a basic pattern of inquiry?—we should acknowledge the difficulty in finding one overall, unified method of science or intelligence. The analysis of ordinary language has shown that there are diverse "logics" or methodologies in different languages, and various procedures of reasoning and inquiry. For example, it is no simple matter to squeeze ethical reasoning into the mold of natural science methodology. The methods of argumentation found in the law cannot be easily subsumed under those found in the theoretical sciences. The techniques employed in the social and behavioral sciences vary from science to science. Hence, there are various styles of inquiry and kinds of validation and confirmation appropriate to different areas of discourse; and any attempt to find a single model is fraught with difficulty.

Nevertheless, one may agree with Hook that there are more or less common features or characteristics applicable to all fields of inquiry: we insist upon evidence, we abhor inconsistencies, we examine alternative hypotheses, we are open-minded, we consider hypotheses as fallible and probable, we judge hypotheses in terms of consequences, our inquiry aims to resolve problems and to satisfy our purposes, and so on. If there is *one* pattern of inquiry, it is so general that unless the differences are noted we can be accused of equivocation. Perhaps people object to the general term "science" as descriptive of what they are or should be doing, when all that they mean is that in any inquiry we employ "critical intelligence," or "reason," and we attempt to be "objective" as defined by the context at hand. This would not be disconsonant with what Hook is proposing when he employs the "knowing how" terminology and when he maintains that all inquiry involves critical thinking in terms of means and ends.

Perhaps the attempt to propose a general definition for "knowledge" must suffer the fate of all philosophical generalities—to be so general that it excludes nuances and subtleties. Although one can give a general definition of "knowledge" or the method of gaining and testing it, and find a basic continuity between inquiry in ordinary experience and science, one cannot ignore the varieties of meanings and uses of "know," and the term is more like a cover term for "family resemblance" than strictly univocal.

## V

The second question is, of course, a key question for pragmatic naturalists as well as for empiricists and positivists, for it concerns the justification and defense of the scientific method, i.e., the method of induction, or, as it has been labeled by Hook, the "hypothetical-deductive method." Hook has devoted a good deal of attention to this theme in articles and books.[9] His argument has many aspects, though two rather fundamental considerations appear: first, that this principle of naturalism, i.e., the commitment to scientific method, does accord with ordinary experience up to a point, and second, that as a proposal this principle has pragmatic convenience.

Hook's first argument in defense of scientific thinking should now be clear from the above discussion. The demand for the total justification of science or reason is illegitimate, for science and reason are simply implicit in our ordinary ways of thinking and in the technological processes of reasoning already involved in practice.

Hook is maintaining, moreover, that the rules governing ordinary thinking are not culturally relative or a predilection of Western civilization—as Zen Buddhists seem to argue when they claim that the scientific method as conceptual and empirical is Western, whereas in Asian cultures there is an "intuitive" and "mystical" way of "knowing." Rather, as far as we can tell from an analysis of anthropological data, the teleonomic means-end way of knowing also applies to primitive culture. Claude Lévi-Strauss's theory of structuralism seems to support the notion of an underlying set of invariant conditions to human mentality.[10] That is, even if the primitive mind is fixated on his mystical religious tradition, this does not undermine or invalidate his commitment to technological reasoning. Rather, it complements it, and is always present as a necessary component of living. Indeed, to deny a minimal level of objective thinking would make life in any culture impossible. Thus again, we cannot deny the important uses of common sense and scientific method in certain areas of life, both for the primitive and the modern: to do so would be to fly in the face of the obvious. The question however is: How far shall we *extend* this method?

To demand a justification of first principles already deeply embedded and functioning in the "life world" or practice is to raise a spurious question. As Nelson Goodman shows[11] in regard to justification of deduction, the justification of general rules derive as much from the particular judgments in which we reject or accept deductive inferences as from an examination of the general rules themselves. Aristotle could only formalize principles of deductive inference which he saw already implicit in the judgments of ordinary men and in the skills of argumentation of the Sophists. Thus, rules and particular inferences alike are justified by being brought into agreement with each other. A rule is amended if it yields an inference we are unwilling to accept; an inference is rejected if it violates a rule we are unwilling to amend. Similar considerations apply to the hypothetico-deductive method and induction: particular hypotheses are justified if they conform to the valid canons of inductive inquiry; and the canons are valid if they accurately codify accepted inductive practices. Thus we can stop plaguing ourselves with illegitimate questions about the justification of scientific induction, and examine actual usage instead. The definition of a general rule relates to such usages and uses. This logical point is important: the justification of scientific methodology is based to a large extent upon an analysis and reflection of what we already do, the rules intrinsic to usages and uses. It is not a meta-rule simply imposed on the subject matter of our ordinary processes of inquiry.

However, since Hook has made it clear that scientific method is at the same time a normative proposal, the appeal to existing usage by itself does not suffice—especially if one wishes to justify an extension of the method to other areas. Hence, additional considerations must be brought to bear on the question of justification.

In this regard, Hook has introduced another important logical point concerning the kinds of questions which are being raised. There are no ultimate questions, he insists, only "penultimate ones," and this applies both to the justification of what we already do, the procedures we employ, and what we ought to do. To demand the justification of first principles by deriving them from still more basic first principles would require either that we reduce them to indefinable terms or undemonstrable propositions, which are ultimate, or that we commit a *petitio principi* by assuming the very principle that we wish to prove. Hence, one does not "justify" first principles; one does, however, attempt to make them seem "reasonable." Here, what Hook is saying essentially is that philosophical "justification" involves a reasoned argument wherein we try to make a case for our general position. The procedure is not unlike that employed in the legal context wherein one attempts to "prove" his case, not simply by deduction from first principles, but by a drawing together, focusing, or converging of considerations, factors, and arguments, which make his defense seem cogent.

Hook introduces a basic contextual consideration here: we never begin such reasoning *de novo* or from scratch. Discussions of justification are forced upon us by the case at hand, by life situations and concrete problems. In human experience there are no first beginnings and no final endings to the succession of moral principles. Rather, different levels of questions can be raised and appropriate responses given. The defense of the first principle of scientific naturalism, i.e., to use scientific knowledge as the ideal, is not unlike the justification given in everyday life for one set of procedures that we wish to adopt rather than another, whether in gardening, cobbling, or mechanics. And similar considerations apply to reasoning in the ethical domain and the justification of other normative principles; they are always related to the situation or context before us. Thus Hook is saying that even for those areas where we do not now use scientific methods and procedures, the kind of justification that we can give for gaining adoption is the kind of justification that appeals to the ordinary man, for it is used throughout life.

What Hook is maintaining is that empirical *consequences* constitute a central consideration: It is not by words, but by deeds or fruits, that we judge. It is how well a principle works out in practice over the long run that is the basis for our decision to continue to use it, discard it, or modify it. Thus he says, although the first principle of scientific naturalism is not necessarily true, it is plausible to the plain man when he inspects the results and effects of its use;

indeed, most human beings tend to judge ideas and ideals to some extent by their pragmatic consequences, irrespective of their philosophical persuasions. And the consequences of the scientific mode of inquiry are such that: (a) it facilitates the development of new knowledge, since its controlled use has led to steady progress; (b) its use enables us to make the knowledge we already possess more coherent; and (c) no matter what our desires, ends, or values, it enables us to fulfill them most adequately, being the most effective instrument that we have for dealing with the world.

Here is the dilemma which the pragmatist always faces when he attempts to vindicate his position, and it is the charge that Plato hurled against Protagoras: Why accept what the plain man does when he takes into account the standards of consequences or effectiveness? Now as I have pointed out, the pragmatic naturalist begins with the plain man and returns to him and to common sense to warrant his position; he does not stay there, but considers his principle a normative *proposal*. The problem again is not simply to justify existing inductive procedures, but to justify their extension where they are not now being used, and to make them a model for all knowledge and inquiry. How judge proposals, we ask? Proposals imply value judgments; does not naturalism thus presuppose a more basic value judgment, which is controlling?

The only answer that can be given here is first to admit, as Mill, Dewey, Hook, and a score of other thinkers have admitted, that there are no discoverable ultimate standards of value by which epistemological principles can be judged. The only argument in appraising key value judgments is a *comparative* argument. In other words, the pragmatic case, in the last analysis, is based upon a balanced appraisal of conflicting claims.

All other positions face a quandary similar to that hurled at the naturalist—though compounded far more so. It is unfair then to burden the naturalist with the "riddle of induction," for there is a "riddle of intuition" or a "riddle of subjectivism" or a "riddle" for any other method. The intuitionist, mystic, and subjectivist can only justify his position by assuming his method to do so, thus committing a *petitio principi*. The burden of proof rests in a sense with these alternative positions. Moreover, insofar as the intuitionist, mystic, or skeptic attempts to justify his method and employs argument and reason to do so, he is already conceding a point to the naturalist. Even to seek a justification is in a sense to presuppose "objectivity" as an ideal. What does the word "justification" mean? In a sense it is equivalent to that employed in the scientific or objectivistic mode of inquiry and in ordinary life where we demand grounds for belief. To even raise the question of justification is to suggest a solution. To say that justification is an open question is to open the arena for an objective examination of all claims to knowledge, which is precisely a key methodological criterion of methodological naturalism. The only response of the nonobjectivist is to refuse to justify his method.

The naturalist asks: Which rules of procedure in the long run appear "better" or more "effective" in gaining results? Naturalism would deny that they are merely stipulating or that their proposal is an arbitrary persuasive definition of "knowledge." If all positions involve some question-begging and are on the same ground in this regard, we may ask: Which is least self-defeating? Which accords best with the facts, with intelligibility as ordinarily understood, or enables us to satisfy our diverse desires? Naturalists have made it clear, for example, that they do not exclude on a priori grounds the reports of mystics, intuitionists, or even those of acidheads under the influence of LSD and other psychedelics; for they do not exclude by definition reference to a transcendental realm, God, or immortality. On the contrary, they examine them with care and caution. But they do insist upon some responsibility in adjudging claims made on behalf of subjectivism or transcendentalism. Naturalists leave open the question. They do not block inquiry by denying on a priori grounds, as do subjectivists and transcendentalists, that such things cannot be known by objective methods of inquiry. On the contrary, as we have seen, all the other methods at some point must presuppose the use of the objective method in addition to their own methods. In other words, the objective method is to some extent *unavoidable* if we are to live and function in the world, and everyone has to assume it up to a point; the same thing cannot be said of most other methods.

# VI

The posture that the pragmatic naturalist takes in defending the use of scientific method can be no more clearly seen than in the sciences of man. The recent developments of philosophical psychology within analytic philosophy and of humanistic psychology within phenomenology and existentialism only emphasize the distinctive position that Hook is taking. The pragmatic naturalist, with the logical positivist and the behaviorist, seems to stand rather isolated in philosophy today by insisting that all hypotheses about man be tested by the experimental method. There are those who maintain that motives and intentions which apply to "action" differ from behavior and that linguistic analysis will suffice to uncover the categories of the "logic" of action. There are those who insist that the idea of a scientific psychology is mistaken and that certain aspects of mind resist empirical or behavioristic treatment.

The pragmatic naturalist is not maintaining a blind faith in scientific methodology, nor is he arguing that the rigorous method he proposes must inevitably succeed. He is not so naïve as to believe that all human problems can be solved or all questions answered. He has, however, examined the chief arguments against the extension of science to man or the development of a complete science, and he questions them. One can imagine in the pre-Galilean days of science someone objecting to the proposal to develop a science of nature as illegitimate, arbitrary, and contrary to our traditional outlook of the world. Similarly, today the appeal to "free will," "consciousness," or a divorce between motives and causes does not seem to be decisive to the pragmatic naturalist. Yet the pragmatic naturalist will concede that whether the first principle of naturalism, i.e., the scientific method, is the most reliable approach in explaining man is still an open question, and that it can only be judged as inquiry proceeds. That it must succeed is not deductively certain. But in the light of fruitful gains that have been already registered in the natural, biological, and behavioral sciences, we have good reason to believe that they will have a range of success in the future. But how much and to what extent remains to be seen. The point is, let us see what the other proposed methods achieve, and if on balance and in comparison they remain programmatic, have bare pickings, and produce meager results, then we have a right to continue to insist upon commitment to a hard methodology. This does not necessarily involve reductionism, nor does it deny that other techniques and methods may be incorporated into the methods of the behavioral sciences—but surely not methods that eschew evidence and ignore data altogether.

# VII

The pragmatic naturalist is perhaps most vulnerable to criticism in his recommended use of scientific method in the field of ethics and politics; and it is here that his first principles have suffered most. Clearly, naturalists had oversimplified the kinds of reasoning involved in normative matters; and it was an unfortunate mistake simply to assert that a science of value or ethics was possible and that ethical judgments or valuations were verifiable in the same way as other empirical judgments. Valuational judgments are not descriptive, and they are not tested in precisely the same way as are descriptive or explanatory hypotheses in the natural or social sciences.

The mistake here is perhaps due to the fact that the term "scientific knowledge" was being overstretched by the naturalist, and there was insufficient appreciation of the fact that ethical reasoning, though similar in many important respects, is unlike other forms of scientific inquiry. Hook and Dewey, of course, were interested in pointing out the continuities of inquiry, that science itself involves value judgments, grows out of problems, is related to our interests and needs, is judged by consequences and results, and that there is an analogy between the hypotheses found in the applied and technological sciences and the value judgments that we make. They insisted that valuation judgments were amenable to empirical treatment. Factual considerations can modify our prizings and transform them into critical appraisals. With all of this said and done it was an unnecessary confusion of the issue to insist upon the application of the univocal term "science," when what was more approximately meant was that the use of "reason" in ethics and value inquiry was possible. All that the naturalist is claiming is that our judgments of evaluations and prescriptions, though not descriptive in function, can be modified in the light of a reasoned analysis of the circumstances and situations under which they arise and in which they function. Thus ethics and value inquiry could be "objective" to some extent.

As a matter of fact, most analytic philosophers in ethics (Hare, Nowell-Smith, Toulmin, etc.) now agree that there is a logic of morality, that there are good reasons for action, and that factual considerations are not irrelevant to our decisions. In this respect they are saying something very similar to what pragmatic naturalists have maintained. And Hook has continuously insisted that analytic techniques are essential to philosophy. Hook is an analytic philosopher in the sense that he wishes to use the powerful tools of analysis to resolve philosophical puzzles.

However, there is a difference between the naturalistic approach to ethics and the analytic approach, and the difference should not be minimized or overlooked. While the ordinary language school claims to find a set of rules governing moral conduct implanted in the language stock, merely awaiting elucidation and analysis by the moral philosopher, the pragmatic naturalist goes a step further. He is a revisionist, never content with the given data of moral experience or moral argument, but always willing to modify and reconstruct moral values and intellectual procedures in the light of new evidence and data that we discover in the developing sciences of man.

Notwithstanding their similarities, the distance between the pragmatic naturalist and the Wittgensteinian philosopher remains—namely, pragmatic naturalism proposes to introduce a set of valuational criteria, as seen in common sense and developed in science, and to extend them, working out and modifying their applications as the subject matter may warrant.

# VIII

The tension between a Wittgensteinian-type and a naturalistic analysis is clearly apparent in respect to religion, religious experience, and religious language. And here the pragmatic naturalist, and especially Sidney Hook, will brook no compromise. There is not, he would claim, a "logic" of religious language or a "method of knowing" which gives us "knowledge" which we cannot get in any other way. Although religious language may be moral and aesthetic in function, and is to be judged by moral and aesthetic criteria, Hook insists that it cannot claim a special kind of "truth" unattainable in any other way. And here the pragmatic naturalist has challenged the Wittgensteinian philosopher in a most telling and provocative thrust. If the proposal that we extend the method of scientific objectivity to all fields in which we claim to have knowledge is unacceptable and illegitimate, then are we not left with the acceptance and enstatement of the whole bag and baggage of religious discourse and the claims to truth which are embedded in ordinary religious language? The consequences of so arguing would be unfortunate and paradoxical; for they will legitimize that which many analytic philosophers may not wish to accept. Thus we are torn between the demands of ordinary language analysis and the demand for scientific objectivity. We must surely enter into the thickets of religious language in order to unravel its meanings and uses, and not pass judgment from without. However, if this type of approach is pushed too far, it might allow for the reintroduction of a kind of "knowledge" that ordinarily is discovered in religious language and a kind of metaphorical "truth." Some Wittgensteinians (but only some) are still attracted by the verifiability criterion of the positivist in regard to cognitive and literal descriptive truth claims. And some have argued that religious language is being "misused" when assertions are made about an alleged special "religious" knowledge or truth. The ordinary man often claims to have a religious experience and to believe in God on the basis of "common sense." The naturalist would dispute this claim and deny that he is properly using the standards of common sense, an appeal to reason, and evidence. One must not confuse what is *commonly* held in a culture on the basis of uncritical grounds with the use of common sense. Here the standards that the scientific naturalist employs against most theistic claims are the criteria of verification and logical consistency. Here I am talking of the methods judging the truth claims that are made in religion, and not simply the meaning and use of the terms employed. If the religionist is to make truth claims, he must, the naturalist insists, satisfy the standards of objectivity as defined above.

## IX

But then a proposed standard or criteria is being used. Who is to say what is a misuse of "know"? For the pragmatist it is an appropriate task of the philosopher to criticize and revise standards and methods. We are entitled to say that although the plain man claims to know certain things in terms of his religious experience and religious discourse, this claim falls down when examined in the light of the methodological criteria of scientific principles and the appropriate or inappropriate uses which they delineate.

In the last analysis, Hook's support of the first principle of naturalism is based upon a comparative method of appraisal; or as I have argued elsewhere, it involves the use of coduction.[12] The pragmatic naturalist attempts to make a case for his position. Although vindication is involved (as Herbert Feigl suggests), it is more than that. For he appeals to a variety of considerations in arguing his brief; he examines the differing claims made by alternative methodological positions; and he selects those which on balance appear to be most plausible and cogent. He does not begin with a fully developed set of first principles which he imposes, but rather in the midst of the world and the alternative positions maintained, he attempts to resolve those which seem most adequate in the light of a continuing argument.

If the first principle of naturalism is accepted, it is accepted because it appears to be the most reasonable as an instrument of our purposes of all those advocated in the present context of inquiry. This principle is not final, necessary, arbitrary, or ultimate. Undoubtedly all human proposals involve decisions and commitments; but there are various kinds of commitments that we make, and some options seem more plausible than others. Thus we need not sink into the well of indecision and skepticism, as the existentialist sometimes suggests, or opt for a leap of faith. There are some choices that appeal to a responsible man as reasonable. The pragmatic naturalist thus places his greatest measure of confidence in the reaches and uses of reason. Perhaps pragmatic naturalism is the expression of the "biased overoptimism" of a "naïve" culture and age, as has been charged. Yet it is a point of view that is not without some reasoned justification by a man who examines its grounds and attends to its consequences, both in ordinary life and in science.

# NOTES

1. Sidney Hook, "Naturalism and First Principles," in *The Quest for Being, and Other Studies in Naturalism and Humanism* (New York: St. Martin's Press, Inc., 1961), p. 173.
2. Hook, "The New Failure of Nerve," *The Quest for Being*, p. 78.
3. Hook, "Naturalism and First Principles," p. 185.
4. Ibid., p. 186.

5. Hook, "Scientific Knowledge and Philosophical 'Knowledge,' " *The Quest for Being,* p. 214.

6. See, for example, Norman Malcolm, *Knowledge and Certainty, Essays and Lectures* (Englewood Cliffs, N.J.: Prentice-Hall, 1963).

7. Hook, "Modern Knowledge and the Concept of God," *The Quest for Being,* p. 119.

8. Hook, "Scientific Knowledge and Philosophical 'Knowledge,' " p. 216.

9. See Hook's *The Quest for Being,* especially "Naturalism and First Principles," "Nature and the Human Spirit," and "Scientific Knowledge and Philosophical 'Knowledge' "; also his *Reason, Social Myths and Democracy* (New York: John Day, 1940), chap. 1.

10. Claude Lévi-Strauss, *Structural Anthropology* (New York: Basic Books, 1963).

11. Nelson Goodman, *Fact, Fiction and Forecast* (Indianapolis: Bobbs-Merrill, 1965).

12. Paul Kurtz, *Decision and the Condition of Man* (Seattle: University of Washington Press, 1965).

# 3.
# Neo-Behaviorism and the Behavioral Sciences

Naturalism is committed to the use of science in understanding both nature and man. In the twentieth century its program of inquiry has been especially influential in the development of the behavioral sciences. Even a cursory examination of the behavioral sciences as they exist today demonstrates the great energy, particularly in the United States, that is being expended in these fields. The behavioristic study of man is an ambitious enterprise and the sheer number of behavioral scientists, journals, institutes, and organizations devoted to the task is enormous.

Yet the whole behavioral science approach stands out in sharp contrast to the methods still being used to study human beings in various parts of the world, i.e., the traditional humanistic study of man. Indeed, the behaviorist approach is widely criticized by philosophers, theologians, classicists, and humanists as fundamentally

From *Pensiero e linguaggio in operazioni (Thought and Language in Operation),* Vol. I, No. 4, (Milan, Italy: Istituto Editoriale Cisalpino, 1970).

misdirected in nature and scope. One hears a great deal about the narrowness of the statistical, or experimental method *vis à vis* the need for theory, or the insufficient appreciation of an historical focus, or more recently the need for a phenomenological approach to probe the *lebenswelt,* and of the importance of linguistic analysis.

In no small measure a good deal of the criticism is based upon a misunderstanding of the nature of "behaviorism," "neo-behaviorism," and the "behavioral sciences." A dramatic revolution has occurred in the twentieth century study of man, with which it would be well for critics of the behavioral sciences to acquaint themselves. However, while the behavioral science approach holds much promise for future inquiry, it need not exclude other approaches to the study of man, particularly the phenomenological and linguistic, which may be incorporated without contradiction within its general program.

# I. BEHAVIORISM AND NEO-BEHAVIORISM

The term "behaviorism" was first used in the early part of the twentieth century within psychology. As a result, "behavioral science" is often mistakenly identified with psychology. This is unfortunate, since the behavioral program of the twentieth century has been extended to many other sciences. Moreover, "behaviorism" was first interpreted in its physicalist and hence most extreme sense; but there is now a nonreductive aspect to the behaviorist program that has a wider appeal. For these reasons it is appropriate to designate the new behaviorism which one finds in the behavioral sciences today as "neo-behaviorism."

Historically two main forms of behaviorism have developed: mechanistic and functional. Watson and Pavlov are chiefly responsible for first enunciating mechanistic behaviorism. All human or animal behavior, it was alleged, was to be accounted for in terms of physical explanations; and all psychological processes were to be correlated with observable physical changes in the organism on the micro and molar level. Introspection as a psychological method was held inadmissible. There was no need to postulate a mysterious "mind" or "subject." Thus psychology was interpreted as a natural or biological science in which only mechanistic causal explanations were admitted.

Functional behaviorism on the other hand was a weaker version of the same movement. It was originally defended by American pragmatists such as James, Dewey, and Mead, and psychologists such as E. S. Tolman and C. L. Hull. These functionalists likewise rejected a mind-body dualism and were critical of any attempt to deal with consciousness as a substantive entity. They cast suspicion on introspective psychological reports which were untested or uncorrelated with observable behavior. But unlike the mechanistic behaviorists, they did not believe that simple physicalist explanations would suffice. Rather, they said that human behavior was goal-directed or purposive, and hence that teleonomic[1] and functional explanations were useful in dealing with human behavior, and that since man was a social animal it was necessary that biological behaviorism be supplemented by social behaviorism. These latter-day behaviorists are sometimes called transactionalists because they have held that human beings transact within a biological and social environment, and that any adequate account of behavior must deal with the full field of interaction. Accordingly, behaviorists became interested in social psychology, sociology, and cultural anthropology as aspects of the transactional field.

The term "behaviorism," originally introduced within psychology, has since been extended to the other sciences which deal with man, so that today the term "behavioral science" has wider application. Indeed, the new behavioral program may now be said to apply to virtually all the sciences and specialities which deal with man; and at least thirteen such fields of investigation can be discriminated. A comprehensive study has shown that all of the older fields now have their behaviorists.[2] Moreover, a veritable breakthrough has occurred in the past two decades by the establishment of a whole set of "newer" fields, which are unashamedly behavioral and which deal with areas traditionally philosophical, such as language, meaning, and value.

Earlier behaviorism had been thought by many to provide a theory of human nature, i.e., a set of general assumptions about the nature of man. And this was probably true to some extent, for behaviorism generally had been allied to a materialistic or naturalistic conception of the universe and behaviorists have been opposed to the postulation of any "subjective consciousness," "mind," "self," or "soul" separate and distinct from the body. Behaviorism had focused on behavior and on the field of interaction, implying that transactive behavior, action, processes, or events are the basic constitutive "reality" of human beings.

Most present-day neo-behaviorists, however, would regard any such theoretical account as premature and metaphysical speculation. Neo-behaviorism, they would insist, should be interpreted primarily as introducing a set of regulative principles which recommend *how* we should go about studying human beings. The neo-behaviorists are interested in proposing prescriptive rules for investigating man, not in offering general accounts of his "essential traits," "nature," or "being." Thus neo-behaviorism is best construed as a strategy of research or a methodological program.

What does the neo-behavioral program involve? Unfortunately no precise platform has been worked out which would be acceptable to all of its proponents. What is clear is that neo-behaviorism cannot be identified simply with the Pavlovian-Watsonian program of physicalist reductionism; nor is neo-behaviorism today to be identified with any one school in psychology, such as the SR conditioned response learning theory. The restricted definition of "behaviorism," which a B. F. Skinner in psychology might employ, would hardly be acceptable to a neo-behaviorist in political science, sociology, or economics. Virtually all neo-behaviorists, including even the most extreme physicalist behaviorists of earlier days, are now willing to deal with psychological areas which were formerly considered *verboten,* such as perception, thinking, and motivation, and they recognize the importance of introspective reports as psychological data to be explained. Some of the recent advocates of neo-behaviorism are also receptive to the use of teleonomic, functional, intentional, and motive explanations. Many do not believe that a reduction of the many sciences of man to a single physical science is at this stage of research possible or even desirable.

Some philosophical critics have interpreted behaviorism as "logical behaviorism," that is, as a theory of meaning in which every statement or definition of a psychological fact is equivalent to or must be translated into some statement of a physical fact. Others have interpreted behaviorism as an operationalist theory of definition whereby all definitions admitted into behavioral science must be framed in terms of a set of operations to be performed. But these interpretations of neo-behaviorism are also far too restrictive and would exclude a great number of inquirers who would wish to be considered as participating in the neo-behavioral program. It is clear that for the neo-behaviorist only a looser theory of meaning and definition is possible. He does not insist that all sentences in behavioral science be directly stated in physicalist or operational terms, but simply that they be related to other sentences which are, thus allowing for the admission of intervening variables and hypothetical constructs. Logical behaviorism and operationalism are wedded to early versions of logical positivism and pragmatism, both of which have been superceded.

We have said what the neo-behaviorist program is not, may we say more directly what it is? What is crucial to neo-behaviorism, is simply the insistence that all hypotheses introduced in science must be *experimentally confirmable and that these verifications must be intersubjectively or publicly repeatable by the community of inquirers.*

While neo-behaviorists stress the role of experimental verification as essential to all scientific inquiry, this in no way precludes the use of mathematical models and theoretical systems, which all but the most extreme empiricists concede to be essential to any developed science. Many behavioral scientists today are reluctant to build high-level, theoretical deductive systems, which they frequently consider to smack of premature philosophical speculation or intuitive guess-work. They prefer to concentrate upon the data and upon detailed experimental observations and statistical correlations. Most take as their immediate goal the development of hypotheses of the middle range, i.e., hypotheses amenable to some theoretical generality, yet closely related to concrete empirical contexts or particular facts. Yet behavioral science, like natural and biological science, has as its eventual goal the development of a set of mutually related hypotheses of wider deductive and theoretical significance. In the last analysis, however, neo-behaviorists insist that all statements that are considered warranted must be experimentally confirmed by reference to publicly observable changes.

## II. THE BEHAVIORAL SCIENCES

The most remarkable fact about the neo-behavioristic program today is that it is shared by so many different inquirers in a variety of disciplines, each of which is considered to be a behavioral science. The traditional fields of science, which have now become in part behavioristic are familiar: anthropology, sociology, psychology, political science, economics, jurisprudence, education, and history. The newer fields which have recently developed are less well known: the communication sciences, including linguistics, cybernetics, and information theory, and the preferential sciences, such as decision making and game theory.

We are faced with the complex question of the definition of the field of each science and of its interrelations with the other sciences. The sciences of man are today dependent upon the division of labor that has evolved, largely in the university context; but this is an historical development which is in part accidental and not based upon viable reasons. The neo-behaviorist insists that the present division of inquiry is in need of fundamental reorganization. Indeed, the definitions of the separate sciences border at times on chaos. Moreover, the duplication of effort between the sciences suggests an inefficient expenditure of talent.

For example, both anthropology and sociology claim to be "integrating" sciences, but the precise differences between them are at times difficult to ascertain. The anthropologist, Ralph Linton, for example, defined his field in general terms as "the science of man," and A. L. Kroeber thought that it aims at being "a coordinating science." Yet the sociologist Stuart Dodd also claims that sociology is a general science which deals "with the general characteristics of human groups in space and time."[3] A similar problem may be raised for the definition of history. Many have defined history very loosely—thus Henri Pirenne says that the "object of the study of history is the development of human societies in space and time."[4] Henri Berr and Lucien Febvre have said, however, that "no branch of knowledge . . . has exhibited more varied modalities and answered to more contradictory conceptions than has history."[5] The definition of economics is also in trouble. For Alfred Marshall, economics is "a study of man's actions in the ordinary business of life."[6] Ludwig von Mises, however, considers it to be "a branch of the more general theory of human action."[7] While for Jacob Viner, economics "is whatever economists do." Among the newer fields of behavioral research the duplication of effort is very noticeable. Game theory is often considered part of decision making, which is interpreted as part of operations research, management science, or administration theory. And communication and information theory are frequently identified with cybernetics or systems engineering. In addition, the lines between the older and the newer sciences are not always clearly drawn. For example, both economics and political science today have incorporated game theory and decision theory as part of their inquiries.

Can any sense be made of the present proliferation of the behavioral sciences? Specialization up to a point may be convenient, but no science can be developed entirely independently of the other sciences without becoming itself an obstacle to further inquiry.

With this problem in mind it will be convenient to provide a list of the basic behavioral sciences. This list is not exhaustive.[8] It does touch on the main disciplines which can be observed in a growing area of research. The list is intended to provide, from the standpoint of the neo-behaviorist, tentative working definitions of the subject matters of the separate sciences, as well as some indication of the interrelations of these sciences with cognate sciences. The interrelationship of these behavioral sciences is a special problem, however, to which I shall return in Section III.

## The Traditional Fields

*Anthropology.* Traditionally "the comparative study of man and his works," neo-behavioristic anthropologists today investigate the biological, and especially the cultural aspects of humans from the earliest origins until the present day. Anthropology may be divided into two subfields: (a) *physical anthropology:* a study of the evolution and present biological properties of human species and the interrelation between biological variability and cultural setting, and (b) *cultural anthropology* (*ethnology* or *social anthropology*): the study of the development and function of customs and techniques, of the organization and functioning of cultures, their stability and change, similarities and differences. Anthropology is also closely related to two others: (c) *archaeology:* the study of past human cultures and the analysis of the relations between culture, environment, technology, and population size, and (d) *linguistics:* the inquiry into human languages as they relate to culture.[9] The relation of anthropology to sociology, biology, psychology, and history is especially close.

*Sociology.* Sociologists study the behavior of humans in social groups and organizations and the way these groups are structured and function. This involves a study of customs, habits, mores, social disorganization, social change, and problems of social roles and statuses. Among the closely related subfields are: (a) *social psychology:* the psychology and personality aspects of social interaction, and (b) *population and human ecology or demography:* a study of population trends and migration patterns. Sociology is closely related to anthropology, political science, history, psychology, and economics.

*Psychology.* As inquiry into both human and animal behavior, psychologists focus on the individual, though relating individual characteristics to the social and environmental context. Psychology emphasizes the complex biological functions of humans, such as perception, learning, thinking, attitudes, aptitudes, emotion, motivation. Among the important subfields of psychology are: (a) *social psychology:* a study of social groups and their effect on variables of individual behavior, (b) *developmental psychology:* the study of processes of development, especially in the child, (c) *comparative psychology:* the study of similarities and differences between animals and human beings, and (d) *psychoanalysis:* a study of unconscious processes as they influence behavior. There is considerable controversy as to whether psychoanalysis is or can be reformulated as a behavioral science. Only a very limited portion of psychoanalytic inquiry can be construed as behavioristic, and most behaviorists reject it on methodological grounds. Psychology is related to biology and physiology, anthropology, and sociology.

*Political Science.* Traditionally the investigation of political institutions and power with emphasis on the structure and functioning of governments, more recently political scientists study the processes of decision and power within a social or intellectual community. A closely related subfield is *public administration:* the structure and function of institutions and their administration, especially those publicly organized. Political science is related to economics, history, jurisprudence, psychology, and sociology.

*Economics.* Originally defined as "the science of wealth," more recently in terms of "scarcity," economists investigate how men and society choose to employ scarce productive resources to produce commodities with or without the use of money and exchange, and to distribute them for consumption. Among the areas for special study are price, business cycles, money and banking, finance, economic growth and development, labor, farm and consumer groups, and international trade. Economics is closely related to politics, jurisprudence, sociology, history, psychology, game and decision theory.

*Jurisprudence.* Traditionally a part of the philosophy of law, jurisprudence today is an inquiry into legal processes, rules, and organizations, particularly of judicial, legislative, and executive behavior. Jurisprudence is closely related to political science, history, economics, sociology, and anthropology.

*Education.* Education is especially concerned with the teaching and learning process and with social means of facilitating this, particularly in terms of the school. Education is intimately related to psychology and sociology.

*History.* Historians concentrate upon the dated sequences of particular events in the past, their correlation, description, and explanation. A special problem that arises is the difference between history and the other sciences. Many think history to be an art, or a form of literature, or so irreducibly concerned with the unique that it cannot provide descriptive or explanatory causal laws. But historians who are neo-behaviorists insist that there is a mutual relationship between history and the behavioral sciences. Historians utilize the tested hypotheses of the behavioral sciences to deal with concrete problems of the past. History is thus closely related to archaeology, anthropology, political science, economics, sociology, jurisprudence, and psychology.

## The Newer Fields

Some of the questions that the newer fields of behavioral science deal with have been investigated for centuries, yet it is only comparatively recently that efforts have been made to apply behavioral techniques. The problems of knowledge and language have traditionally been considered philosophical questions. In the past two decades a great deal of attention has been devoted by behavioral inquirers to the formulation of testable hypotheses.

## The Communication Sciences:

*Linguistics.* Linguistics historically was considered a subject for classicists, philologists, and grammarians. Today there is a small group of intensive inquirers concerned with developing descriptive linguistics. This entails an inquriry into language structures, the relationship between languages and their historical change. Linguists study the principles underlying the organization of languages, the system of sounds, and the ways in which words and sentences are formed. Linguistics has a special affinity with anthropology.

*Cybernetics.* Cybernetics is an inquiry into the regulative processes of physical, biological, and behavioral systems, with special emphasis on feedback mechanisms in nervous systems and machines. According to Norbert Wiener, the founder of cybernetics, it is concerned with "the entire field of control and communication theory, whether in the machine or in the animal."[10] Cybernetic engineers have been successful in applying electronic techniques to the creation of automatic systems. In regard to humans, the chief explanatory hypothesis that is used is the notion that the brain and central nervous system operate like these machines. Thus complex machines can be constructed which parallel human functions: they can play chess, detect and correct their errors, store and sort information, etc. The basic explanatory hypothesis introduced is that of negative feedback, i.e., the work done by a feedback mechanism, opposes the direction of the brain system and thus serves to regulate it. The brain thus operates something like a thermostat or governor on a machine. Cybernetics is closely connected to biology and physiology and provides a foundation for computer technology.

*Information Theory.* This is sometimes used synonymously with "communication theory." Information theorists inquire into the most effective ways of coding, transmitting, and receiving messages in communication systems. They are especially interested in the technology of speed, accuracy, and economic cost of transmission. They believe that quantitative and statistical measurements can be applied to communication channels and signals and that this information will be of use in explaining human knowledge. This field is a highly developed part of natural science and computer technology.

**The Preferential Sciences:**

*Game Theory.* An inquiry into human situations which are analogous to games and in which choices are made among alternative strategies by "rational" individuals in conflict or competition. There is special effort to formulate mathematical models which are supposed to explain and predict human conduct in such specialized situations. This inquiry is now being used within economics and political science.

*Decision-Making Theory.* An investigation of those aspects of human behavior in which choices are made among alternatives. Efforts are made to (a) describe and explain the decision-making process, and also (b) to develop criteria for measuring the relative importance of goals by considerations of probability, effectiveness, and value. This field is sometimes identified as Value Theory, Operations Research, Systems Engineering, and Management Science. Decision-making inquiry is related to all the sciences, but especially to psychology, economics, and political science.

## III. THE OVERLAPPING OF THE BEHAVIORAL SCIENCES

As is apparent from the above, there is so much overlapping among the behavioral sciences that one may ask: Is there one science of human behavior, of which these various fields are only parts, or are these fields necessarily separate and distinct?

The same problem had been raised during the development of the social sciences, and there are, of course, several suggestions. A nineteenth-century basis for the distinction between the social sciences was in terms of institutions. Thus it was alleged that political science is distinguished from the other sciences by the fact that it studies "the state" and "the government," whereas economics deals with "the economy," education with "the schools," and sociology with "the family," "the church," and other social institutions as they interact in society as a whole. This division, while suggestive, is nonetheless fraught with difficulty for the neo-behaviorist, who is especially disturbed about the vague concept "institution," a notion which he considers to be in some of its formulations an Hegelian abstraction incapable of precise behavioral definition. Moreover, he asks, where would this analysis leave psychology, the communication and preferential sciences, many of which do not in all of their inquiries deal with the institutional setting?

Another suggestion is that all the sciences, including the natural and biological sciences, be divided up in terms of "levels" of organization. The general system theorists are especially sympathetic with this view: the natural sciences, they claim, deal with micro-particles on the level of subatomic and atomic events, and the biological sciences with the cell and the organ. Psychology studies the individual as he functions in an environment. Each of the separate sciences treat various forms of higher-level organizations and groups: political science with governmental organizations; economics with specialized organizations that produce, market, and consume; sociology and anthropology with the interaction of these groups in society or in the culture as a whole. The communication and preferential sciences could find appropriate levels in this scheme. Information theory could view messages in terms of "information quanta," linguistics would deal with language as a cultural phenomenon, and decision making might be construed both in biological and sociological terms. Most behavioral scientists are dubious of basing the division of inquiry upon this ground, for it would seem to commit the behavioral sciences to an imprecise and unverified *a priori* metaphysical theory of emergent levels. Neo-behaviorism, on the contrary, would prefer to be neutral as far as possible in its ontological presuppositions, which it believes are not relevant to the practice of inquiry.

Some have suggested that the behavioral sciences might be distinguished empirically by the fact that they focus on different aspects of behavior: political science on the processes of decision making and the exercise of power by governmental officials; economics on producing, marketing, and consuming behavior; sociology on familial, religious, and educational processes and functions; psychology on certain highly specialized processes of the individual, such as motivation, perceiving, thinking, etc. But this division, while more attractive than the institutional or level theories, may pose similar difficulties. Individual and social behavior can *not* be easily dissected or abstracted, since the subject matter is continuous; any such division presupposes a general theory before inquiry, which may prejudice inquiry.

For the neo-behaviorists, the overriding consideration of how to divide inquiry is that of *convenience:* which strategy of research is most likely to be most fruitful in achieving the aim of explanation and prediction. All recognize that while some degree of specialization of the sciences is surely useful and necessary, in actuality any hard and fast line that may develop may do much to impede behavioral research and the lines between the sciences must be constantly redrawn. Most behaviorists would insist that the present division of inquiry is neither sacrosanct nor infallible. The great danger is that the definitions of the sciences in one age may become ossified by tradition and oppose new departures in inquiry in the future.

The basic consideration should always be: What is the best strategy for organizing cooperative research? Today the most promising organization of research energy seems to be not simply in terms of separate disciplines, but in terms of *common problems.* Thus the neo-behaviorist recognizes that the immediate imperative for him is to bring to bear the combined talents and resources of many separate sciences to the treatment of those problems which are interdisciplinary in character.

## IV.  INTERDISCIPLINARY PROBLEMS

As one examines the literature, one finds indeed that there are a number of interdisciplinary problems, which have emerged and which are common to many behavioral sciences. I can only list some of the most significant.

(1) *Study of language and communication.* The established sciences such as psychology, social and political science, and anthropology have turned their attention to the investigation of symbolic and verbal behavior. In these inquiries they have been aided by the newer sciences of communications, especially by linguistics, cybernetics, and information theory. Many areas of thinking and cognition have been explored as aspects of verbal behavior. B. F. Skinner's book, *Verbal Behavior,*[11] is typical of one such approach to traditional questions of meaning and significance. The point is that the study of language and communication is not the private province of any one science, but of many. A great number of techniques have been used, includ-

ing the use of computer technology, statistics, comparative analyses, cross-cultural inquiries, and field studies.

(2) *Personality, acculturation, socialization, learning.* Similarly, social, clinical, and experimental psychology; anthropology; psychoanalysis; biology; sociology; and education have all focused on the problem of personality development: What are the factors and characteristics involved in personality learning and development? There have been extensive inquiries of child development and animal behavior employing mathematical statistics, projective tests, comparative analysis, cross cultural and field studies.

(3) *Social structure, function, and mobility.* Sociologists have introduced the concepts of structure, function, role, and status in an effort to explain social systems. These concepts have also been used by anthropologists, social psychologists, and political scientists. Various techniques have been used such as statistical, scaling devices and comparative studies to study specific situations: the government, the school, the community, the church, the economy, the military, etc.

(4) *Small group interaction.* This area of social interaction provides a rich field for cooperative research. Social psychologists, sociologists, educational inquirers, and organization theorists have turned to such topics because of the greater facility for controlled laboratory situations and the testing of hypotheses.

(5) *The policy science, decision, preference, value.* The newer behavioral sciences are concerned with decribing how human beings make decisions and choices and in also offering guidance in policy formation, rule and prescription making. Linear programming, systems engineering, decision, organization, and game theorists have suggested that there are mathematical-logical models for predicting choices and guiding policy. They have introduced high-level probability and statistical models, and have employed computer techniques. The older social sciences have attempted to use these methods, particularly economics, political science, and sociology; and they, along with education and jurisprudence, have been called, not inappropriately by H. D. Lasswell, "the policy sciences."

(6) *Administrative and organization theory.* This is a growing area, largely under the influence of Herbert A. Simon, which deals with

organizations, their administrative structures and the way they function. Political scientists, sociologists, and economists have participated in this inquiry.

(7) *Attitudes, opinion, consumer wants.* A major advance has been achieved by the use of public opinion polls, sampling, interviewing techniques, scaling devices, models, etc. in describing and accounting for public attitudes and opinion. Political scientists, sociologists, economists, and psychologists have especially contributed to the inquiry.

(8) *Biological basis of behavior.* A veritable breakthrough has been achieved in molecular biology and in uncovering the physical-chemical basis of behavior. Thus research into DNA or RNA, the electrical stimulation of the brain, and the use of drugs to modify behavior has had great impact in psychology, psychiatry, medicine, and indeed in the study of group behavior in sociology.

The above is only a partial list of the convergence of interest among many behavioral sciences on a broad frontier of problems. But, of course, behavioral science continues to focus on problems more particular in character, such as economic growth and development, population control, demography and human ecology, juvenile delinquency, urban planning, international relations, and conflict resolution. The prospect in the behavioral sciences is that there will be greater team work and cooperative inquiry in the future. In this sense twentieth-century behavioral science is following a pattern which has already become a strong force in natural science where teams of researchers from many fields contribute to the solution of particular problems.

There have been a great number of gains in the behavioral sciences in recent decades by means of cooperative inquiry, much of which is unknown to those outside of the field. Among some of the most interesting have been: the use of Carbon 14 dating in anthropology, archaeology, and history to verify the age of artifacts and fossil remains; electrical and chemical stimulation of the brain as a means of modifying psychological and group behavior; the creating of computer machine models as clues to the functioning of the human brain; the use of statistical techniques in linguistics and anthropology for analyzing languages and rates of changes ("lexico-statistical dating"); the building of econometric and game models as indices to economic behavior; the effective statistical characterization and prediction of public opinion attitudes; and the development of teaching machines and programmed instruments in education.

# V. IS A UNITY OF THE SCIENCES POSSIBLE?

A fundamental issue often raised in the behavioral sciences is whether the remarkable convergence of interest and focus of the many different fields suggests that a single behavioral science of man is an achievable ideal. The unity of the sciences ideal has aroused the imaginative dedication of many of the best scientific minds, at least as far back as the sixteenth and seventeenth centuries. This has meant for many not only a unity of the behavioral sciences but of all the sciences, with the reduction of the behavioral sciences to the biological sciences and of these sciences to the natural sciences. This program, often called *reductionism,* has as its eventual goal a unity of language, but also, and more fundamentally, a unity of the hypotheses and laws of the sciences. Thus, for example, laws derived in biology, psychology, or sociology are alleged to be only subinstances of more general laws.

Most of those who have defended reductionism have been physicalists in that they have conceived of the basic laws and propositions of science as ultimately definable in physical terms. There have been, however, other nonphysicalist advocates of reductionism. Methodological individualists have argued that the laws of the social sciences were translatable into psychological and biological laws governing the individual. Those defending a sociological interpretation of history seem to make sociology or economics the dominant science. And organicists opt for biology.

Important advances have been made in the direction of reductionism, particularly of physicalist reductionism. For example, physics and chemistry have been closely interrelated, as have psychology and biology in many important areas. But no one would affirm that the reductionist ideal has been fully achieved as yet. Reductionism is not primarily a tested theory of the universe, so much as it is a *methodological ideal or program.* That is, like neo-behaviorism, reductionism may be construed as providing a set of prescriptive rules and recommendations that a certain line of inquiry be undertaken in the future.

There have been strong criticisms leveled against this program from a variety of fields. Organismic biologists have resisted the reduction of biology *in toto* to chemistry or physics, claiming that the principle of organization of an organic system is not explainable entirely by reference to its simpler parts. Holists have maintained that the body functions as a whole are not reducible to its components. Gestalt psychologists have insisted that the holistic interpretation of perception is essential to our understanding of it. Sociologists and anthropologists have objected to the reduction of sociocultural concepts and hypotheses to methodological individualism or to the psycho-biology of the body; for social relations or the functioning of social systems and organizations are not to be understood simply in terms of the properties of separate individuals.

What is at stake in this controversy is the relationship between the conceptual language *and* laws of the various sciences. Which is correct: the reductive model, which insists that both the language and the laws of the sciences can be reduced to one basic science, or the holistic model, which denies that this can be fully achieved?

The answer from the standpoint of the neo-behaviorist, I think, is that *both* are correct in part and in relation to different aspects of science. If one examines the present state of the behavioral sciences, perhaps only a third model, which I have labeled *coductionism,* accurately describes the present state of inquiry and seems the wisest strategy of research to pursue in the immediate future.

Thus, for many questions that arise in behavioral research, rather than insisting upon the reduction of all explanations to one, *or* upon the autonomy of separate explanations, a variety of explanations from many different sciences may be relevant, and some of these may be reducible, but not all. There is in the behavioral sciences a convergence of mutually supportive concepts and hypotheses from the separate sciences, each of which may provide some aid in explaining one aspect of a situation, yet none may have priority. For example, the problem of economic growth and development is one that concerns a number of behavioral sciences. What are the factors which contribute to the growth and development of an area or nation? Economists analyze aspects such as the amount of capital available for investment, natural resources, technology, and market potentialities. But this in itself is hardly sufficient. One must call upon the political scientist who points to the political structure, the attitude of the government toward economic development, whether it encourages expansion or not, or the policies of the various political parties contending for power. But a sociological analysis of public opinion and attitudes or of the class structure is an essential ingredient necessary to understand the growth rate. Similarly, the level of development of educational facilities or the influence of psychological and value attitudes toward economic growth rates are relevant. Hence the total situation is a function of a variety of causal conditions and each of the behavioral sciences introduces relevant factors. There may not be a single causal explanation, which is ultimate and decisive in regard to economic change. The logic of *coduction* suggests that what is needed are mutually supportive explanations from many contexts of analysis rather than a single deductive model.

Interdisciplinary work thus is essential to behavioral research. Yet I do not wish to suggest that this reference to autonomous explanations of the sciences precludes the reductive ideal. Coduction is a regulative principle of inquiry allowing a variety of explanations—but this does not mean that it is more sympathetic to holism—for it allows for the ideal of both reductionism and holism at the same time.

There are no simple rules which tell us which explanations are applicable in any single inquiry; and the criteria of relevance are situational and contextual. One can not say beforehand what to include or exclude. This is a function of the concrete problem at hand. That is why the attempt of either reductive or holistic programs to exclude the other from consideration is legislative censorship, which, I suspect, is based in some measure upon metaphysical poetry of what behavioral science must be like in terms of a preconceived notion of the universe. Only an experimental test of an explanation can determine for the behaviorist what is relevant in regard to any particular frame of reference.

As is clear from our discussion, interdisciplinary inquiry is the lifeblood of behavioral research today, but such research falls short of the call for a unity of the sciences or the disciplines which study man or of the reduction of these sciences to one science.

Yet if it is to be carried on effectively two prerequisites would seem to be necessary. First, even if one cannot as yet have a unity of the concepts and language of all the sciences, there is some need for the standardization of terminology and concepts across the behavioral sciences. If behavioral scientists are to be able to communicate effectively with each other, then one of the obstacles to this, namely, the development of isolated literatures and different conceptual foundations, must be overcome. It is usually very diffcult for one outside of a field to penetrate its jargon, yet similar problems are often faced within other behavioral sciences which have different sets of terms and concepts. Accordingly, as far as possible efforts should be made to translate cognate terms and concepts into standard usages.

Second, there is a need to concentrate upon the development of hypotheses of the middle range, as Robert K. Merton and Thomas H. Marshall have suggested. Rather than place all reliance upon a quest for high-level integrating theories, it may be useful at this stage of behavioral science to concentrate upon hypotheses which I have some theoretical generality yet have some relationship to observable and testable data.

One final problem often raised, which I wish to treat briefly, concerns the relationship of the neo-behavioristic program itself to other seemingly different approaches to the study of man. I am thinking here of the phenomenological and the linguistic-analytic programs which have been introduced within philosophy in the twentieth century and now have advocates in many of the sciences which study man. Following Husserl, the phenomenologists reject the behavioral method as inadequate for treating the *lebenswelt* and accuse it of psychologism (or sociologism), insisting that only a phenomenological account of the given can suffice. Following Wittgenstein, many (but not all) philosophical analysts believe that the key to mentality is language and that language analysis is not reducible to behavioristic methodology.

It is important to see that due in part to this challenge the neo-behavioral program has been modified: it need not exclude phenomenological reports or linguistic analyses. Indeed, present-day neo-behaviorists have come such a long way from the early strictures of behaviorism that many now *insist* that an important and indeed essential part of the data of behavioral inquiry is the phenomenological given, which cannot be ignored, and linguistic behavior, which is at the center of human behavior. To exclude either on *a priori* grounds is to impoverish and distort at their inception the sciences of man. The principle of coduction, I submit, would allow the behavioral sciences to draw important findings from both phenomenological and linguistic inquiries.

The chief point of difference with phenomenology and linguistic analysis, and it is a serious one, concerns *how to deal with* the phenomenological given and language and how to test assertions about them. The behaviorist insists that all statements about this range of data must be testable by publicly observable inquiry and that a subjective or intuitive approach to either is hardly scientific. He believes, however, that it *is* possible to develop techniques for correlating such subject matter with observable phenomena and of testing assertions about it as a form of behavior.

In Europe and other parts of the world the behavioral sciences have not reached the level of specialization and development that they have in the United States. Sociology is often related to history and psychology to philosophy and these are humanistic rather than scientific in approach. Morever, the lines between the various disciplines that study man have not been clearly drawn and the specializations are in an underdeveloped state. The behaviorist considers all of this to be seriously deficient.

The rapid specialization and development of the behavioral sciences in recent years, however, have presented a serious problem to the behavioral sciences, which the humanities at least do not face: How to draw together what has been dissevered? How to unify the language and the hypotheses of the separate disciplines? The challenge to the behavioral sciences is to become more interdisciplinary by focusing on problems of common interest and by employing a principle such as coduction which will enable them to do so. This implies that the challenge is also to draw upon the findings of phenomenology and linguistic analysis and to incorporate them into its program. If this is accomplished, it will mean an enrichment of behaviorism, but also a further modification of its original program.

# NOTES

1. A form of teleological explanation, yet devoid of traditional metaphysical overtones.

2. *A Current Appraisal of the Behavioral Sciences,* by Rollo Handy and Paul Kurtz (Behavioral Research Council, Great Barrington, Massachusetts, 1964). Revised edition by Rollo Handy and E. C. Harwood, 1973. I wish to thank the Behavioral Research Council for permission to draw

on portions of that study, especially George Lundberg, E. C. Harwood, Stuart Dodd, Alfred de Grazia, and Rollo Handy.

3. *Systematic Social Science: A Dimensional Sociology* (Beirut, Lebanon, 1947), p. 2.

4. Quoted in Berr and Febvre, "History," in *Encyclopaedia of the Social Sciences.*

5. Ibid.

6. *Principles of Economics,* Vol. 7 (New York: Macmillan, 1890), p. 1.

7. *Human Action, A Treatise on Economics* (New Haven: Yale University, 1949), p. 880.

8. There are other fields that may qualify as behavioral. For example, *Geography* studies environments as they relate to man. Moreover, some of the subfields of the traditional behavioral sciences may become separate fields. Some may also consider *General Systems Theory* to be a behavioral science, though others would exclude it since it is more theoretical than experimental.

9. Linguistics is treated separately below.

10. *Cybernetics* (New York: Wiley, 1948), p. 19.

11. New York: Appleton-Century-Crofts, 1957.

# 4.

# Coduction: A Logic of Explanation in the Behavioral and Social Sciences

I

In Shakespeare's *Othello* Desdemona is murdered by her husband, Othello. Let us imagine that some one comes in at the end of the play and asks, How did she die and why? And let us provide a possible explanation of her death in contemporary terms. A doctor, first called to the scene, provides a medical diagnosis: the immediate cause of death of Desdemona was a lack of oxygen. He appeals to a general law: whenever an antecedent condition of this kind is present, death ensues. The coroner issues his report: the cause of death was a compression and constriction of the throat due to suffocating; and he estimates the probable degree of physical force exerted in suffocating her. A detective from the homicide squad hypothesizes that Othello, found dead at Desdemona's feet probably

Originally published in the *Proceedings of the Thirteenth International Congress of Philosophy* (Mexico City, 1964).

committed the crime, and then took his own life. Questioning of Cassio and other witnesses confirm this supposition. Why did Othello stifle his wife? Investigation indicates the presence of motives of jealousy and anger fed by suspicions of infidelity. And a psychologist or psychiatrist submits that whenever general motives of this kind are present (constructed as dispositional conditions), intentional decisions of this sort frequently result. Why was Othello jealous? A social psychologist indicates that a third person within the social context, Iago, attempted to arouse Othello's suspicions. And a political scientist suggests that a struggle for political power was at stake. A sociologist, examining the situation, points to the fact that Othello, as a Moor, was a member of a minority group which was discriminated against, and that this condition might explain Iago's actions and also Othello's unfounded resentment. Last, a neurophysiologist insists that if only he had electrodes implanted in the brain, he could have detected the intensity of Othello's anger and predicted the consequent results.

In the above fictional reconstruction of Shakespeare's *Othello,* biomedical, physical, psychological, and social explanations are offered. The death of Desdemona is explained by reference to various antecedent conditions, any one of which affords some explanation of the event, yet by itself is incomplete. Taken in conjunction these conditions provide a more complete account of the event in question. Here is an illustration of what I shall call, for want of a better name, "the logic of coduction," the kind of logic of explanation that we frequently use in human affairs, in historical inquiries, and in the social and behavioral sciences. To coduce an event is to bring to bear a number of supplemental hypotheses. There may be many factors relevant, and many conditions applicable. Coduction refers to mutually reinforcing accounts of how and why an event occurs. To coduce is not to reduce to *one* explanatory principle, law, or theory, but rather to sets of correlative principles. There are many factors which will explain the above event and many levels of interpretation.

Now it might be argued, on the contrary, that each event follows in causal sequence. First, Iago provoked Othello. This stimulated changes in Othello's brain waves, built up rage, and resulted in the strangulation, the lack of oxygen, and the eventual death of Desdemona. Thus to understand an event we merely trace sequences of occurrences in serial order and reconstruct situations in historical terms. This analysis is not entirely correct; for many events are concurrent; moreover, in the sciences of human behavior particular sequences of events are explained by applying previously tested generalizations and laws. Thus statements describing an event to be explained (the *explicandum*) are subsumed under (testable) statements of general laws and statements of the initial conditions present (the *explicans*). An explanatory causal law states that whenever C is present, D occurs; and x, an instant of C, is present, therefore y, and instant of D, occurs. This hypothetical-deductive model is used whenever singular conditions or complex sets of logically related conditions ($C_1$, $C_2$, $C_3$ ... $C_n$) are found to be applicable. But the coductive model applies to those cases where there is a conjunction of mutually supportive explanations, but the sets of conditions have no apparent logically connected relationships. Hence explanatory laws drawn from many sciences may point to conjunctive antecedent conditions ($C_1$ ... $C_n$), which are disconnected conditions in the sense that they are drawn from many different universes of discourse or levels of explanation, and at present have no theoretical order or unity.

## II

Coduction applies not only to the explanation of singular events, but to classes or kinds of events. For example, economists frequently ask *why* prices on the stock markest rise (or fall) (a problem no doubt restrictcd to capitalist societies). A sample set of explanations[1] which many economists find relevant are: stock prices tend to rise whenever there are ($C_1$) prospects of increased earnings or dividends, or ($C_2$) an oversupply of funds and a limited supply of stocks available, or ($C_3$) strong inflationary pressures, so that owning common stocks is considered to be a hedge against inflation. $C_1$, $C_2$, and $C_3$, as observed regularities, together form a conjunctive statement, and the events of this kind are coduced from the conjunction of three factors, all of which tend to contribute to the rise in the stock market.

Of course, it may be argued that $C_1$, $C_2$, and $C_3$ are only sufficient conditions which are deducible from a more basic covering law: e.g., ($T_1$), investors generally tend to bid up the price of a stock whenever there is an expectation of increased profits in the form of dividends or capital appreciation, or more fundamentally, stocks generally tend to rise when investors are motivated to purchase them. Here we have $(C_4)$ a general psychological explanation of the behavior of investors in terms of a rational model. But are we to be satisfied with motive explanations? Recent behavioral inquiries have found correlations between chemical changes and psychological behavior; different portions of the brain can be related to different functions; changes in electrical brainwaves accompany changes in psychological motives. Why not deduce motive explanations from more basic biological, chemical, and/or neurological laws ($T_2$ or $C_5$)? Thus in the above situation we have various sets of possible explanations—economic, psychological, physical-chemical. But there are many more available, for the subject matter is highly complex. There are other possible economic explanations, for example, $(C_6)$ perhaps there are speculators at work manipulating the market. There may be noneconomic factors: political conditions $(C_7)$, such as the fiscal policies of the administration, sociological factors $(C_8)$, the recent status symbol of owning stocks has sent additional people scurrying into the market, and so on.

To what extent are the explanations of one science reducible to those of another? This problem has been hotly debated within the behavioral and social sciences. For example, in psychology there are the advocates of both micro and molar explanations, and in economics of micro- and macro-economics. Micro-economists (such as F. A. Hayek and L. von Mises) seek to explain changes in the whole economy by reference to the laws governing individual economic agents or individual firms (by using, for example, "marginal utility" theory). Classical models postulated rational individual decision-makers, but some critics claim that the facts indicate widespread deviation from these models, and that emotional, institutional, and other factors enter in. Macro-economists (such as J. M. Keynes) have approached economic events not by reference to individual agents or firms, but by reference to the observed relationships or cyclical fluctuations among large-scale aggregate units or statistical averages (national income, gross national product, etc.). They claim that many large-scale economic trends (for example, unemployment crises) can not be handled by reference to individuals alone. Institutional economists emphasizing the historical method would go still further. The point is that in the above illustration stock market activity involves a complex combination of individual facts taken in the aggregate over a period of time, and are to be characterized partly as such. Some economists, for example, have attempted to correlate aggregate odd-lot and short-interest purchases (as indices) inversely with the rise and fall of stock market prices.

This points to another kind of explanation that is widely used in the behavioral and social sciences: some kinds of events are described as occurring with statistical probabilities, i.e., with long-range relative frequencies. The relationship here between *explicans* and *explicandum* is inductive in character. In both the hypothetical-deductive and the probability-statistical models there is an attempt to account for a particular event or kinds of events by reference to general laws, though in the latter case the conditional statements are framed in statistical terms. What is important for our purpose is that coduction applies in this latter case as well.

At least twenty specialized sciences and disciplines[2] have recently developed to deal with various aspects of human behavior so that a plurality of descriptions and explanations are today available. Coduction at the very minimum, I submit, is an account of the logic of explanation currently being used here. The deductive-inductive models of explanation function in any particular science. But these models do not, I submit, do full justice to the kinds of approaches actually employed in those areas where explanation is not strictly or largely from covering law or probability-statistical induction in one science, or from logically integrated theories and laws in several. The relationship thus between a set of conjunctive statements ($C_1 \ldots C_n$) and a statement of an event (e) is not of strict entailment, but operates more closely related to probability-statistical explanation, though it goes beyond even this to a convergence of probable explanations. In other words, the logic of coduction describes the current situation where many scientific explanations are brought to bear on an event, and it is a logical account of the relations between various disparate explanations and sciences. This account leaves room, however, for some laws in one or more sciences being related, but not all laws in all sciences are so related.

# III

Many writers deplore the present underdeveloped state of the behavioral and social sciences. The ideal we are told is to develop a basic science (or sciences) to which all of the separate sciences can he reduced, and from which all of the separate laws can be derived. This, of course, was the goal of the classical mechanists. It was thought by many (for example, Hobbes and d'Holhach) to apply to human nature as well. There are today impressive areas in the physical and biological sciences where significant reductions have been made, giving considerable credence to reductionism as the model of scientific explanation. There have been many different versions of reductionism: it is (1) a methodological or logical analysis, (2) a prescriptive ideal, and it may imply (3) quasi-empirical or metaphysical presuppositions about the nature of the universe.

(1) Methodological or logical reductionism may assume an (a) strong, (b) moderate, or (c) weak form. (a) In its strong form it takes as its model the unified sciences, where all the subsciences $(S_1 \ldots {}_n)$ are derivable from a basic science (B). Given the comprehensive theories of the basic science, the separate laws in the other sciences are considered to be subsets, deducible or derivable from the basic theories, and having an internal order and connection. (b) In its moderate form, reductionism is an attempt to derive the laws of one or more sciences from one or more basic sciences $(B_1 \ldots {}_n)$, or at the very least, it is an attempt to apply the theories or experimental laws, confirmed in one domain of inquiry to other domains. (c) In its weak form reductionism seeks a unity of scientific language, and it attempts to correlate terms from one domain to the next, to relate them systematically, or perhaps only to standardize usage.

The chief point of methodological reductionism is that the laws or terms of the derived sciences are alleged to be logical consequences of the theoretical assumptions of the basic science or sciences. Here the laws or theoretical terms of the derived sciences are connected to the fundamental science(s), either logically or factually. In the latter case the linkage is looser than in the former, and the coordination may be solely empirical. Thus whenever an event (e) occurs, and condition $C_1$ in one science explains it, other regularities in other sciences $C_2$, $C_3$, etc., may be noted to be applicable, and to be in some sense related, perhaps by $T_1$, a broader theory. What appears to be crucial is the general theoretical structure which connects explanations across the various sciences. Thus thermodynamics was reduced to statistical mechanics in terms of a more comprehensive theory applicable to both domains.

It might be pointed out that such connecting theories have frequently been introduced within the psychological or social sciences, and that they are sometimes called one-factor theories. For example, many psychoanalytic and sociological explanations have functioned as connecting theories, to which subexplanations were allegedly related. Durkheim finds the incidence of suicide to be explained primarily as a social phenomenon; and Marx and Engels consider the "ultimate," "basic," or in each case "decisive" cause of historical change to be economic (the forces and relations of production). Unkind critics believe that these explanations are "seductive," for they elevate explanatory laws to a higher level of science. Yet such explanations may also satisfy a form of the reductionist model (aside from whether or not the above hypotheses are true); for there is an attempt to relate changes in one or more domains or sciences to the explanatory theories and laws of another science considered to be basic (B).

Clearly this is not what is typically meant by reductionism. For the reductionist generally expects that a macro-science (S) could be explained in terms of a micro-science (B); and that wholes described in (S) are reducible into the parts explained in (B). The kinds of micro-reduction defended classically have assumed two major forms: (i) *physicalism:* where the explanations of physical-chemical science are taken to be basic, and the biological and psychological sciences are reducible to them, or (ii) *methodological individualism:* where the social sciences are said to be reducible to invariant biological and psychological conditions, and according to Mill must be ". . . resolved into the laws of individual men."

What is central to methodological or logical reductionism is that it is a meta-analysis of the formal structure of explanations. This analysis, I believe, is a reliable account, as far as it goes, of *certain* kinds of explanation found in *some* sciences; but it is not a complete account of all explanations in all the sciences.

(2) Reductionism thus is more than a meta-analysis of our existing theories. For it is also a prescriptive ideal, proposal, or rule, which is designed to direct future inquiry; and its efficacy is judged

on grounds of pragmatic convenience. No one would claim, I assume, that the reductionist model has been fully realized; accordingly, reductionism, if it is anything, is a strategy of research. The notable achievements of subatomic physics, the gene theory, DNA research in biology, etc., are thought to augur well for the continued expansion of the reductionist program, even the reduction of parts of macroeconomics to micro-economics is held to be a favorable sign.

(3) Reductionism, however, has frequently implied certain presuppositions about the universe, the most common of which has been metaphysical materialism. The classical materialists took the kinetic principle, matter in motion, as the primary constituent of the universe, and more recently reductionists have suggested that mass, energy, and the micro-particles of physics and chemistry are fundamental. All "wholes" are decomposable into the sums of their parts. Scientific reductionists are dubious of metaphysical conjectures, yet quasi-empirical assumptions *may* be lurking in the background of some of their protests; and their insistence that *only* micro-reductions will suffice may he based upon a special conception of "reality."

If this is the case, then methodological individualism contradicts some important features of physicalist reductionism. Indeed, methodological individualism seems to wreck havoc with extreme physicalism's (2) program of research, and its (3) implied micro-theory of "reality." The methodological individualist recognizes the complexity of social events and the practical difficulty of reducing his psychological explanations to lower-level physical-chemical concepts and laws. For example, the stock market cannot very well be explained in terms of the present laws of physics and chemistry. One would not even know where to begin. The standard of pragmatic convenience suggests that it is not necessary to demand a purist reduction to elementary particles in order to explain or predict changes in economic phenomena. The physicalist reductionists insist that this is only a half-way house, and that someday we will be able to advance to the most elementary level. But this, it should be patently clear, is conjecture. Is it grounded in metaphysical anticipation?

The methodological individualist may not be without his own metaphysical presuppositions. He may tend to be a nominalist, claiming that individuals, not universals are "real"—or at the very least he considers talk about "institutions," "groups," or "classes" to be reified nonsense. Nonetheless, the methodological individualist is in closer touch with his subject matter (though his critics might say, not close *enough*) than are his erstwhile physicalist bedfellows, who are about as far removed from social phenomena as one can get.

# IV

Now allied against both the physicalist and methodological individualist is the holist, who maintains the thesis that there are autonomous levels, which are not reducible to lower levels of explanation and analysis. His position is shared in part by functionalists, phenomenologists, and even linguistic analysts.

Holism likewise has three versions: (1) It is a methodological or logical thesis based on an analysis of special kinds of explanations; for example, in studies of perception, the use of molar and motive explanations in psychology, homeostatic and teleological explanations in biology, functionalism in anthropology and sociology, and linguistic and semantic studies. The holist claims that each science introduces theoretical terms and laws appropriate to the level of phenomena under observation, and that some, but not all, are derivable from more basic sciences. The holist claims, moreover, that the whole may influence and be greater than the sum of its parts, and that new principles of organization must be developed appropriate to the higher qualitative level. Here then the terms, concepts, and laws of one science are taken as independent, logically and empirically, from those of another.

(2) Holism is not merely an analysis of certain kinds of explanation, it may also be regarded as a prescriptive ideal, which is designed to direct the strategy of inquiry, particularly in the human domain. Do not worry about physicalist or reductive explanations, or a unified theory, say the holists, but try to see how the materials under investigation fit together and function in their own ways. Holism is especially taken seriously in philosophical studies of language. Although a behaviorist such as B. F. Skinner deals with verbal behavior, he does not give an account of the internal relationships of meaning which symbols, words, and sentences sustain. In other words, logic and epistemology are not reducible to psychology—a form of psychologism. Many holists take seriously the claim of Sir Charles Sherrington that although we can trace the paths and routes that

an electrical impulse takes in the nervous system and observe some of its effects in the brain, we are no closer today to understanding *how* it becomes a percept or idea, or functions as "mind." Not all inquirers accept the idea of "wholes," but they do accept the idea that there are strata of analysis.

(3) It is thought possible by some to accept a modified form of the holist methodological program (phenomenologists and linguistic analysts would fit into this category), but to reject metaphysical holism. Many holists, however, do express quasi-empirical or metaphysical views, and presuppose emergent evolution and a theory of levels. Some even extend the level theory into the physical domain, claiming a gradation of levels in nature; micro-particles, molecules, cells, organs, persons, social groups, cultures, etc. Some holists are sympathetic to a creative, indeterminate, and pluralist universe.

Reductionists have criticized holism on three grounds. First, they claim that methodological or logical holism is not an adequate account of the logic of scientific explanation. And they are dubious of the "special" character attributed to holistic, teleological, and functional explanations.[3] Many areas which the holist thought were irreducible *have* been explained on the micro-level—witness the breakthroughs in micro-biology, which holists (Woodger, E. S. Russell, etc.) only thirty years ago had diagnosed as not feasible, or the startling experiments in the neurological and chemical control of behavior. What right have we to think that the erroneous limiting appraisals of the past will be any more valid in the future? Second, reductionists attack holism's prescriptive program, maintaining that it is premature to reject the reductionist ideal, and reiterating its fruitfulness as a working hypothesis.[4] Third, and most drastically, reductionists attack holistic metaphysics as unverified conjecture. To say that something is an "emergent" perhaps may only be a confession of our ignorance, or the inability of our present laws to predict—not an inherent fact of nature.

In rejoinder the holist maintains: First, that reductionism is not an accurate account of all scientific explanations; it is based largely on natural science (even here there may be levels of explanation) and it does not take sufficiently into account the data of the biological and social sciences. Second, holists believe reductionism to be a narrowly conceived prescriptive program, which if pushed too far may inhibit significant scientific explanations already useful in the biological and behavioral sciences. Methodological individualism shows the inconvenience of excessive reductionism and implicitly recognizes that there are levels of analysis—the question is not *whether* there are levels, but *which* ones should we focus upon. Third, professions of metaphysical purity by reductionists all too often veil undefined and unverified metaphysical assumptions—materialistic, monistic, and deterministic—which ignore the data from the life and human sciences: whereas holism seems a more accurate character-ization of what we know and do not know about the universe. The reductionist accuses the holist of stifling research and engaging in metaphysical speculation, and the holist counter-charges the reduc-tionist with normative faith, unconscious metaphysics, and refusal to examine the actual data under study.

Both reductionism and holism provide partial methodological analyses, their prescriptive ideals are disputes about how best to con-duct future research, and their metaphysical conjectures, when pres-ent, extrapolate beyond the present data of the sciences.

## V

Now there is, I submit, some merit to both sides of the argument; and coductionism can accommodate the double claim. First, as we have seen, coduction is a logical and methodological analysis based upon our current explanations in the social and behavioral sciences.[5] It is grounded on the descriptive observation that we have many theories, laws, and generalizations in the behavioral and social sci-ence, some of which are internally related, but many of which are not, and that we usually believe that a full recount of an event or class of events should draw from many different levels of explana-tion, even though we do not always know how to connect them.

Second, coduction is also a prescriptive rule, incorporating the best of the reductionist and holist programs, allowing for the con-tinuing search for micro-explanations, yet also admitting the feasi-bility of molar explanations. Coduction thus does not deny that we may be able to find comprehensive theories in a basic science, nor even that connecting theories on higher levels might not be attain-able, but it does not prejudge either directive on *a priori* grounds. I say this when I suspect that the most daring advances in scientific research in the near future will probably be developed on the micro-level, and that this kind of research must be encouraged. But I do not know that we can say beforehand that *only* this line of inquiry should be pursued. The puzzling character of both reductionism and holism is the tendency of each to legislate for the total universe.

Within philosophy today one of the major points of contention is between behavioral, phenomenological, and linguistic approaches to man. If coduction makes any sense within behavioral science, then it may also apply to the current dispute in philosophical method. For example, in the area of language study, coduction allows for physicalist reduction, phenomenological description, and linguistic analysis at the same time. We understand language by seeing both its antecedent physical and behavioral conditions and its actual functions in the context of linguistic usage and discourse. This suggests that "explanation" may be far more complex than our traditional accounts allow.

Does coduction presuppose quasi-empirical assumptions about the universe? I would prefer to interpret it primarily in neutral (1) methodological and (2) prescriptive terms. I must confess, however, that I am dubious of any attempt to categorize nature in simplistic terms, such as the monistic materialist is prone to do. Even though I suspect that mass and energy are "primary" in nature, and that whatever *is* probably has a material basis, yet I hold that to explain something, it may not be sufficient to know its elementary constituents, but also the way it is organized and functions, its plurality and historicity. This, I suppose, inclines me to both a physicalist *and* level view. I do not wish to deny the *possibility* that physico-chemical science may some day be able to expand its concepts and laws so as to include higher levels (it would be brought up to the data); nor do I wish to exclude the *possibility* that we may not be able to integrate our knowledge completely because things manifest themselves on various levels (a level would not be a critical turning point or sharp dividing line but a mid-point on a scale of qualitative change). Anyone who is committed to a scientific methodology must take into account data from all the sciences (not only the physical); and critical reflection upon our diverse scientific knowledge today may suggest some evidence for a general physicalist-holist view of nature.

But I reiterate that coduction may be viewed primarily (1) as a methodological statement—as such it is a more accurate account of the *present* logical status of our explanations in the social and behavioral sciences, and (2) as a prescriptive program—which is open to the claims of both the reductionist and holist. In this sense coduction is most receptive to the spirit of scientific inquiry. If either a reductionist or holist were to insist that his thesis be construed in methodological and not quasi-empirical terms, then I would reply that the merits of either claim remain an open question and are dependent upon success in future research, and that coduction makes this point explicit.

## NOTES

1. I am not here interested in the merits of any of these hypotheses.

2. Psychology, sociology, anthropology, political science, economics, history, jurisprudence, linguistics, archaeology, psychoanalysis, education, demography, communication theory, management science, systems engineering, operations research, decision making, game theory, semantics, general systems theory, cybernetics.

3. See Ernest Nagel, *The Structure of Science: Problems in the Logic of Scientific Explanation* (New York: Harcourt Brace & World, 1961).

4. Thus two defenders of reductionism claim: "The emergent theory of levels . . . encourages an attitude of resignation which is stifling for scientific research. No doubt it is this characteristic, together with its theoretical sterility, which accounts for its rejection." Carl C. Hempel and P. Oppenheim, "The Logic of Explanation," *Philosophy of Science,* 15 (1948). And again: ". . . Can unity science be attained? . . . We believe that this hypothesis is *credible;* and we shall attempt to support this . . . by providing empirical, methodological, and pragmatic reasons in its support." P. Oppenheim, and H. Putnam, "Unity of Science as a Working Hypothesis," *Minnesota Studies in the Philosophy of Science,* Vol. II, *Concepts, Theories and the Mind-Body Problem,* ed. H. Feigl, M. Scriven, & G. Maxwell, (Minneapolis: University of Minnesota Press, 1958), p, 8.

5. Whether or not coduction also applies in the physical sciences is not at issue here, although it *may.*

# 5.

# Meta-Metaphysics, the Categories, and Naturalism

John Herman Randall, Jr., was one of the leading naturalistic historians of philosophy that America has produced. Randall's interest in metaphysics was a constant theme of his philosophical work; and it is an aspect of his position that distinguishes him from the age. For at a time when metaphysical inquiry had been in eclipse, Randall had pursued a basically metaphysical interest in philosophy. As a former student of Randall, stimulated by his bold and provocative lectures, I am in a quandary similar to that faced by Aristotle when he felt called upon to analyze the theory of the Forms of his teacher. Aristotle noted that the Forms had been introduced by his friends, but he asked whether his devotion should be to truth or to his friends—and he concluded that, while both are dear, piety required that truth should be honored above his friends. I take it

From *Naturalism and Historical Understanding: Essays on the Philosophy of John Herman Randall, Jr.,* edited by John P. Anton (Albany, N.Y.: State University of New York Press, 1967). Reprinted by permission of the publisher.

that Professor Randall would want me to make the same choice and that he would prefer that I submit his metaphysics to detailed critical analysis rather than polite compliment. It is incumbent on naturalists interested in metaphysics to conduct their inquiries with caution. Although I am impressed by the sweep of Randall's philosophical net, I am concerned with its lack of precision on key points, which I think are in need of clarification by someone sympathetic to his general naturalistic approach. Moreover, I am troubled by what I detect to be a modest deviation from an empirical and scientific naturalism.

# I. RANDALL'S META-METAPHYSICS

In an early paper[1] and again in *Nature and Historical Experience,*[2] Randall provides an account of the nature of metaphysics, as he views it. Metaphysical inquiry has been in disrepute in modern thought; and Randall agrees that certain kinds of metaphysics in the Western tradition deserve their bad reputations. Thus, he argued quite effectively that the quest for "Being" as "Totality" or as a "Whole," or the attempt by metaphysicians to provide an overall unification of knowledge, is mistaken. Empirical thinkers have judged these claims premature, presumptuous, and to have employed mythical means to achieve supposed unities. Moreover, he also shows that the search for "True Being" or "Reality" as distinct from "Appearances" is illegitimate, for nature is irreducibly plural and the so-called theories of "Reality" are generally masks for underlying moral biases in terms of which metaphysicians seek to exclude parts of nature as "unreal." Everything which can be encountered is in some sense real, says Randall, and to denigrate or exclude part of the world is to impose one's value judgments upon what one finds.

There is another conception of metaphysics, the Aristotelian, which Randall does mean to defend as meaningful and legitimate. Indeed, he believes that metaphysics, as the "science of existence," is one science among many, distinguished not by its methods but by its own specific subject matter. According to Randall, the goal of Aristotle's metaphysics is to analyze "the 'generic traits' manifested by existences of any kind, the distinctions . . . in any universe of discourse drawn from existence" or exhibited in any "existential subject-matter."[3] And

Randall maintains that present-day empirical naturalists concur in this inquiry. Such a metaphysics, for Randall, is "empirical" because the "primacy of the subject matter" is its basic principle, and the beginning of any "sound" metaphysical inquiry is the world "as initially encountered." However, this empirical inquiry is not to be merely identified with the findings of the sciences, as so many other contemporary empirical naturalists have attempted to do. Metaphysics is, for Randall, as we shall see, much broader in scope.

Metaphysics, says Randall, is also "analytic"; though his use of the term "analytic" is specialized and distinct from the prevailing view, which considers analyses to be of terms, concepts, propositions, their meanings and logic, and not of things in the world, where descriptive or synthetic statements more appropriately apply. Metaphysical inquiry, for Randall, is "analytic of natural existence" in that "it lays bare those generic traits and distinctions which terms can formulate."[4] It is "analytic" in the "further sense that it seeks to disclose the traits of existence and to trace their implications."[5] According to Randall, although metaphysical reflection of the world as intellectually experienced begins with existence formulated and expressed in language and discourse, it soon leads beyond this to the world as directly or immediately experienced. The metaphysical analysis of any specific subject matter is for Randall the "critical analysis of the distinctive traits of that subject matter, of the intellectual instruments, the concepts and distinctions for dealing with it and of its implications for the nature of experience."[6]

Many philosophers today might agree with Randall's critique of those abstract metaphysical systems which seek "Reality" or the "Whole" of existence. They also might agree that a limited kind of metaphysics is possible. Randall's metaphysics, however, does not appear to be "empirical" or "analytic" in the usual sense of those terms; it seems to go beyond what most other twentieth-century descriptive metaphysicians are willing to do.

For example, Randall maintains that his "empirical" and "analytic" metaphysics inquires into science and language, their methods, concepts, and implications; but he claims that it also includes "an analysis of other types of human experience besides those primarily cognitive."[7] Without "the religious dimension of experience" accounted for, says Randall, metaphysics is incomplete and hardly "imaginative and comprehensive." Moreover, metaphysics for him must include an account of art, morality, and other basic types of human activity, which are all responses "to the generic traits of existence." Such responses, he maintains, "have metaphysical implications for the nature of the world that generates and sustains them."[8] Each, according to Randall, can be analyzed in itself, and can be seen "as revealing the traits of existence that call it forth."[9] Philosophical theories of religion, art, and morality thus lead to our "seeing" them in their contexts. These "theories" enable metaphysics "to serve" as "a method or instrument of criticism and clarification."[10] But they also provide a form of "intelligibility" and "understanding." Thus, although metaphysics has a critical function—it is a "critique of abstractions"—it also has a theoretical function, for it enables us to see things in their widest range of relationships, and as such seems to provide a form of "synoptic vision."

Randall also seems to share the view, widely held today, that metaphysical analysis entails the introduction of "categories," at least this is one interpretation that Randall lends himself to. Thus Randall is interested in presenting a list of "ontological" categories or "predicates," which he calls different "ways of being" or "ways of functioning." These categories, he says, do not denote different kinds of things, but rather, "different ways in which the same thing (or factor) can function."[11] " 'To be' anything means to function, and hence to be, in one of these . . . ways."[12] Thus it is the task of metaphysics to provide a set of highly general intellectual concepts that apply to *any* existential subject matter, thing, or factor. Although the quest for "categories" is not the whole of Randall's metaphysics, nonetheless it seems in some way to be an important part of it—as it was in Aristotle, which Randall draws upon so heavily. And it is that aspect of his metaphysics which is perhaps most open to criticism, for Randall does not provide us with a detailed account of what he conceives the categories to be.*

---

*In a letter received from Professor Randall in response to this paper, after it was in press, he replied that he completely rejects the notion of "categories" and that any analysis which attributes such a theory to him is mistaken (though he has not written up this part of his thought as yet.) Inasmuch as this paper is based upon Randall's published writings, and since the concept "categories," or something similar to it, has brooked large in the literature on metaphysics and the metaphysics of naturalism, I have decided to publish this chapter substantially in its original form, in the hope that it may help to clarify the concept "categories." If one examines Randall's writings, one can find quotations which support the claim that he has a theory of "categories." Thus he writes:

# II. WHAT ARE THE CATEGORIES?

There have been many lists of categories in the history of thought. Most frequently these have been based on an interpretation of the sciences of the day. For Aristotle the categories presented both a logical and ontological distinction about the nature of existence and of our manner of thinking about it. The categories were predicates, one or other of which must be affirmed of any subject, if we inquire as to what it is in itself. These state the mode of essential being of any subject that exists. For Aristotle, the ultimate subject of predication or primary existence was substance and the other categories ("quantity," "quality," "relation," "place," "time," "position," "state," "action," or "affection") were secondary and predicables of this. The important point was that there was nothing which was not either a substance or some other category, and that the categories cannot be further reduced. It is important to see, however, that Aristotle's categories were not definitory of the whole of Aristotle's metaphysics, for metaphysics involved a quest for the first principles and causes of being, and Aristotle introduced many other important concepts: the four causes, matter and form, potentiality, and actuality. Moreover, to the list of categories he later added five other key predicables: *genus, species, differentia, proprium, accidens.*

Kant adapted Aristotle's doctrine of the categories to his own

---

Now since these five "ways" are five different ways in which factors can be *said* to function, or *said* to be, they might be called five "predicables" or five "categories." . . . In terms of the functional realism of the present analysis, there would be no objection to calling them "categories," since that position implies that ontologically, they are ways of functioning in Substance before they are formulated as ways of stating: they are definitely ontological or metaphysical categories. (*Nature and Historical Experience,* p. 177)

This analysis has so far been led to distinguish five fundamental ways in which factors can function in Substance, or the Situation. . . . Since these are five ways in which factors can be *said* to function, or *said* to be, they might be called five "predicables" or categories. But since the ways of functioning are prior to the ways of stating them, they are ontological categories. (Ibid., p. 271)

In any case, Professor Randall may have decided not to employ the term because it is misleading and confusing; nevertheless, he talks of "ways of functioning," "ways of being," or "traits of existence"—and I believe that much of my criticism would continue to apply to those concepts no matter how they are designated.

use in the *Critique*. He was not interested in "the metaphysics of being," but in "the metaphysics of experience." He asked, what are the modes of synthesis on the part of the mind through which objects are apprehended and known? The categories, he claimed, were *a priori* and presupposed in all thinking. Kant's twelve categories were deduced from a study of logic, and were based upon a fourfold structure: "quality," "quantity," "relation," and "modality." The point was that the categories denominated the conceptual characteristics which *any* object must possess to be thought, much the same as the forms of intuition, space and time, denominated the *a priori* and necessary characteristics which any object must possess to be experienced.

P. F. Strawson, in his influential work, *Individuals: An Essay in Descriptive Metaphysics,* has also provided a categorial scheme.[13] "Descriptive metaphysics" for Strawson is supposed "to describe the actual structure of our thought about the world" and "to lay bare the most general features of our conceptual structure."[14] And Strawson focuses on "particulars," "material bodies," and "persons." However, his analysis is based more upon ordinary language than upon contemporary science, and it is distinguished from what he calls "revisionary metaphysics" in that it simply describes our concepts embedded in language, and does not propose a radically new way of looking at the world.

There is obviously a confusion in the literature on metaphysics between different senses of "category." It has been used as a synonym for "predicable," "trait," "presupposition," "assumption," "invariant condition," "basic reality," "methodological principle," "first principle," "rule," etc. Some writers, for example, have interpreted materialism as providing a set of categories: "matter in motion," "mass," and "energy" are said to be fundamental in nature. But this is an extended conception of categories, and according to Randall's view, it presents a reductive account of basic "reality" rather than a categorial metaphysics. Whitehead's organismic metaphysics may seem to provide another list of categories. But this approach for Randall is a speculative metaphysical account of the whole of reality rather than a limited statement of key categories.

For a descriptive and categorial metaphysics not concerned with the "reality" or "totality" of being, at least six different interpretations of "category" seem to emerge.

1. In the "metaphysics of being," (a) a "category" may be said to be that which applies to *any* object or subject matter that exists. This is the Aristotelian notion, and it is apparently what Randall means when he says that metaphysics is an inquiry into the characteristics that appear in every existential field of inquiry and in existences of any kind. These categories appear to be "universal" in the sense that they state the characteristics that *every* thing in the world which allegedly *is* possesses. This conception of metaphysical category is open to criticism by empirical metaphysicians, who wish to focus their inquiry on observable data, for universal assertions apply to analytic, not descriptive sentences. (b) Thus the term "category" has also been used to refer to "generic trait." Such categories are not universal assertions, but only probabilistic generalizations about some of the properties and characteristics that nature seems to manifest. They do not apply to any and everything, but only to many or most things, and they are drawn primarily from an interpretation of the data of the sciences.

2. In the "metaphysics of experience," (c) a "category" may refer to the underlying presuppositions of experience and knowledge, such as the Kantian categories of the understanding and the forms of intuition. This interpretation again has been questioned by empiricists, who are dubious of absolute presuppositions that are said to apply to *all* experience and knowledge. (d) Empirical metaphysicians have transposed this inquiry into an inquiry into the categories of "transaction," i.e., an account of the generic (though not universal) characteristics and traits of human interaction as revealed by the biological and social sciences. Dewey's *Experience and Nature* would seem especially to fall under this interpretation, for it is a generalized account of human transactions within nature (though Dewey was no doubt also interested in "the generic traits of nature"). (e) The term "category" may refer to the basic methodological rules and principles which govern inquiry, or in Randall's language, the "ultimate intellectual instruments," "concepts," and "distinctions" for dealing with nature. Such an inquiry is an inquiry into the "logic of inquiry" and the basic criteria found to be most effective in empirical investigations in science and practical experience. (f) A "category" may refer to the key concepts uncovered in the "logical geography" of a language system, i.e., the key rules governing the uses of language. This apparently expresses Strawson's conception of de-

scriptive metaphysics. It is similar to Kant's quest for presuppositions, but it is unlike Kant's, in that it is not a metaphysics of Mind or mental forms but of linguistic rules underlying usage.

In my judgment the interpretation of "category" as 1 (a) predicables of any object, and 2 (c) *a priori* presuppositions of experience, are most open to criticism, especially if these are construed in universal terms as applicable to *any* or *all* objects. For a descriptive metaphysics, only categories in sense 1 (b) generic traits of nature, and 2 (d) generic traits of human transactions are meaningful. "Category" as (e) methodological rules, is an extended sense of "category," and perhaps the term "metaphysical" does not really apply here. 1 (b) and 2 (d) can only be based upon a close reading of the conceptual framework and conclusions of the sciences, and 2 (e), where investigated, upon the methods of the sciences. 2 (f) the analysis of fundamental linguistic rules, is an important inquiry which is based upon a careful analysis of the rules of use, primarily of our natural languages. I do not see how an examination of the concepts employed in ordinary language (Indo-European primarily) can be divorced entirely from an examination of those used in the sciences. A fuller analysis of Strawson's metaphysics, however, is an appropriate topic for another time.

Now Randall's conception, of category seems to involve 1 (a), (b), 2 (d), and (e). He appears critical of 2 (c), the Kantian approach, and 2 (f) of ordinary language unrelated to an ontological or instrumentalist framework. Randall however talks continuously of the metaphysics of experience in generic or universalistic terms, and he has a theory of language, so that although (c) and (f) are called into question by him, they are not necessarily excluded from his inquiry.

## III. THE CATEGORIES OF RANDALL

I submit that aspects of Randall's meta-metaphysics and his categorial scheme as outlined above can be questioned, and on the following grounds: First, because it moves back and forth between, and identifies or equates, a metaphysics of being (1) and a metaphysics of experience (2), without recognizing the differences between them. Second, because it does not properly distinguish the different conceptions of the categories, and in particular blurs category 1 (a) and 2 (d). Third, because it does not actually employ the methods or conclusions of scientific observation and generalization in its account of the categories.

Randall's metaphysical position is in accord with the classical Aristotelian quest for the basic categories applicable to any subject matter 1 (a). Like Aristotle, Randall begins with "Substance" as "primary existence." However, he introduces an entirely new list of five categories or predicables: (i) "operations," (ii) "powers," (iii) "ways of operating," (iv) "kinds of powers" and (v) "connectives."

"Substance" is first interpreted by Randall in (1) the Aristotelian language of being to mean (a) "the operation of powers" found in any existential subject matter. But Randall then extends the classical conception of "Substance" to (2) the language of experience. For although Substance refers to "the facts encountered," "the field inquired into," "the forces worked with," "the material manipulated,"[15] in the last analysis it applies to "the context of interaction" 2 (d). Randall finds that "Aristotle's analysis of Substance as the operation of powers, and Dewey's analysis of the situation, mutually illuminate each other."[16] It is Randall's extension of the concept "Substance" to Dewey's transactional situation, however, that is at once the most distinctive and yet most puzzling aspect of Randall's entire approach.

Randall refers to his theory as a kind of "functional realism," and he also says that it is a "behavioristic," "operational," and "contextual" view of being. But it is here that the most profound difficulty of Randall's metaphysics arises. His transition from a metaphysics of being (1) to a metaphysics of experience (2) has him talking in two ways. He says that "Substance is encountered as 'activities' or 'operations' taking place in various determinate ways—as acting and interacting with us and with other activities, as co-operating with us and each other, as doing things to us, as something to which we do things in return."[17] But it is not clear if he is interpreting Substance *entirely* as a human transaction within a context (in the language of experience), or if Substance applies to "real things," in Aristotle's sense, independent and in their own terms (in the language of being).

Randall distinguishes Substance from Structure. The latter refers to "form," or that which linguistic or reflective experience formulates in the situation at the end of a process of inquiry. Structure is not apart from Substance, but within it. Substance includes both reflection, as the introduction of terms and distinctions in science, and experience, as a transactive cooperation of an agent in nature. Randall is no doubt intent on showing that metaphysics should be concerned, not merely with language or the world of intellectual formulations and discourse, but with the world as immediately encountered and directly experienced. He is saying that our contact with the world is active and dynamic, not merely passive. In this regard Randall's philosophical outlook is consonant with a theme pervading much of twentieth-century thought.

But Randall on the other hand claims that his is an *ontological* account of nature, not merely an account of human transaction. He states that his behavioristic and operational way of formulating the nature of primary existence is ontological, that "it applies to the behavior and operation of whatever is encountered, and not to human behavior and operations alone"[18]; and that Substance is encountered and known "as a complex of interacting and cooperating processes, each exhibiting its own determinate ways of cooperating, or Structure."[19] He illustrates the realistic and ontological foundations of his theory when he asks: "What is motion? What is electricity? What is light? What is energy?" And he answers that "the statement is always a formulation of how it 'works,' acts, cooperates, or behaves."[20]

But what does it mean to say that motion, electricity, light, or energy "behave," "work," "act," or "cooperate," or are "the operation of putting to work" of their powers, or the actualization of their potentialities? Or what does Randall mean when he says, "In an isolated system, like the planets, we can predict with complete success: we know exactly how all the masses will cooperate."[21] One might reply that organisms can be said to "behave" and human beings to "cooperate," *not* natural objects.

The point is that Randall, like F. J. E. Woodbridge, is committed to a form of "natural teleology." If we examine what Randall has written in his book on Aristotle, concerning the relevance of Aristotelianism to contemporary science, we find Randall talking as if contemporary science has rediscovered Aristotle and virtually reinstated his teleology over the errors of Newtonianism:

> In the twentieth century, the physicists themselves found their billiard balls, the Newtonian mass-particles following the simple laws of motion

of molar masses, dissolving into complex functional systems of radiant energy. They discovered that the subject matter of physics itself must be treated in functional and contextual terms, in terms of concepts appropriate to "the field." And what this means is that in his basic concepts the physicist himself must think like the biologist. . . . Today, the concepts of Aristotle's physics, those notions involved in his analysis of process, have been driving those of Newton out of our theory. . . . Far from being obviously "wrong," it seems today far truer and sounder than the basic, concepts of Newton. . . . This holds true of many of his analyses: his doctrine of natural teleology (etc.) . . .[22]

But Randall surely overstates the case. Although there has been a revolution in twentieth-century physics and Newtonian concepts have been modified in important ways, I do not see how this leaves room for the reintroduction of Aristotle's physics or of his teleology, however illuminating the study of Aristotle may be.

Randall also seems to overstate the case for teleology in modern biology. Although holistic and functional explanations are employed in the biological sciences, they are not sufficient in themselves, but are only among many kinds of explanatory devices used by modern biologists. Thus I think that Randall perhaps overemphasizes their use when he says: "Functional and teleological concepts are just the notions that modern biologists, no matter how 'mechanistic' their explanatory theory, actually have to employ in describing the subject matter they are attempting to explain."[23] Or again, it is very hard to claim that modern theories of evolution involve teleological assumptions when the exact opposite seems to be the case:

It is to be noted that for Aristotle the world is not a process of processes, it is not an "evolution." Aristotle is not thoroughgoing enough, he does not exhibit enough "natural teleology" in his conception of the world, to satisfy our own present-day evolutionary thinking. Far from being too much of a teleologist, to a post-Darwinian Aristotle does not seem to have been enough of a teleologist.[24]

Randall thus seems to approve of Aristotle's reading of functional and teleological means-ends relations into nature; and he seems to accept without dissent Aristotle's analogy which I find dubious, that nature behaves, like art, and that in both, means-ends relations can be found:

The teleology found in processes that take place by art is not radically different from the teleological order found in processes that take place by nature. There is no gulf between natural processes and processes of human production, but rather a continuity. Art is actually a cardinal illustration of natural processes. . . .[25]

Randall's "natural teleology" raises a special problem in regard to value, and whether it, too, can be read into nature. He writes that:

Substance . . . is shot through with "directions," "ends," "powers now coming into operation," "vectors" . . . (and) exhibits a great variety of functional and teleological structures, of relations . . . between power and their operatings . . . just because it is literally teeming with directions and ends, because it exhibits so much natural teleology, Substance is shot through and through with "values."[26]

Now if what Randall means by this is that *human beings* in their behavior presuppose ends or purposes, and in their inquiries institute operations and evaluate hypotheses in terms of them, I would have little difficulty in understanding what he is saying. Under this interpretation, Randall would simply be an instrumentalist in science, and his teleological concepts would apply to *man* and the goals he introduces in the course of inquiry, and not to nature independently. Randall's metaphysics could then be construed as providing an ontological basis for pragmatism. (Though I might add that such an interpretation of science as behavioral and operational is too general. While Dewey's instrumental philosophy of science does account for much experimental inquiry, it is hardly adequate for mathematical or theoretical physics.) However, the key point is that although the purposes of an inquirer are involved in any context of inquiry (second order) these purposes surely must be distinguished from the data under study (first order), and these purposes are *not* simply identifiable with the data. To say that Substance is "shot through and through with values" only confuses matters, for it is hard to see how values apply to interactions which are not human.

If Randall's metaphysics is to be construed solely as a metaphysics of human transactions, 2 (d), then in a sense it is primarily a theory of human behavior and not of nature. That human transactions are in and *of* nature, and not merely subjective, that they involve objects and factors in the environment, and that human beings introduce means-ends relationships and values is an important point. But if this is what Randall is saying, then why the need for the language of Substance or of being? It is true that man is part of nature; but it only clouds the issue by talking in the language of being and interpreting the categories as an account of *any* subject matter, 1 (a), or even as an account of the generic traits of nature, 1 (b).

Randall's distinction between Substance as primary existence and the other five categories likewise presents some difficulties. Randall does not seem to talk, as far as I can determine, of Substance as a "category." Yet it is a key, and highly general, concept, and it may function, as a "categorial type" in that it distinguishes common features of the world as experienced and known. Thus Randall should have at least six categories, not five. But what of his other five categories?

*(1)* "Operations," according to Randall, "are what we encounter directly in Substance or the Situation."[27] But in regard to the language of being or nature such a notion is dubious. Do we, in the natural and biological sciences, encounter "operations," or rather do we not observe processes of change, a far different matter? That operations are instituted in the course of inquiry as one experiments and tests, I am not disputing, but that operations are present in the data under observation is another matter. Randall rejects the language of "events" as phenomenalistic, yet "events" or "processes" seem more neutral to me than do "operations." The term "operations" seems to apply only to the language of transaction, but even here its use is not accurate, for many kinds of human behavioral transactions occur which can not be considered as "operations." Operations seem to involve conscious purpose, but many forms of human behavior are nonconscious.

*(2)* "Powers," for Randall, refers to the factors responsible for an operation, "the factors that are operating as means and mechanisms in the process."[28] "Powers" however is a vague term. If "powers" apply to the language of being, then they may invoke a whole closet of teleological ghosts. Randall seems to overlook the discussion of counterfactuals: merely to read "powers" into nature seems to provide little by way of explanation, particularly in view of Randall's recognition that "all knowledge of those powers is derived from operatings."[29] If "powers" apply to the metaphysics of transaction, then

"dispositional properties" would perhaps raise fewer problems, i.e., under certain observed conditions certain things in interaction with men have certain observed properties.

Randall's categories (3) "ways of operating" and (4) "kinds of powers" are difficult to interpret precisely. "Ways" are defined by Randall as "functional structures, as something discriminated in concrete operations, and cooperations."[30] They refer to "how" things behave. "Operations" function as "particulars," and "ways of operating" function "universally." "Kinds" are "a different type of structure" on the generic level applicable to powers. Thus Randall implies that although the situation as encountered is particular, we do generalize; hence "ways of operating" and "kinds of powers" are introduced as ontological categories. But I fail to see why "ways" or "kinds" are not subsumable either under "powers" (i.e., "dispositional properties"), or under Randall's category (5), "connectives," which I shall touch on shortly.

Randall's categories are also interpreted by him as methodological criteria or principles of explanation, 2 (e). He distinguishes the internal or "formal structure" from the "functional structure." And he suggests that in our inquiries, both a reductive structural and a functional explanation are used. He says that the functional structure of operations and behaviors can be formulated equally as the properties of powers, and he indicates that the same structure of behaving discriminated in processes "can be expressed equally as 'ways' of operating, or as 'properties' of 'kinds' powers." Although it is the same structure, "it is that structure functioning in two quite different ways."[31] What Randall seems to be saying is this: functional explanations are necessary and useful to inquiry—but to say that is to refer to a methodological rule, not a fact of nature and least of all inanimate nature. We begin, according to him, with observed processes (functions), we read back structures (powers) as explanations of them.

Why does Randall choose this language? Because I suspect he is really intent in preserving the Aristotelian system of matter and form (the noun language), potentiality and actuality (the functional verb language), and of its teleological underpinning. But Aristotle's categories, even in the revised form that Randall gives them, and his use of teleological explanations do not provide an adequate account of present-day scientific inquiry. I restate my point: although functional explanations may have *some* use in biological and behavioral inquiries, they seem to have little relevance to inorganic or physical-chemical inquiries. Hence I believe that a list of categories so thoroughly based upon an Aristolelian foundation is today questionable.

But what is omitted from Randall's list of categories disturbs me more than what is included. *If* metaphysical analysis is supposed to uncover the chief traits of *any* subject matter, then there are surely two further categories that Randall seems to leave out. After comparing Randall's statements concerning the nature of "history" with his conception of a metaphysical category in sense 1 (a) predicable and 1 (b) generic trait of existence, one concludes that "history" certainly would qualify as a category:

> Everything in our world has *a* history, and the man who wants to understand any particular thing or field is well advised to inquire into *its* history. Everything that is, is historical in character, and has an existence that can be measured in time. And this historical aspect which any particular thing has and possesses is an essential part of what it is. . . . History is not a "thing" at all, it is not a noun, a "substance." It is rather a character, an adjective, a predicate. . . . It is rather at once a trait of all subject matters.[32]

Similarly, Randall excludes mass, energy, and physical-chemical processes from his list of basic categories; yet it is difficult to see on what basis one can do this, for physical-chemical structures seem to be present in every process in some way. Randall himself is the best source for this view:

> This "internal" or "formal" structure of the means and materials of processes—the way in which they are put together—is ultimately "physical-chemical" . . . (and is) involved in all natural processes and actions. . . . Physical-chemical behaviors . . . are invariant through a range of contexts.[33]

If physical-chemical processes are invariant in the internal structure of all things, then does this not qualify matter as a "generic trait of existence" and hence as a fundamental category? I see no sense in attempting to subsume history under "operations" (a genetic account is more than an account of an operation), or to subsume matter under "powers." Both "history" and "matter" seem to be "generic" in their own right. Moreover, one can ask upon what grounds Randall excludes from his list of categories "function," "relation," "level," "continuity," and similar concepts which seem to have a kind of "generality."

This leads me to consider the last category of Randall, which I find to be the most puzzling, (5) "connectives" or "conjunctions." Randall defines "connectives" as "factors functioning in Substance," and he includes under it not only all the linguistic signs and symbols of language but also the symbols of mathematics, logic, theology, *all* the hypotheses and theories of science, moral and legal codes, human and social ideals, and metaphysical and historical myths. Connectives, he says, are "operations functioning in Substance," organizing and unifying them. Although nature is plural, according to Randall, it is "a fundamental metaphysical fact that Nature can become unified in human vision."[34] Connectives are "functionally real," though they are "not operative or 'actual' in the absence of the participation of *human* activities."[35] There is no ultimate Substance or context for Randall: what we encounter is a particular Substance or situation; however, we do try to relate, connect, and fuse together our various experiences into unified perspectives. Nature itself is not so unified, but she lends herself to human unification. However, such unifications in the last analysis are "myths." This does not mean that they are meaningless, says Randall, for they have a definite function, they have deep roots in human demands, and they provide meaning to life. Although such connective myths are objective facts about the human condition, they make no truth claims about the universe.

My basic concern about "connectives" is similar to that which I have raised in regard to the other metaphysical categories. It is still unclear to me whether "connectives" apply both to (1) a metaphysics of being, and to (2) a metaphysics of human transaction. If it applies to (2), as would appear to be the case, then many issues can be raised. "Connectives" would hardly qualify as a category, for they are not universal factors functioning in Substance, and they are not present in any and every subject matter. They only seem to come into play when certainly highly sophisticated and cultural human interests are operating, and they are not present in all behavioral transactions. Furthermore, there would appear to be, using

Randall's own terminology, other highly generic characteristics, which seem to be present in most human contexts. For example, "value" and "purpose," according to Randall himself, seem to be invariant in every transactional situation. Why are these not "categories"?

If, on the contrary, the category "connectives" is construed as applicable primarily to (1) the nature of being, then it would be a mistake to consider scientific "connectives" in the same way as other connectives, such as religious myths. Although it is the case that attempts at unified physical theories or comprehensive biological or overall social theories have been open to question in the history of science, yet surely there are integrating conceptual hypotheses on lower levels that "connect" explanations from various ranges of data. Thus it is an overstatement to interpret as "myths," for example, micro-bacterial explanations of disease in biology, electromagnetic theory in physics, or S-R theories of learning in psychology. Although scientific theories do not provide total unifications, they do provide "unifications" of sorts on a lower order. However, many scientific hypotheses and theories seem to function more like "ways" or "kinds" in Randall's terms, than like "connectives."

It is of course the case that human language, art, religion, morality, and science all have instrumental functions within human experience—as Randall has astutely pointed out. But I should insist that their functions differ. Cognitive "connectives" within science are of a different logical order than noncognitive ones; they tell us more about the world than do the others, for they are testable in terms of the data. That Randall does not emphasize sufficiently the *differences* between scientific "connectives" and other connectives weakens the claim that his general philosophical orientation is thoroughly naturalistic; for naturalists insist upon the priority of scientific method in the area of knowledge.

This is no place to enter into a detailed analysis of Randall's theory of noncognitive aesthetic and religious symbols. But I would like to indicate that I am somewhat hesitant about an aspect of his treatment because I think that it may deviate again from empirical naturalism. Although Randall maintains—correctly I would urge—that noncognitive symbols do not provide a form of knowledge, as do cognitive symbols, nonetheless, he also indicates that they

Can be said to "disclose or "reveal" something about the world in which they function. . . . This revelation can be called "knowledge" or "truth" only in the sense that it is equivocal or metaphorical . . . it resembles what we call "insight" or "vision." Such religious symbols do not "tell" us anything that is verifiably so; they rather make us "see" something about our human experience in the world.[36]

Randall further explains his conception of the function of religious symbols in his book *The Role of Knowledge in Western Religion*.[37] Here he maintains that what religious symbols "disclose" can best be seen analogically by analyzing the "insight" into the character and nature of another human personality. He agrees that external observation of a human being's behavior is useful, but he also says: "Intimate acquaintance with another human personality acquired through a long experience of friendship or of love, can give us an 'insight' into the essence of the man that cannot be won by any merely external observations of his behavior."[38]

Randall, unlike most other naturalists, does not appear to be fully committed to the behavioristic scientific program. Indeed, Randall maintains that a man is not exhausted in his behavior, but rather in the "possibilities and powers latent in his nature"—and that these are known by a kind of *verstehen*. Randall generalizes from this analogy of personality to the "Divine"—thus increasing his distance from empirical naturalism. He claims "that a religious symbol unifies and sums up and brings to a focus men's long and intimate experience of their universe and of what it offers to human life."[39] Thus he claims that religious symbols disclose or reveal powers and possibilities "inherent in the nature of things," and that they serve as instruments of insight and vision. Now perhaps I am overemphasizing one aspect of Randall's theory. For he does stress the pragmatic and functional side of religion and he is thoroughly naturalistic in focus here. Moreover, he also indicates that the "Divine" is a symbol of human value, an ideal. But I am somewhat concerned about this aspect of "vision" that he seems to add.

For Randall, religious symbols enable men to discern "Perfection shining through the world's imperfections in a dimly reflected splendor."[40] Thus, although religion involves practical commitment and know-how, it also provides a "vision of the Divine" and of the "order of splendor."[41]

In his discussion Randall suggests that scientific hypotheses and theories are no longer "true" in modern science, but merely "warranted" or "tested." If this is so, he asks, then how do we adjudicate the claims of religion and science? Religious symbols are tested by their adequacy—even though they cannot be confused with the warranted knowledge of science. Perhaps, he says, "it is now the visions of the unified possibilities of the world—of the Divine, of the 'order of splendor'—that we are once more permitted to call 'true.' "[42]

These latter remarks of Randall should bring to a head what has been implicit in my discussion thus far, and what is in a sense my major reservation about Randall's metaphysics. He transgresses from what I consider to be a basic methodological principle of philosophic naturalism, i.e., the commitment to the methods of science. This principle, fundamental of course to Dewey's naturalistic metaphysics, is a key assumption of the collected volume *Naturalism and the Human Spirit,* where Randall recognizes this commitment when, in the Epilogue, he says the "insistence on the universal and unrestricted application of 'scientific method' is a theme pervading every one of these essays."[43]

If one asks, How does one judge or appraise Randall's metaphysics? an answer seems to emerge. Here is a kind of "vision," a "seeing," a "perspective," which Randall has and which he is attempting to communicate. Randall's categories perhaps thus function, to use his own language, as unifying "connectives" or "myths." These may provide a kind of "insight" in Randall's sense much the same as all other metaphysical theories; but they seem incompatible at times with contemporary sciences—even though he may not intend such to be the case. Thus, in the last analysis, I am forced to conclude that Randall's categories are not an entirely reliable guide of what a naturalistic metaphysics should include. Randall's categories appear to function as a generalized account of "human transactions" (*sans* the behavioral sciences); they do not say enough about the "generic traits of nature" or of the world as viewed by contemporary science.

# IV. THE CATEGORIES AND NATURALISM

What of meta-metaphysics and the search for the categories from the standpoint of naturalistic metaphysics? My own position should by now be clear. I reject the Aristotelian notion that metaphysics is a "science of existence" with a distinctive subject matter of its own. And this involves a rejection of other aspects of the Aristotelian program which Randall fortunately also rejects—the view that metaphysics gives us a "special" kind of knowledge that we could not possibly get in any other way, or that it gives us knowledge of Being independent from beings in concrete contexts. I also reject the search for categories which are universal, 1 (a) in the language of being, or the Kantian search for universal and *a priori* presuppositions, 2 (c) in the language of experience; for I do not know how one would go about testing such categories by empirical observation and generalization. The whole notion of a universal category which applies to *any* subject matter or of a universal presupposition violates the principle of verification, so essential to an empirical naturalism. Universal statements are analytic, not synthetic; they are based upon logical analysis, not empirical observation. And an appeal to the synthetic *a priori* is surely not an option for an empiricist.

Does this mean that I consider all metaphysical inquiry nonsense? *No.* For I think that metaphysicians of science have a useful job to perform, though on a *limited* scale. Empirical metaphysicians can, as I see it, bring to light various sets of general concepts which function in different subject matters and areas of inquiry; they can thus uncover the categories of "the middle range" (to borrow a term from the social sciences). A generalization based upon probabilities is not the same as a universal statement. In this more modest sense, metaphysicians can examine 2 (b) "the generic traits of nature," if this inquiry is construed as a distillation of the assumptions and conclusions of the natural and biological sciences. Aristotle's categories are, in the last analysis, a reflection of the scientific view of his day, much the same as Kant's categories bring out the presuppositions of the Newtonian world-view. A categorical analysis which is not related first and foremost to the philosophy of science hardly has a claim to our attention. This, however, should be viewed in historical terms, as R. G. Collingwood points out, for our presuppositions are constantly being modified. In any one age, we can help to interpret how the sciences approach nature, and we can help to interpret and sum up what they are saying about the cosmos; we can generalize and take inventory. The metaphysician in this sense is a "middleman."

Although he does not himself engage in an experimental test of his concepts, he does seek to analyze, explicate, and clarify the key concepts and hypotheses which are used by the sciences of nature and have been tested. A category would be a generalization from our tested theories; it would not itself be a scientific theory or law or a substitute for it. Moreover, a metaphysical category would not be equivalent to any and every law, theory, or concept used in the sciences; but it would rather refer to the most fundamental concepts which seem to play a key role in the body of our knowledge at any one time in human history. Unlike Aristotle and Kant, I would say metaphysicians of the "middle range" seek categories based upon cognate concepts and generalizations from several sciences, but they do not necessarily apply to *all* the sciences. Thus, for example, similar concepts are today used in physics, chemistry, and the natural sciences: "mass," "energy," "particle," and "field." It is important to interpret their meaning and function. Difficulties emerge however when such categories are simply stretched by the metaphysician or universalized as applicable to all the sciences. I am not saying that "universal" or generic categories are logically impossible, only that they depend upon the development of a unified scientific theory which we do not have at present. Metaphysicians do leap ahead of scientific theories, and they find clusters of concepts that bear "family resemblances," which they label "categories." The danger in metaphysics is always that such categories may be extended so far that they become simply "root metaphors," analogical, and equivocal, and that in the process they lose their precise cognitive significance.

Such metaphysicians of course should not restrict their inquiries to the natural or life sciences. They can also investigate 2 (d) the generic traits of human transactions; they can provide generalized conceptual accounts of the sciences of human behavior, i.e., summary statements of what we do and do not know about man from the standpoint of the biological, behavioral, and social sciences. Although drawing of analogies between 1 (b) and 1 (d) is useful, these inquiries should not be equated or confused. Nor does this imply that man is bifurcated from or not a part of nature. In regard to 2 (d) the generic traits of human transaction, there are a great number of concepts that may be fruitfully investigated : "behavior," "function," "intention," "value," "decision," "evolution," "culture," "society," etc. The quest for a single set of categorial concepts which is either universal, exhaustive, or complete, hardly seems to do justice to the wide range of data and knowledge that we have about human beings. We are far from a unified theory of human behavior, and thus any categorial scheme of human interaction would be incomplete. In dealing with human behavior, we must surely take into account all of the varieties of human experience; and philosophers need to develop conceptual analyses appropriate to the special subject matters of art, religion, and morality, among others. However, I should say that the moral, religious, and aesthetic dimensions of human experience are *not* candidates for truth in any special way—surely not about nature and not perhaps even about man—but, rather, that they provide us with *data to be explained by the sciences.* They are not sources for generic metaphysical categories. The key principle of naturalism should not be compromised here: all claims to truth must be examined by the same responsible methods of empirical observation and test; and intuitive "insight" or "vision," whether from art, religion, or morality, is no substitute for experimental verification.

In metaphysical contexts, the term "category," as we have seen, has also been applied to (e) methodological principles of inquiry and (f) linguistic rules of use. Methodological investigations and analyses of the logical grammar of our language are both vital and necessary to philosophy. An analysis of the methodological principles and criteria that are employed in scientific inquiry, and of the language that is used in ordinary life, may shed further light about the nature 1 (b) of the world, and 2 (d) of human beings. These analyses, however, while significant in themselves, can be carried on without a primary "metaphysical" interest or concern. They are not distinctively or peculiarly "metaphysical"; for they are presupposed in all philosophical investigations of art, morality, religion, politics, education, history, science, etc. Thus, to stretch the term "metaphysics" so that it applies in some special way to (e) and (f) invites either the charge that "metaphysics" is here being used in an equivocal and metaphorical sense, or that it has become a kind of superphilosophical inquiry involving virtually the whole of philosophy.

The chief conclusion that I wish to draw here is that, for descriptive and empirical metaphysics, the term "category" may be applied fruitfully, in the qualified way that I have suggested, to an account of (b) the generic traits of nature, and (d) the generic traits of human transaction. Insofar as Professor Randall's metaphysical interest does this, I think that his work deserves serious attention and that he has made a *notable* contribution to metaphysics, especially naturalistic metaphysics, and particularly at a time when many other philosophers have forsaken her. But insofar as there is an attempt to introduce, under the heading of "category," other inquiries, then I think that we need further clarification of the nature of this questionable enterprise.

# NOTES

1. "The Nature of Metaphysics: Its Function, Criteria, and Method," *Journal of Philosophy* 43 (1946): 401–12.

2. *Nature and Historical Experience* (New York: Columbia University Press, 1958), chap. V.

3. *Nature and Historical Experience,* p. 124.

4. Ibid., p. 144.

5. Ibid.

6. Ibid., p. 137.

7. Ibid., p. 135.

8. Ibid.

9. Ibid., p. 136.

10. Ibid., p. 137.

11. Ibid., p. 177.

12. Ibid., p. 176.

13. London: Methuen, 1959.

14. Ibid., p. 9.

15. Ibid., p. 147.

16. Ibid., pp. 148–49.

17. Ibid., p. 150.

18. Ibid., p. 152.

19. Ibid.

20. Ibid., p. 151.

21. Ibid., p. 175.

22. *Aristotle* (New York: Columbia University Press, 1960), pp. 166–68.

23. Ibid., p. 229.

24. Ibid., p. 129.

25. Ibid., p. 188.

26. *Nature and Historical Experience,* p. 155.

27. Ibid., p. 177.

28. Ibid., p. 183.

29. Ibid., p. 186.
30. Ibid., p. 177.
31. Ibid., p. 187.
32. Ibid., pp. 27–28.
33. Ibid., pp. 164, 174.
34. Ibid., p. 195.
35. Ibid., p. 197.
36. Ibid., pp. 265–66.
37. *The Role of Knowledge in Western Religion* (Boston: Starr King Press, 1958).
38. Ibid., p. 116.
39. Ibid., p. 117.
40. Ibid., p. 118.
41. Ibid., p. 121.
42. Ibid., p. 134.
43. "The Nature of Naturalism," in Y. H. Kirkorian, ed. (New York: Columbia University Press 1944), p. 358.

# Part II

# Naturalistic Ethics

# 6.
# Naturalistic Ethics and the Open Question

## I

Naturalistic ethics is an attempt to provide an empirical basis for ethics, including the definition of ethical terms and concepts. This effort has not been without its sharp philosophical critics. Many nonnaturalists who have objected to the naturalistic definition of ethical terms raise the "open question" argument. Because naturalism cannot, as they allege, meet this question, they accuse it of a fallacy (or "mistake" in William Frankena's revised phraseology). The general criticism runs something like this: you cannot offer an empirical definition of "good" or "value," since any definition offered is open to the question, "but is *this* good or obligatory?" Any proposed definition is said to fail since it does not count for the normative element, the intuitive apprehension of a quality, or unanalyzable property, the emotive meaning, or the persuasive appeal. There is nothing whatsoever which we could substitute for "good" in every instance. Thus, it is held, an "ethical" definition cannot be derived from "nonethical" subject matter.

From *The Journal of Philosophy,* 52, No. 5 (1955): 113–28. Reprinted by permission of the publisher.

But many of those who appeal to the naturalistic fallacy may be guilty of it themselves. At least there is an implicit agreement among nonnaturalists as to the function of definition and the starting point of ethical inquiry, namely, the analysis of common usage. But in the objections raised by intuitionists, emotivists, and linguistic analysts a definition of normative has been presupposed. Anything outside of these tautological limitations is antecedently excluded. The very construction of the "open question" form of the naturalistic fallacy does not permit of conceivable resolution. Further, it is not consistent with "common usage." Hence, many analytic philosophers are inconsistent with their announced intention of expunging from philosophy and science questions resulting from "verbal confusion."

Now in this chapter I wish to contrast two possible approaches to ethical inquiry. The first applies to a kind of philosophical position which I shall call the "nonnaturalistic, analytic, or linguistic position." Although it may not completely characterize any one particular philosopher, I think that it is generally descriptive of a recent trend in philosophy. I am not here as interested in textual interpretation as in pointing out mistakes which I think many philosophers make in common. I do not wish to deny the value of twentieth-century anti-naturalistic arguments. They have no doubt pointed to fundamental issues overlooked by many overzealous naturalists. But I think that it is time to analyze more carefully the presuppositions of the nonnaturalistic viewpoint. I hope that some sort of positive compromise between the naturalists and their critics, although not totally devoid of some skepticism, may be reached. Hence, I wish to submit a second approach to ethical inquiry. It is a naturalistic program revised in the light of the nonnaturalistic position, and it includes "a behavioral science of value" and "a theory of decision."

I think that we must grant many of the nonnaturalistic criticisms of one type of naturalism, viz., that type of naturalism which describes human psychology in order to find a standard of value or good which will necessarily entail obligation. But this does not leave naturalism without a program. For if the nonnaturalistic objections are true of overzealous naturalism, they are also true to some extent of nonnaturalism as well. Nonnaturalism maintains that the explanation and analysis of language is possible without committing the naturalistic fallacy. I think that this is not completely so; however, it is true in a restricted sense. Hence, I wish to argue that to the extent to which linguistic analysis is possible, to the same extent the analysis and explanation of human behavior is equally possible within a delimited field. This is the role for the behavioral sciences approach to value, which I shall outline in Part IV. Briefly, such an enterprise is interested primarily in the description and explanation of human behavior—value is related to the laws of behavior—and only secondarily to the question of application and obligation. I am not arguing necessarily that there is a sharp split between behavior and obligation. Indeed, most likely an adequate science of man will find obligations implicit in social behavior as empirical facts. I simply want to argue that one may analyze human nature, or specify "goods," or recommend action in specific contexts with relative degrees of impartiality—and without committing the "naturalistic fallacy" in its extreme form.

## II

Now ethical naturalists have suggested many definitions of "value."[1] But to any definition offered there is always the retort: "But is it really good?" or "Why ought I to follow this definition?" This objection, I submit, is in error. It is surely too sweeping. The usual procedure in ethics is to try to refute one definition by criticizing it in terms of another definition. G. E. Moore is highly critical of this method, and this is one of the reasons for his pointing out the naturalistic fallacy. But Moore and company themselves hold an *implicit* definition of good. Indeed, the question itself presupposes such a prior definition of "good" and "ought." The actual reason why the proposed naturalistic definition of good is rejected is because it is inconsistent with their own assumed definition of good. In other words, the so-called naturalistic fallacy is a fallacy by definition.

I should like to analyze the open-question argument to indicate the essential confusion involved. I submit that this question is a bad question, which, if taken in its extreme form, cannot be answered. But there is no reason why it need be asked in this extreme way. Although there may be other meanings involved, the open-question argument may be broken down into two more fundamental types of questions.

First, when one uses this objection one may mean the following: "But is it good?" or "Why ought it to exist?" It is convenient to discuss "Is it good?" as roughly similar to the question "Why ought it to be?"—notwithstanding some differences. Moore explicitly interprets "good" as a simple, intrinsic, indefinable property. He has not been able to characterize such a nonrelational quality without illustrating by means of some relationship to human beings; however, I will assume his nonrelational interpetation in order to see the significance, if any, involved in this statement. Further, I shall interpret the term "ought" as most nearly equivalent to "normative," especially since intuitionists and emotivists, among others, seem to stress this meaning.

Second, and more importantly, the open question may mean "Why ought *I* to do or accept it?" or "Why ought our *social* group to do it?" The relevance of such a question to the social group is usually not raised by recent writers. But knowledge of ethical significance to the individual cannot simply be translated intact to the social context. I shall largely omit consideration of social ethics in this chapter even though I believe it to be as important as psychological considerations. It is only because others have dwelt on the egocentric predicament in ethics that I wish to analyze this meaning here.

First, then, what is meant by the question "*Why* ought something to exist?" (or "Is it good in itself?"). Somewhat analogous questions were raised at one time in nonethical domains. Hume asked *how* we come by the idea of causation. His familiar reply was that from habit and custom we come to expect that certain events will occur in the future as in the past.

But it is possible in this context to ask the question *why* instead of *how*. Here we may either be searching for (a) a descriptive explanation, or (b) an "ultimate" justification of causation and/or induction. Ever since the seventeenth century, science and empiricism have thought question (b) to be irrelevant to the scientific enterprise. Science in general has been most effective with question (a). This type of explanation involves subsumption under a more comprehensive theory or law which has been verified. Science is usually willing to accept the proposition "$B$ follows $A$" (or "If $A$, then $B$") as reasonably warranted on the basis of relevant evidence. This evidence, though limited, is acceptable to normal scientific procedures without calling into account the whole nature of existence or without trying to find a complete deductive justification for epistemology. Science simply accepts *B* following from *A* as a natural or theoretical fact.

True, many philosophers (analysts excluded) consider it perfectly meaningful to suggest philosophical interpretations of causation or induction (b). For instance, realistic theories attribute the possibility of prediction to the "natures" and "powers" of things, and conventionalistic interpretations base prediction upon "theory construction." However, neither philosophical explanation need refer to deductively certain first principles nor end in infinite regress. At the very least, one is compelled because of the demands of living to accept pragmatically the fact of nature and life. At any rate, even philosophical explanations refer finally to something given as the ground of prediction.

Now it may be possible to ask still another type of question: (c) "Why ought *A* to follow *B*?" (or "Is it good that something exists?"). Here there is a search for a conclusive axiological basis for existence. But it is very difficult to raise this question seriously in relation to nonhuman matters, since there is scarcely a meaningful reply that could be given. Indeed, it is difficult to conceive of *any* sort of reply which could possibly satisfy this question. When we are asked "Why *ought A* to follow *B*?" or "Is something good *in itself*?" we can only resort to scientific explanation of why or how it occurs; at most we may refer to an epistemological explanation of why *A should* follow *B* in the future. But to ask "ought" in any Pickwickian sense and expect a meaningful answer is seriously to stretch the realm of imagination.

Let us apply this general analysis to value theory and ethics. We will suppose for the moment that we have considerable inductive knowledge of the laws of human behavior. Here of course we are assuming that there are *some* such laws (which empiricists do not necessarily deny). What these laws are is inconsequential for now: humans may be beings striving for pleasure, interest, the fulfillment of type, etc. Many naturalists have attempted to define value in terms of human behavior. They chose the term "value" instead of "good" because "value" seemed to be a broader term relatively free from the special connotations which accrued to the latter (although, unfortunately, "value" has since acquired its own special connotations). Thus naturalists have freely stipulated a meaning for "value," where "value" is generally taken as equivalent to "the theories of laws of human behavior." The chief question among naturalists concerns the adequacy of their theories of human behavior. For freedom of definition is justified by its fruitfulness within the context of inquiry.

Now what if someone asks "*Why* ought the human species to function in the way that our theories indicate that it does?" or "Why is it good for human beings to live for the basic ends that they do?" If what I am saying is in some sense true, then the only possible answer can be in terms of the meaning of "why" in sense (a) as explanation, and possibly in sense (b) as a philosophical theory, but never in sense (c).

In matters of scientific fact, most empirical philosophers have refused to deal with the question *why* where it has demanded an ultimate deductive justification for descriptive law or definition. Such definitions are accepted as adequate within an object language on the basis of normal scientific procedures (or clearly stipulated philosophical meaning). To ask if "*A* ought to follow *B*" is to argue an *irrelevant thesis,* to commit a form of the fallacy *ignoratio elenchi.* Yet, paradoxically, similar questions are still raised by empiricists in objection to naturalistic definitions of value. Accordingly, if "*Why* ought *X* to be?" is one possible meaning of the open question and if it is taken in sense (c), then I am arguing that it is a mistake to ask it in ethics or value theory in any but the restricted senses above.

The second possible meaning of "ought," however, is closer to what is usually meant by those who raise it. It asks of any definition: "Why ought *I* to accept and act upon this; why is it good for *me*?" The wide acceptance of this meaning shows the great influence of our cultural experience on our theories. The whole tenor of the Judaic-Christian heritage on the one hand and the "individualistic" theme in society on the other has to a great degree held to the undue emphasis on "ego-centered" problems and categories. Thus it is generally held that the normative meaning of an ethical term refers to its imperative function. Ethical terms are supposed to move an individual to action and to deal with the control of attitudes and activities. And it is said (especially by emotivists) that because of this the open question can never be answered sufficiently; all attempts to do so commit the naturalistic fallacy. But, as it has been pointed out,[2] the reason why it cannot be solved is because the connection between a definition and an action or belief is only *psychological* or *social*, not logical. There is *no* final guarantee or proof that any one individual always will be sufficiently persuaded to accept a definition or proof. One cannot even be sure that a person will want to accept the methods of verification and proof. Human beings frequently behave irrationally. Surely, if we have learned anything from our cultural experience and its overemphasis on romantic love, it is that in matters of the heart it is difficult to act cognitively. One does not always know whom he will fall in love with; and once he has, all the argument in the world may not convince him that he ought not to. There is no guarantee that an individual will abide by the strictures of logic. Thus, of any definition of "good," you can never be positive that anyone will be sufficiently motivated to approve of or accept it.

Pointing out the presence of an ultimate imperative element in ethical language is the lasting contribution of the emotive theory. But I do not know if ethical naturalism ever really seriously denied this, or needs to, for that matter, to preserve its theory. The instilling of conviction and motivation is a question of application. This is the task of psychology, sociology, education, etc. Why individuals refuse to accept scientific evidence requires detailed investigation; the causes lie deeply embedded in the funded mass of socio-psychological influences that have conditioned individuals to see, feel, believe, and act along culturally predetermined channels. Thus *why* people believe the way they do is a problem of psychology, psychiatry, etc. *How* to get them to believe is a problem for the mechanics of human behavior and control. *What* they should believe is a problem for the scientific enterprise in general.

Actually the objection is really akin to the traditional arguments of religion. Religion stresses the existential dilemma of life conscious of itself: the soul of man cries in the wilderness of the universe for certainty, but it can find no compulsive guarantee for any way of life.

But once again I wonder in what sense the egocentric type of objection to naturalistic definition is relevant. It is hardly relevant in the scientific context—but here, too, there is an "imperative" element. One can imagine an individual (supposing for purposes of discussion that he has a gastric disorder) crying unto himself, "Why ought my enzymes to digest my food?" The question is exasperating. How would we go about replying to it? We might begin by explaining how our digestive system functions. Most of the operations of the body seem to follow definite laws that do not come under conscious control. There are, of course, some areas that do seem to come under our control. At one time people thought that disease was punishment by God for evil works; now we know that it can frequently be prevented and cured. Research is continually revealing new possibilities to man. We may, for instance, discover that this man's gastric disorder is due to a diet deficiency and prescribe certain vitamins to rectify it. Here the individual has the choice of taking the vitamins or not. Suppose, however, that this individual, being a doubting Thomas at heart, asks his doctor, "But why are vitamins good; why ought I to take them?" A conscientious doctor will most likely attempt to reply by first referring to the problem at hand. He might tell the individual that our scientific knowledge indicates that vitamins will probably cure him. If Thomas is not satisfied and asks "But why ought I to be cured?" the doctor may point out to the individual that this will contribute to satisfaction or fulfillment in the long run or the maintenance of life itself. This presupposes, however, that the individual finds life itself worthwhile. If he says he does not, further appeal may not be possible.[3] You may tell him that life *can* be worthwhile if he will satisfy certain basic needs. You may suggest to him that life is really good since most normal human beings strive to maintain it; and the very fact that he is questioning suggests that he at least nonconsciously finds life of some value. But if he still persists, rational arguments *may not* induce belief or motivation that is initially absent. The individual (or martyr) who does not rationally want to accept the fact of life perhaps is somewhat like the individual who does not want to accept the facts of nature or existence. "Why ought I to behave in a certain way?" (this refers to those activities which are law-like) is like the question "Why ought Mars to revolve around the sun?"

But after all, what would be our reaction to a person who, when confronted with two contending theories, e.g., that the movement of Mars around the sun can be explained in terms of scientific laws (law of gravitation, theory of relativity, etc.) ($X_n$), or the God of War, selects the latter in spite of overwhelming evidence to the contrary? Actually the proposition "The revolution of Mars about the Sun can be explained in terms of $X_n$" has two parts: "$X_n$ is true," *and* the imperative: "You ought to believe and act in accordance with this truth." But this is my point—if a person *refuses to believe,* there is little that you can do. He may reject wholesale your definition and methodology. If so, you may argue and bring evidence to bear *ad infinitum* and you still may not be able to *prove* to him the facts of nature and life and that he should believe them.[4]

In the light of the foregoing discussion I should like to summarize the conclusions that may be drawn. First, if the question "*Why* ought *B* to follow ultimately from *A*?" is not relevant in respect to natural science, then it is not relevant in the science of man. Second, if "Why ought *I* to do or believe *X*?" is not relevant in science, then it is not relevant in ethics or value theory. In other words, if empirical ethics fails, so does empirical science. Thus, in respect to first principles, science no less than ethics and value theory needs to be defended. Propositions *about* natural facts, like propositions *about* human behavior, propositions which state that we ought to believe something, like propositions which state we ought to do something, both require "justification." Empiricists and naturalists at least have rejected any ultimate justification in science. The reasons why we are more apt to agree in natural science is that we know infinitely more about natural processes than we know about humans (this is precisely the interest of naturalists such as Dewey and Perry who want us to learn more about human behavior). Presumably, any deductive justification of science and knowledge fails; the best defense of science may be a pragmatic one. Science is "justified" simply because of its instrumental value to society: it enables us to predict, explain, and control better than any other method.

Similar considerations apply in ethics. If once we reveal the facts of human behavior and anyone still refuses to accept the truth of these facts because he does not have sufficient "reasons" for belief, we might ask him what he means by "reasons," and why anyone should be interested in reasons in his sense of the term. Actually the open-question demand is a rationalistic one. It usually means by reason "logical conclusiveness" or "deductive justification." But, as I have been trying to argue, "reason" or "evidence" is not used in this way in science (or in ordinary life, for that matter) when people claim to have a reason for a prediction or explain human conduct (or argue for a course of action). And if the chief difference between natural science and behavioral science is that the subject matter in the latter concerns conduct and propositions about conduct, then it is irrelevant in behavioral science, value theory, and ethics (if value theory and ethics are related in part to behavioral science), no less than in physical science, for a person to appeal to the open-question argument.

## III

Most nonnaturalistic ethical theorists, however, remain convinced that any naturalistic definition of good is in error. Hence they hold themselves to a restricted program. They are concerned with the analysis of language. Russell aptly characterizes the general emphasis of these writers when he says that "the aim [of ethics] is, not practice, but propositions about practice."[5] Stevenson's program is a limited one. "Its first object is to clarify the meaning of the ethical terms 'good,' 'right,' 'just,' 'ought,' etc. Its second object is to characterize the general methods by which judgments can be supported."[6] And Ayer on occasion agrees with this attitude. His concern "is only to analyze the use of ethical terms, not scientifically to explain" them.[7] Although in some circles there is a vague desire to achieve a "realistic" interpretation of ethical terms, the literature generally indicates the commonly accepted assumption that an appeal to ordinary usage frequently provides a test of ethical analysis. Oxford philosophers (Ryle, Hare, Strawson, Toulmin, etc.), influenced by Moore and Wittgenstein, have defended explicitly the analysis of common usage. The meaning and function of ethical terms in everyday language thus has evoked considerable debate and has become the center of ethical analysis.

Now this type of inquiry is useful. No doubt an analysis of how people actually employ ethical language is interesting. On the basis of this understanding some clarification even of practical action may be achieved. Unfortunately, however, common usage is notoriously obscure, confused, indeterminate. People use ethical terms in a variety of ways, making all sorts of appeals, rational and nonrational (to emotion, tradition, authority, etc.), to support their ethical convictions.

Hence, to accept common usage as a reliable guide may be a great error. Many ethical naturalists also have concerned themselves with common usage. They have thought it necessary to argue, in order to defend their position, that ethical terms as a matter of fact *are* used descriptively in ordinary language. They frequently have held that common ethical predicates simply refer to rational or empirical criteria. But an all-out defense of the cognitive basis of ordinary language is largely unnecessary from the standpoint of the naturalist's own program, since (as the nonnaturalists point out) most of the naturalistic definitions of ethical terms which have been offered do not refer to how people presently use terms, but how they *should* use them in the future. The naturalist might better support his position by admitting once and for all that ethical terms are frequently used irrationally. But he needs to make it clear that his definitions do not simply describe common usage. The naturalist is making a proposal; he is suggesting a theory for interpreting human behavior. What he needs to defend is the thesis that it is logically *possible* and scientifically *plausible* to use terms in the way he recommends. The use of these terms, however, is relevant strictly *within* the context of scientific or philosophical inquiry, and not necessarily to everyday life. It is true, however, that the scientific naturalist who is interested in the science of values has made an initial personal value commitment to scientific objectivity.

Actually many ethical nonnaturalists are proceeding in a similar fashion, at least for one part of their program. Although they claim to be impartially observing the meaning and use of ethical terminology, they are obligated to "objectivity"; they are *interpreting* how people use such language and are suggesting how philosophers (and everyday people) *ought* to use such terms once they are clear about the *real* function and meaning of ethical language (to evoke emotions, etc.). The emotivists, for instance, argue that many people who think they are using terms descriptively are really misguided; hence they offer a theory in the place of simple description. The nonnaturalists in ethics generally assume that the starting point and proper task of ethical inquiry is the impartial analysis of ethical language. But while their meta-ethics is supposed to be distinguished from normative matters, they actually are making an implicit normative commitment. For they (like the naturalists in their field) are committed to the activity of analysis as a problem and accept it as a proper and valuable activity.

Now the nonnaturalists berate the naturalists for their "value preference," i.e., to explain behavior scientifically. We are told that we should not prescribe how terms are used, but only describe. But if we are to take the analytic program at its face value, the analytic program itself becomes suspect. Let us for the moment proceed in the way they recommend. We shall be concerned with the meaning of the terms "philosophy," "analysis," and "philosophical analysis." These terms are used in many contexts, in ordinary life and by professors of philosophy. Ordinary people usually mean by the term "philosophy" the "love of wisdom," "the seeing of life steadily and whole"; and professors of philosophy interpret "philosophy" in many ways: "the criticisms of practice," "the formulation of a general speculative theory," "the analysis and formulation of categories of existence," etc. Philosophical analysts, however, do not remain consistent with either criterion, for they emphatically hold such definitions of "philosophy," etc., to be incorrect. True, they will admit that "philosophy" has had these significations, but those who hold to these meanings, we are told, would not do so if they were sufficiently versed in their particular theory of knowledge. But must not consistent analysts refuse to go along with the *re*definition of the terms "philosophy" and "philosophical analysis"? After all, since the above is the way people use the terms, are the analysts justified in proposing a change?

This raises fundamental issues analogous in a sense to those raised in ethics where redefinition of ethical terms is held to be inadmissible because it flouts common usage. But here is the rub— are they not committing a type of mistake similar to the naturalistic fallacy in ethics? They proceed from common usage (and/or philosophical usage) to a theory or a proposal, a redefinition of the term "philosophy." But might we not say that the *definiens* and the *definiendum* are not equivalent, that there is a type of "persuasive definition"? If so, there can be no conclusive defense of philosophical analysis without begging the question: those who engage in analysis do so because they want to. But where then does this leave the analysts' program? Earlier analysts, at least, seemed to believe that they could present reasons for their theory of analysis. But if we are to take their theory seriously, then this phase of their enterprise is nothing more than an attempt at poetic persuasion.

One way out is to hold that mere consistency with common usage (and/or philosophical usage) is not a proper test of correct definition. Such a test is not used in the natural or biological sciences. It is really rejected by analysts when they attempt to redefine a program of philosophy. Hence, a similar rejection, perhaps, is necessary in ethics.

Because an appeal to common usage is not rejected, another serious mistake in meta-ethical analysis may be involved. For there seems to be an implicit agreement with the Greek sophists who defined "justice" in terms of what is usually meant in traditional usage. Thus they seem to argue that the only way we know that something *means* "good," "right," "ought," etc., is that people use terms that way. This simple description implies a form of acquiescence. (Although even simple description presupposes certain principles of selection.) There is little or no willingness to criticize the given. The "good" is interpreted in terms of the given; it is only revealed in the speech of humankind. Our modern-day analysts are also somewhat like the Hellenic skeptics who affirmed, "We skeptics follow in practice the way [language] of the world, but without holding any opinion about it."[8]

But the procedure they employ in philosophy and ethics is somewhat similar to that adopted by some of the naturalists they criticize. Mill, for intsance, thoroughly at odds with absolutistic Kantian ethics, wishes to *describe* human psychology. He hopes that from such an explication of human behavior people will be better able to guide themselves in terms of the standard he proposes. The linguist's meta-ethics is derived from the language of humans. It is hoped that this analysis will enable clear-headed people to eliminate verbal misunderstandings and confusions. But language both reflects behavior and is a form of it. Hence, if it is a fallacy to derive ethics from descriptive psychology, then the derivation of the meaning of ethical terms from a description of common usage (as an implied standard) is also a type of mistake. And if it is not a fallacy in the case of linguistic analysis, then it is not a fallacy in naturalistic psychology.

The difference, we will be told, is this: Naturalists not only describe human behavior but explicitly define what is "good" and then prescribe it for practice; whereas analysts simply describe the usage of terms without defining what is "good" or recommending action. That the latter in some sense implicitly define good and recommend analytic action is one of the points of this discussion. For any type of human activity involves an initial value commitment. But there are *degrees* of involvement. Hence, it is possible for naturalists to explain in an impartial way how people behave (defined as "value") *without* making an immediate recommendation for practical behavior. Most recent naturalists, at least, have attempted to avoid Mill's overoptimism and have abandoned the attempt to frame a general standard of value.

But this is *not* what is usually meant by ethics, object Ayer and others. It is psychology or sociology and is a redefinition of "ethics." They affirm that only the analysis of language is permissible in philosophy and ethics. Actually, however, what we have are two separate programs: the analytic program is the linguistic program; the naturalistic program (one part at least) is the value program. The one calls for a redefinition of "philosophy" and its problems; the other for a redefinition of "ethics" and its problems. The first is interested in the analysis of human language and the second in the explanation of human behavior. Both types of behavior are useful in terms of their contexts and their problems.


## IV

If my analysis is correct, then the naturalistic attempt to define "value" or "good" is not *a priori* bound to fail; and the question to be asked of any definition is not "Is it good or obligatory?" (in the senses indicated), but "Is it true or warranted?" What, then, are the tests of true definition? First, a philosophical definition must be distinguished from a scientific definition; in no sense can philosophical definitions replace scientific definitions. Philosophical definitions have important pragmatic functions. They act as catalysts in the intellectual community, giving insights and suggesting fruitful hypotheses for other scientists to investigate. They are intended to be generally consistent with experience; yet they frequently leap ahead of existing empirical knowledge. (Philosophers try to relate their concepts to experience chiefly by the method of illustration and example.) Both analysis and synthesis are the tools of philosophy. Ethical definitions are organizing concepts which help us to understand how human beings behave.

But a definition is not merely required to follow common usage. There are no unalterable reasons why philosophy should continue to retain the terms "value," "ought," "good," etc. Such terms are not subsistent entities. True, philosophers usually intend their ethical concepts to apply to "real" properties; they prefer using terminology which has some commonly understood meaning. Yet, if definition is to overcome the difficulties of past inadequate interpretations, and if it is to avoid the confusing emotive effects of traditional teminology, some stipulation of new meaning must be admissible. Further, it may not be necessary (as Moore points out) to give a *single* definition to any ethical term. Human behavior may be so complex that only plural definitions are possible. Philosophical definition, however, is at most general, not universal. Yet its very generality is useful, since it serves as a focus for interpreting an intellectual enterprise and suggesting problems for future inquiry.

But the basic problem for value theory and ethics is to explain human nature. This is the specific problem of science—philosophy can only generalize from it. Two approaches are possible here. The first is a simple statistical description of human behavior, without any attempt at explanation. The second view emphasizes typological norms, which have the status of explanatory law, and searches for potentialities already implicit in human behavior. Whether you decide to apply the honorific term "value" to the conclusions of simple description (value$_1$), ("prizings"), or to explanatory law (value$_2$) ("appraisings") is secondary, since neither entails any necessary connection with obligation or action. Many naturalistic philosophers have emphasized value$_2$ over value$_1$. The difference between value$_1$ and value$_2$ indicates in part the difference between the linguistic approach to ethics and the behavioral approach. The linguists are willing to consult common usage to determine the meaning of ethical terms; the naturalists, however, feel it necessary to investigate the underlying causes of behavior, not simply their final expressions. Thus there may be good grounds for defining value in relation to the laws of human behavior (value$_2$), since all behavior, including language, only has reference to the broader context of human activity—but this is not crucial.

What I am suggesting as basic—namely, the continuity between ethics and behavioral science—is not so far from Ayer's accusation that naturalists turn ethics into psychology or sociology (I want to admit it); or from Moore, who insists that the province of ethics is "casuistry" (the search for intrinsic goods or, as I prefer to call them, the conditions of life); or from Dewey and Perry, who want to investigate the causal regularities of behavior. This position does not unduly flout the traditional meaning of the term "ethics." Indeed, it is consistent with the Greek view of ethics—an attempt to characterize the nature of humankind. The chief question for the science of value then is the question "What is life?"; value will be defined in terms of it. Thus the definition of value is equivalent to the definition of man.

But it is well known that the value program has bogged down. One of the reasons for this morass is due to fears of naturalistic fallacy. I hope that I have in part dispelled these fears. Another reason for the lack of progress is simply that most of the definitions offered thus far have not been sufficiently framed in terms of scientific knowledge. Indeed, the definition of ethical concepts has usually been carried on in an *a priori* fashion. I suspect that the definitions offered thus far are incomplete because they have been uncritically framed in terms of "individualistic" assumptions and are usually predicated on psychology or biology alone. Not enough attention has been paid to the other behavioral sciences. Since human life is to a great extent socio-cultural, any explanation of humankind must take account of the full context, including anthropological, cultural, economic, political, and sociological factors. Yet few have attempted a definition of value in terms of these materials.[9] Behavioral science has suggested concepts—adjustment, homeostasis, equilibrium, etc.—that may provide an important beginning both for individual personality and social structure. But we msut be cautious. What is necessary is a more comprehensive behavioral science, including a detailed theory of social science.

Thus the explanatory sciences of man, and not necessarily the criticism of actual moral problems of practice, is the direct problem of the science and philosophy of value. The principles of behavior become the principles of value, *without any ultimate or egocentric connotations.* It is my thesis that it is a mistake for the nonnaturalists to raise here the open-question objection. But this still leaves the problem of application, practical wisdom, or art. This is in large part the task of applied social mechanics. It is conceivable that there are two types of solutions, "ideal" and "actual," to problems of behavior. One may indicate the theoretically correct solution of a problem, but any solution may be inadequate if it fails to recognize the character of the empirical subject matter. It is here, in respect to *actual conditions,* that the "theory of decision," or "logic of practice," is so vital, for it must outline the methods of dealing with practical problems.

Is the open-question argument here relevant? Does one in every problem of conduct have to raise ultimate "why" questions? I can only suggest that as a matter of fact we do not always do so, neither in everyday problems or in problems of applied science and art: in medicine, law, psychiatry, engineering, education, etc. A theory of practice can formulate "prescriptions" relevant to specific contexts without calling into question for that problem those contexts themselves (much the same as an analyst in his context or a scientist in his). Some progress has been made along these lines: situational criteria frequently give guidance for action and limit the range of relevant evidence; one cannot consider ends (as revealed by scientific explanation) without considering knowledge of means and techniques (as invented by the mechanics of human engineering).

But the problem of application is ultimately taken out of the hands of scientists and philosophers and is the direct obligation of society itself. The laws and potentialities of society, like those of nature and life, are given. While philosophers may propose Platonic Utopia in the sky, human beings live with what they have. Any successful solution of the problems of practice must be in terms of existing structures which the sciences do not control. And it is time that philosophers cease requiring of other philosophers absolute standards to solve practical problems. It just cannot be done. Yet there is a significnt role for ethical philosophy—to understand the nature of human life and the laws by means of which it continues.

## NOTES

1. For purposes of this discussion I shall use "value" (value theory) and "good" (ethics) synonymously (notwithstanding some possible differences) because similar objections have been raised against both.

2. See H. A. Prichard, "Does Moral Philosophy Rest on a Mistake?" *Mind* 21 (1912): 21–37; H. D. Aiken, "Evaluation and Obligation: Two Functions of Judgments in the Language of Conduct," *Journal of Philosophy*, 47 (1950): 5–22; Asher Moore, "A Categorical Imperative?" *Ethics,* 63 (July 1953): 235–50.

3. John Dewey has something pertinent to say here: "Why employ language, cultivate literature, acquire and develop science, sustain industry, and submit to the refinements of art? To ask these questions is equiva-

lent to asking: Why live? And the only answer is that if one is going to live one must live a life of which these things form the substance. The only questions having sense which can be asked is *how* we are going to use and be used by these things, not whether we are going to use them. Reason, moral principles, cannot in any case be shoved behind these affairs, for reason and morality grow out of them. But they have grown into them as well as out of them. They are there as part of them. No one can escape them if he wants to. He cannot escape the problem of *how* to engage in life, since in any case he must engage in it in some way or other—or else quit and get out." *Human Nature and Conduct* (New York: Modern Library Edition, 1930), p. 81.

4. Thus to say that "the only reason why $X$ is desir*able* is because it is desired" is to mean that it can be desired, or that it most likely *will* or *should* be in the future, not that it "ought to" in any special sense.

5. "The Elements of Ethics," in *Philosophical Essays* (London: Allen and Unwin, Ltd., 1910), p. 1.

6. *Ethics and Language* (New Haven: Yale University Press, 1943), p. 1.

7. "Analysis of Moral Judgments," *Horizon* 20 (1949): 174–75.

8. Quoted from Bertrand Russell, *A History of Western Philosophy* (New York: Simon & Schuster, 1945), p. 238.

9. There have been exceptions to this. See articles by C. E. Ayers and George R. Geiger in *Value: A Cooperative Inquiry* (New York: Columbia University Press, 1949).

# 7.

# Human Nature, Homeostasis, and Value

Each age has sought to give a definition of human nature. This definition is usually in accordance with the state of knowledge, peculiar problems, and needs of that age. The definition of humankind has been of central importance to our "moral" life. Each age has prescribed action in terms of its conception of human nature. But we are witnessing a sustained criticism of this whole procedure. From many quarters comes the view that humanity does not have a nature, and that, even if it does, one cannot derive either a moral philosophy or a value theory from human nature.

It is the thesis of this chapter that it is possible to attribute a nature to the human species and to derive a restricted theory of value—if not a moral philosophy—from such a theory. In order to demonstrate this thesis, I will have to deal with three separate topics. In Part I, I raise the question, Does man have a nature? In Part II, I attempt a tentative theory of human nature. In Part III, I argue that value may be defined in terms of human nature.

From *Philosophy and Phenomenological Research*, 17, No. 1 (September 1958): 36–55. Reprinted by permission of the publisher.

# I

The underlying assumption of the classic tradition is that there is a universal essence or nature of the human species. Life, it was held, carries its own tendencies and intrinsic ends. The problem for humankind was to reveal its ends and to provide the conditions which will enable their fulfillment. Thus Greek philosophy held that if we could define human, we could then say something about the "good life." This definition was to be in terms of *genus* and *differentia*; the distinguishing characteristic of the species indicated the *teleos* of humankind. The Stoics agree that humans must live in accordance with nature. Human nature participates in the natural scheme of things. The problem is to discover the "natural law." The Augustinian philosophy of history has humans playing a role in a still larger "divine scheme." But again the universal human, his happiness, blessedness, or destiny, is an entity distinct from the particular individual.

In the modern period there is a rejection of teleology and the Greek and scholastic viewpoint. Yet thinkers like Machiavelli and Hobbes still continue to investigate human nature through the development of a new science of humans. They are more concerned with a descriptive search for basic laws of motivation than ideal ends. Hobbes changes natural law to include the "law of self-preservation." Humanity is held to be desire-seeking, or for other utilitarians, pleasure-seeking animals, who may use reason to maximize self-interest or pleasure. This definition of human nature is largely in terms of the autonomous, self-sufficient individual in his biological capacities independent of the social group. From it a normative theory is derived: satisfaction, pleasure, or happiness is the good.

The eighteenth and early nineteenth centuries, too, everywhere contain the idea that humans have a human nature, a nature found in all men and women. Each person is a particular exemplification of the universal concept human.

In the nineteenth century, however, Darwin gives the classic picture of man a well-deserved jolt. Evolutionary categories destroy the notion of fixed species and forms. Human life is a product of evolution, due either to the struggle for survival; or later, with Mendel, to genetic mutations. Moral and political recommendations follow restatements of human nature in biology.

Marxian dialectic attempts to combine both Hegel and evolution. Human history is said to be a product of socio-economic forces and historical laws. Man has an original nature. But this is corrupted by an evil economic system. Change the system and you change man.

In the early part of the twentieth century behavioristic psychologists suggest theories of human nature which stress the role of conditioning rather than immutable biological forms. "Stimulus-response," "conditioned response," "habit," "afferent-efferent," "nervous system," etc., are leading conceptual explanations. But these, too, are said to be applicable to the entire species, *homo sapiens*. Great optimism prevails: If the environment is responsible for what humans are, a reconstruction of the environment will lead to a better man and woman.

Freudian psychoanalysis, however, has tended to obscure the classic view: Do humans have a nature; can we relate to it? Each person is a product of complex causal influences which operate deep within the self. To understand an individual's neurotic conflict we must reconstruct the materials that create tragedy. In one sense universal human "being" gives way to individual case study, and psychology becomes an art; but in another, psychology is still a science, since it is interested in developing general hypothetical concepts, "id," "ego," "superego," "libido," "the unconscious," etc., which apply to all men and women. The implications of Freudian psychoanalysis for value theory are not always clear. According to Freud, we must understand the basis of abnormality, not condemn it. Freud does suggest that orthodox notions of sin, responsibility, reason, and the soul, are wrong. There seem to be implicit assumptions that recognition of one's real self, the avoidance of repressions, integration, and adjustment are good, since such things constitute a cure. This raises the question whether there are norms implicit in human nature from which value categories may be inferred. This is an important issue that I want to discuss in the last section of this chapter. The main point that I want to emphasize now is that the prevailing view historically is that humans in one way or another possess a nature. True, different things have been meant by "nature"; and there have been different ways, philosophical or scientific, of approaching the problem of definition; yet generally there is the attempt to characterize the behavior of the human species.

The Western tradition has not lacked opposition to the attempt to define human nature (or to derive a value theory from it). But recently such criticisms have increased. Man, we are told, does not have an "essence" or a nature; there can be no science of humankind. Hence, all attempts to ground value on human nature are bound to fail. There has been a chorus of dissenting voices coming from diverse philosophical sources.

Empiricists and nominalists maintain that there is no universal man. The word "man" does not denote a class; it merely applies to each of a number of individuals. There are no basic properties descriptive of the entire species. To understand man, they argue, one must study the summations of diverse additive characteristics; averages and deviations must replace types. The use of probability curves about attitudes and behavior of groups is the only method available. Thus nature (and law) gives way to statistical enumeration and description.

Nineteenth-century historicism has led to the view that human beings do not possess a universal nature, but only a *past*. We are the product of diverse influences. We are the residue of a multiplicity of past events. Hence, we can only understand ourselves by exploring the complex origin and drama of civilization as it plays its role upon the vast stage of history. History is concerned with the unique; this we are told can not be reduced to scientific equation. A precise definition of human nature in terms of strict explanatory law must be replaced by historical method. Only an account of human history suffices to give an insight into human nature.

Still another view finds humanity's *future* to be the overwhelming fact of human life. Emergent evolutionsts tend to undermine optimism in the definability of human being. It is not possible to predict the emergence of future qualities. Life, mind, society are held to be complex developments from lower levels, yet are not reducible to them. Hence humans do not have a fixed nature, but an evolving one.

Pragmatism is also prospective in its interpretation of humanity. It believes that the future can be controlled. Humans are creative beings capable of adding forms to nature and inventing new constructions. Hence, human nature is neither fixed nor follows strict law. It is in a process of becoming dependent upon what humans decree or create. It is neither the past nor a given nature that is decisive, but rather what humanity makes of these materials in the future that is important. It is the promise of what humanity may become that teaches us most about ourselves. For pragmatism, humanity's supreme moral obligation is to resolve problematic situations; the possibilities of human intelligence are held to be virtually unlimited.

But this optimism of only a generation ago has now been replaced by what many have called the "age of anxiety." Contemporary ethical philosophers have perhaps unwittingly contributed to this anguish. The emotivists recommend the need for ethical "sophistication" and skepticism. They have directed a verbal blast at all attempts to modify our values in terms of our increased knowledge of humanity and society.

The theme of anguish is widespread in contemporary existentialism, both atheistic and religious. Sartre maintains:

> Man is nothing else but what he makes of himself. Such is the first principle of existentialism. It is also what is called subjectivity . . . if existence really does precede essence, man is responsible for what he is.[1]

For Sartre, each individual is what he conceives himself to be. He creates his own essence. There are no values external to man and no fixed human nature which he is obligated to fulfill. Each person both chooses his values and creates an image of himself and humanity. Man's subjectivity only reemphasizes the dilemma of his aloneness. Each individual is a distinct being, conscious of his own existential plight. It is the *present* moment which defines life, not any laws of history. Man is free—to be a different person if he wishes. "Man . . . is condemned every moment to invent man."[2]

This theme may lead to a reformer's attitude, yet it may also lead to the exact opposite: a morbid concern with failure, disorder, anomie, chaos, fear, and death. This form of disillusionment has captured much of the literary imagination. T. S. Eliot appears to express the "longing" of our times when he says: "We are the hollow men;/ We are the stuffed men;/ Leaning together;/ Headpiece filled with straw. . . ."[3] Such attitudes have resulted in part in a return to "the fold"—with a mass migration back to religion. Poets and theologians claim to have the answers, even if philosophers do not. Some say that it is man's "eternal spiritual plight" freshly recognized that is responsible for this psychological anxiety. But the contemporary scene bears too many similarities to the later Hellenistic period and the causes then present to be merely eternal and unconditioned by social and cultural factors. Hence, it is the peculiar character of the contemporary climate—its disorder and confusion—that is responsible in part for the view that naturalism fails, that man's behavior has no natural explanation, or that there is no human nature.

Thus we are confronted with a challenge: Does man have a nature? Is he simply to be characterized in terms of approximate averages and deviations from them? Does his past (history), or his future (evolution and creativity), or his present (subjectivity) mean that he cannot be defined, as critics allege? I submit that he does have a nature. *What* is his nature is largely an empirical matter; *whether* he has a nature is a problem for philosophical analysis. Hence, before we can attribute a nature to man, it is necessary to analyze the meaning of the concept.

"Nature" is a highly ambiguous term to which many meanings have been imputed. For Aristotle "nature" or *physics* referred to the internal source of motion or rest in an object; it was the principle of change intrinsic to the thing itself. The nature of a thing could only be understood in terms of the essence and end of the species class, what a thing was in itself aside from its accidents. The pitfalls of Aristotelian logic are well known. Fixed "natures" and "essences" are concepts limited by Greek science and logic.[4]

I think that it is possible to interpret nature in still another more fruitful way. When we use the concept nature we may be referring to the *definition* of a class of entities (within limits), and to the *explanation* of this class of entities in terms of a more comprehensive theory. By definition I do not mean a nominal or dictionary definition. Definition in the sense here used may be described as a scientific description of a class of objects; that is, the definiens refers to a range of observable properties. Things, attributes, or events may be explained by reference to their classes, or their conditions, or laws, or regularities; and laws and regularities may be similarly explained by reference to still other more comprehensive laws, from which they can be derived. It is this latter phase, i.e., explanation, that is the ideal of inquiry and that best affords a basis for prediction; and it is this phase which most theories of man heretofore have failed to emphasize.

I should like to illustrate "nature" by reference to the definition of minerals in the natural sciences. That there are great variations in minerals—and not "fixed" characteristics—is now accepted by all mineralogists. Recognizing continuous variation, it is nonetheless possible to create names for the different portions of a continuous series without maintaining that each name is that of a distinct mineral. Hence a mineral may be defined as a substance which *varies* in chemical composition and physical characteristics *within natural limits.*

But we cannot stop here. In addition there must be a search for more basic explanation: These limits seem to be determined by the variations which are possible without destroying the crystal structure. Thus by reference to the crystal or molecular structure we begin to afford an explanation in terms of a theory.[5]

I maintain that the complete statement of the dispositional predicates used to define a class of entities (such as coal) and to explain it is equivalent to the "nature" of that class. Here "nature," as a general term, refers *either* to classes of entities, their order and structure, *or* to the *statements* used to define and explain such classes within the context of inquiry (since such statements in principle may be translated into the conditional form). The ontological basis of scientific explanation, whether realism (powers and potentialities) or conventionalism (convenient conditional statements), is not here at issue. (Although there is some element of freedom in definition, the fact of verification nonetheless seems to me to imply a real structure.) I am merely saying that the "nature" of a subject matter may be determined (if at all) through a process of inquiry; and that the most adequate definition and explanation of that subject matter is equivalent to a statement of its nature, such that, if X (the subject matter), then a, b, c, (experimental consequences) should follow. Thus, if any substance is coal, then it should under standard conditions have specific properties (volatile, etc.) and a structure (carbon, etc.) which analysis and testing will confirm.

It may be argued that to apply the concept nature in this way to coal is a distortion of meaning. The definition or explanation of coal may be attained without introduction of the surplus term "nature." I agree that within the scientific context, the term is unnecessary. But the use of "nature" does, I think, have important philosophical implications. It is a concept useful in interpreting the meaning of a subject matter. "Nature" in this sense is primarily a *philosophical* or *meta* category. It is in the human context, however, that I am especially desirous of employing the concept. Here the nature of man may be used as stated above. It is not an inner essence or end; nor a fixed faculty or instinct. It refers rather to a general statement of the fundamental definitions and explanatory theories employed in the sciences of man (assuming that some such theories are possible) whatever they may be.

Now with this in mind it is possible to offer a tentative answer to those statisticians who argue that man has no nature but only a point on a curve. Statistical investigation is neither the ideal nor end of inquiry, neither establishing a law nor disconfirming a nature for man. It is only an initial attempt at characterization of human behavior—beyond that nothing conclusive may be generalized about man.

There is frequently a rejection of the concept nature because nature is supposed to apply to standard individuals as representative of the species; and obviously there are wide *deviations* from the standard case. But we should not overlook the similarities within natural limits of members of a species. Men and women may differ among themselves, but their differences are less than those with members of other species. Perhaps man's nature does not simply refer to the standard individual, but is to be further characterized in the context of society and culture. In other words, laws of human behavior are *not* simply biological and psychological, but may also be anthropological, economic, sociological, and political. Hence human nature does not merely refer to the nature of discrete individuals, but to men collectively as revealed in their socio-cultural dimensions.

Moreover, the concept nature is theoretical. It is in a sense an ideal concept. It has the signification of dispositional property and may be expressed in an "if, then" statement. Hence a thing will not reveal its properties, if standard conditions are absent. Thus coal will not ignite at $10°C$; and human nature is not always discovered by statistical descriptions: both require the presence of normal conditions.

In reply to the historicists who maintain that man only has a past, not a nature, I submit that the same thing may be said of *every* entity. All things in the universe have unique "careers." Any one thing has a specific irrecoverable space-time locus; its individual constitution is a result of a set of previous events that it has undergone. *This* coal in a Pennsylvania field has a distinctive history unlike that of its Saar counterpart. Yet, the unique history of a particular piece or vein of coal may not be the most important part of its definition and explanation in general.

This does not mean that we ought to dismiss history. We may be concerned with history in two ways: first, with the unique history or a particular entity; second, with the limiting general laws which apply in the evolution of a class of entities. In some cases knowledge of an individual's history may be useful. What the particular history of Pennsylvania coal is may be an important question. Similarly, the unique history of a particular star, planet, atom, or flower; the time, place, and events formative in the career of any one thing may be of importance in understanding the full "being" of that thing. The multifarious history of individual human beings and societies is a genetic fact that cannot be overlooked. But if we are to be concerned with historical reconstruction, we must also be concerned with the general laws which apply in the evolution of a class of entities. Indeed, general knowledge of this kind is presupposed in any particular historical inquiry, since such inquiry rests on interpretive assumptions. Thus man has a past, but this does not prevent him from also having a nature.

But further, he still has, as has been pointed out, a future. But does man's future imply that he has no nature? Only if it applies in the same way to all other things. For other objects, stars, flowers, or coal also have futures. The development, growth, and cooling of a sun; the sex life and adventures of a rose; what happens to *this* piece of coal in *this* fireplace—these things are contingent. Existence manifests real precariousness; what will happen to any one thing in all of its manifestations is unpredictable. Even knowledge of the general may change in the future as we discover new uses and properties of things. Evolution and futurity are facts of both animate and inanimate objects. But to say beforehand that the future is unconditioned by causal laws (of structure or evolution) is to deny the whole basis of science, social and natural.

The pragmatic recognition that we are presented with a variety of possibilities in attempting to solve our problems opens the door to challenge. Man *is* a creative being; the future *is* open; but not completely so. Man may have a role in making himself. But while the universe may leave room for adventure, it also provides some of the basic rules of the game. Even the situation is circumscribed by its structure and organization. The difference between the pragmatists and the existentialists on this point is a real one: the former attempt to ground knowledge upon science; the latter are overly subjective. The chief defect of pragmatism is that it does not sufficiently emphasize conditions external to the observer as a basis for scientific prediction or valuational judgments. The existentialists do not tell us how science is possible. Even *if* existence precedes essence, it cannot be understood without it and is not separate from it. Man may make choices; he is free to want what he wills. But whether he is free to will what he wills in every case is another matter. Although he may not be compelled, his actions nonetheless presuppose causal conditions—else his actions would be entirely fortuitous and capricious.

The above mentioned critics of the concept human nature have abstracted one category or another applicable to man and emphasized it all out of proportion to its relevance. On the basis of this they have denied that man has a nature. If we are to have complete "intelligibility" of any subject matter, we must reconstruct the full context: past, present, future, and law. This is true whether it applies to our particular solar system (in astronomy), our earth (in geology), or to a particular society (in sociology), or person (in psychology). Yet such investigations of the individual can best proceed in terms of a general explanatory theory. Thus to deal with our solar system or earth, one must apply general concepts and laws derived from the natural sciences; and to characterize a society or individual, knowledge derived from the behavioral sciences and biology is essential.

In a sense, this view is in accord with those classical theories which also attempt to define or describe man. It differs from the classical view because its theory of man is grounded on the empirical sciences. It differs from those modern views which deny that man has a nature in the sense that, although it incorporates statistical and historical methods in inquiry into man, it holds that only a general empirical theory can best afford an explanation of human conduct.

# II

Is it possible to suggest such a theory of human nature? First, a question must be raised: Is there today one field of inquiry which is basic, and from which the fundamental definition and explanation of man must be derived? Psychologists have argued that psychology has priority in any explanation of human conduct, since psychological reactions are present in all human contexts. Biology has also claimed precedence for the organic or evolution, sociology for social structure, and anthropology for culture. Similar claims have been adduced by political science, economics, physics, and chemistry.

In one sense all of these claims for ultimacy may appear to be true. Each discipline investigates an aspect of man that may be present in most or all frames of reference. Each may get hold of a strand that is intricately involved in the fabric of life. Specialization has seemed unavoidable. But, as has been pointed out, there is no reason to believe that the existing fields of inquiry must remain unalterably fixed. These diverse perspectives are only partial ways of looking at man. Human life manifests a continuity of processes. Thus, there must be a steady attempt to amalgamate within science these separate perspectives into a more general theory of human behavior.

It has frequently been the role of philosophy to suggest what such a comprehensive picture may include. Philosophers must be aware of the difficulties involved in such a procedure. At present only a tentative outline—an approximate explanation of human behavior—may be suggested. Such a philosophical statement cannot be substituted for scientific explanation; it does not seek to reduce any field to a lower level; it is not a final conclusion. It grows out of and is limited by the findings of the sciences of man. By taking inventory of our present-day knowledge, pointing out conceptual analogies, and raising daring hypotheses, philosophy may possibly function as an intellectual catalyst stimulating further inquiry.

The concept *wholeness* is a dominant theme running through the social and behavioral sciences. This concept has a familiar ring to historians of philosophy. It emerges once again as a pivotal conception. What does it suggest? That the whole (the organism, man, economy, institution, etc.) may be greater than the sum of its parts; that the functional unity of certain entities displays properties only revealed in an actual process of full operation; that some entities manifest systematic organizations which are more than the separate elements involved. This has been called the organismic hypothesis. It is based principally on two sorts of evidence: empirical observation and the methodological fact that many interrelated factors are involved in the explanation of certain complex entities.

The concept wholeness is not static. It refers to dynamic processes of activity and becoming. *Activity* refers to any discernible change in the behavior of an organic context. Such activity occurs on various levels: in the simplest cellular changes, in motor-affective, perceptual, or cognitive processes, on the socio-cultural scale. It implies that for the behavior of life there is no inherent opposition between structure and function. The functional unity of diverse structures is a cardinal feature of activity. Structures are only names for more stable processes of long duration; and functions are rapid processes of shorter duration.

Can operational definitions be given for "activity," "wholeness," "functional unity"? They have had a more technical formulation in terms of the concept *homeostasis*. This idea is familiar to philosophers who have seen it employed as "equilibrium" by the Greeks, and in nineteenth-century economics and sociology; yet it has been significantly rediscovered in the life sciences.

Claude Bernard first expressed the germinal idea in biology. And the late physiologist, W. B. Cannon has developed it even further. Cannon writes about how the body preserves stability for its own functioning.

> Our bodies in their functional organization show activities that can be distinguished as internal and external. . . . One of the marvels of biology is the remarkable effectiveness of the regulative processes of the body's department of the interior for maintaining constancy. . . . This adjustment goes on through all the stages of growth, despite powerful alternative forces operating from within and without.[6]

Some of the states of steadiness maintained are body temperatures, mild alkalinity of the blood, water, sugar, salt, calcium, fat, and protein reserves. Natural defenses of the organism, processes of storage and release, the nervous and sympathetico-adrenal systems, enable the organism to maintain homeostasis at all times, including times of danger and alarm. The organism is able to direct processes to the restoration of balance. These biological processes are largely automatically controlled. However, as Cannon suggests, in more complex aspects of human life, reason and society also contribute to the achievement of homeostasis. In any event, it is the functional organization of processes or activities that enables the continuance of life and the revealing of germinal tendencies in all phases of ontogenetic, phylogenetic (and socio-cultural) development. A static state of equilibrium is never achieved; homeostasis is only an ideal condition applicable to *dynamic* processes of change and growth.

This suggests two important factors present in organic behavior. First, certain phylogenetic limitations—structures for development and growth (orthogenesis, morphogenesis, etc.)—are repeated in all normal members of a species. Second, structuralized processes or activities of internal and external homeostasis are also found. Metabolism is possible because of the existence of systematic structures of autonomous processes. These have been built in after a long process of evolution. External activities of the organism also contribute to a type of homeostatic adjustment through the development of conditioned response and habit systems.

The species seems to have fairly determinate "tendencies," or dispositional properties (which may be expressed in hypothetical form). But how these are utilized by the organism depends upon particular conditions of the context of interaction. This indicates the importance of the concept *field*. "Field" refers to the fact that many factors may be responsible for the total operation of an organic system. Logically, a "field" is defined when we can indicate the necessary and sufficient conditions relevant to its explanation. Empirically it refers to a scene of activities, both internal and external (organic, psycholgoical, or socio-cultural) where there are mutual interactions of elements in the maintenance of the total organized system.

Fields have different dimensions. In biology field may refer to the matrix of internal activities: an organism is a hierarchical organization of many different functional systems. Or field may refer to the broader environmental scene of interaction: to understand an organism one cannot stop at its skin. Blood stream and lungs depend upon oxygen from the air; and digestive system upon food. Both are products of complex cooperating internal processes and external activities. The organism is an open system in which processes of exchange are continually going on.

Lewin, Murphy, Sullivan, and others have employed the concept of field in psychology and psychiatry. Here field is not necessarily physiological, motor, or neurological, but may be perceptual, emotional, cognitive (real or imagined). (For gestalt psychologists perception is holistic in character.) Thinking and learning presuppose sign, symbol, language, or communication as objective factors in a field. Interpersonal relationships are basic to the life of men and women. Reproduction is bi-sexual. The child is dependent upon the mothering care of another. Personality is the relatively enduring pattern of recurrent activities structured by the society and expressed by the culture.[7] Since man interchanges with an environment which includes society and culture, knowledge of the total field is necessary for understanding him.

The concept *anxiety* seems to have captured the imagination of many psychiatrists.[8] It functions as an explanatory mechanism—the drive to avoid anxiety (and frustration) is said to be a basic factor in the motivation and formation of personality. Is this avoidance of anxiety merely a negative reaction? It would seem to suggest the converse, i.e., the quest for a form of homeostasis, adjustment, "euphoria" seems to be the guiding positive stimulus. Here adjustment or homeostasis must be interpreted in a variety of ways in terms of different sociocultural materials. Yet there seems to be certain basic needs in all cultures; food, air, security, warmth of another person, power, recognition, self-assertion, function as controlling tendencies which graded anxiety mechanisms strive to realize.

Simlarily, Parsons and Merton in sociology have referred to the functional organization of institutions, to "latent and manifest functions" within a society. An institution here is interpreted as a relatively stable pattern of activities contributing to the functioning of the whole field. There appears to be a need for some integration (homeostasis) of these separate functions. Further, all societies appear to require the performance of certain basic functions (e.g., the production and distribution of food, education, defense, etc.), even if different structures are possible.

Cultural anthropologists such as Malinowski and Benedict have also used functional categories. Religious, esthetic, ideological aspects of experience, etc., have a cultural basis in that these are shared symbolic meanings. Such cultural materials have meaning only within the complexus of a civilization and are not readily understood if abstracted from it.

In classical economics the search for "natural harmonies" of supply and demand in the marketplace is an illustration of the use of static equilibrium. This notion was largely borrowed from Newtonian physics, where the idea of a static equilibrium of mechanical forces was widely employed. In recent years, however, economists have begun talking about *dynamic* equilibrium. This is more akin to the use of homeostasis in contemporary biology, where evolution, development, growth is the controlling idea.

Similar considerations, I think, apply to the theory of evolution. The course of evolution is due first to genetic structures and mutations; second, to the differential reproduction of individuals who transmit these heredity characteristics; third, to the adjustment and survival value of such characteristics to the individuals and groups which possess them; and fourth, to the species, population groups, or socio-cultural systems which determine who shall transmit such characteristics. In man the rules of marriage, reproduction, and group "adjustment" are now determined by the society and culture.

Am I permitted to draw an initial definition of man and possibly an explanation of his behavior? First, life may be defined as a hierarchical order of open systems which maintains homeostasis, grows, and reproduces through the exchange of components by virtue of field conditions. The field is essential in defining life, since living things are interactive or transjective beings. Living things display metabolism. They are endowed with undifferentiated genetic structures, or systems of ordered processes which guide growth and behavior. (For man these are not ready-made instincts or faculties.) But life is also controlled through homeostatic adjustment to the internal and external environment.

This definition of life is only an outline. But what about man? What is human nature? There is no one distinct property of man. However, there is a complexus of dispositional properties which in part distinguishes the human species from other species. Thus the human animal has paired grasping organs fully in his field of vision of stereoscopic sighted relationships. He is a fetalized, hyper-mammal, with protracted oral dependence, and intensified all-year-round sexual traits (especially the male). And he has a brain which alone is sufficiently large to enable it to cope with and learn from high-level symbolic meanings and communication.[9] This biological endowment is the result of a slow process of evolution. Whether it is expressed, actualized, or changed depends upon whether man can maintain sufficient homeostatic organization and adjustment. The unique fact of man is that he has constructed complex *external* homeostatic systems of activity (society, the family, the state, the economy, etc.), and that *he has created culture.* The evolution of socio-cultural field structures has enabled both the individual and the social group to express more complex avenues of creative organic activity, in art, religion, philosophy, science. It is an instrument of both expression and repression. A qualitatively distinct way of life is adopted as the socio-cultural context itself channels patterns of behavior (through the mechanism of conditioned response) along habitual lines. Particular societies and cultures have histories. They manifest orders over and beyond that of the individual. They are themselves limited by determinate laws governing their organization and expression. These considerations, I think, begin to explain in part *why* man is human. It is not, in any sense, a complete theory of man. It is a beginning which points out a basic feature of organic fields.

To what extent does this statement involve teleological assumptions? If by teleology is meant entelechies, ideal purposes, or final causes, then this definitely excludes all such reference. If, however, by teleological explanation is simply meant a functional interpretation of a dynamic interrelated system, then by all means this statement is teleological; that is, it implies a "natural teleology."

Some have argued that functional explanation may be translated into other terms. Thus far, however, the life and social sciences have found it useful to employ such functional language; and there is no reason to assume, other than on the basis of faith, that purely mechanistic or physical-chemical explanation will replace it. Indeed, simple efficient causation has itself encountered obstacles in the natural sciences, where the concept field is also employed. But I think that here field has a somewhat different meaning than that found in the above account. Therefore, insofar as it remains fruitful in the sciences of man to interpret the total behavior of an organized system in terms of tendencies toward dynamic homeostasis, I see no reason to attempt a retranslation into physicalist terms.

# III

This has important implications for value theory, for it allows for the readmission into value theory of the essential point of the classic position, i.e., *that value may be defined in terms of human nature.* In Part I, I have argued (along with the classic position) that it is possible that man has a nature. This nature can only be determined through the definition and explanation of man in the scientific context. In Part II, I have even suggested a tentative outline theory of his nature. I now want to argue that human value (or good) may be taken as equivalent to the laws of human nature as revealed by the sciences of man. I hold that this may be so, even if the particular theory of man that I have suggested in Part II is false.

This view differs from the classic view in the sense that it refuses to make value theory universal, necessary, or absolute. It is simply an empirical rule for inquiry. It is not concerned with moral theory, obligation, or prescription. Value theory as here interpreted is primarily an explanatory investigation.

But what is the relationship between the specific theory of human nature I have suggested and value? The implications are as follows. The basis of life is the principle of homeostasis. Life refers to any organic order of open systems in field relationship expansively directed to its own dynamic furtherance. Given an organic field, the valuable then refers to the dynamic homestatic continuance and expansion of that field. Whatever contributes to the field of life is valuable. Since the basic laws of human nature enable life to continue they are good. But the question must be raised: which systems of activity best lead to such an ideal condition? Only those field organizations (biological, psychological, in the species, the society, the culture) which satisfy basic needs of fields, which are based upon conditions of health, and which permit the maximized actualization of life are best. What are the basic needs, health, and the potentialities of life? This question may only be resolved empirically in specific contexts. I have suggested that basic needs of man refer to those conditions found essential for the functional maintenance and growth of life activity in all of its dimensions, that health is dependent upon dynamic homeostasis, and that the potentialities of life may only be revealed in biological and elaborate cross-cultural analysis.

Naturalistic philosophers generally have attempted a relational definition of value. The difference, however, between the view here proposed and the recent naturalistic position is that naturalism has largely defined value in terms of the individual—becoming involved in the ego-valuational predicament, confusing value with obligation, and omitting essential field conditions—whereas I do not. For the naturalist something is good because it is desired by the individual; whereas for the classic view something is desirable because it is good; and for my own, the desir*able* (as obligation) is irrelevant to the good. I still consider the position here outlined to be naturalistic, however, both in the Aristotelian sense that good is derived from human nature; and in the utilitarian equation of good with descriptive referents.

Most contemporary naturalists take man as they find him, as an experiencing being; his likes, desires, interests, pleasures, and immedicacies are the locus of value. But this has raised the spectre of subjectivism: how do we get from one individual's values to the next; how do we relate value to the society and culture?

There have been attempts by behaviorists, especially Dewey, to ground value on the conditions and consequences of behavior. Unfortunately, Dewey did not *sufficiently* emphasize the conditions of experience as the tests of consequences. There is the danger of becoming enmeshed in the sticky stuff of private experience, with no way of getting free. The picture of man that I have suggested might well avoid subjectivism, since value is explicitly defined in terms of the causal conditions and laws of life.

I should like to consider four possible objections that may be offered to the derivation of value from human nature: first, that it violates the usual definition of value; second, that it is a "persuasive definition" and vulnerable to the "open question" argument; third, that everything is "natural" including the unnatural; and fourth, that it elevates mere biological survival of the species to the highest pinnacle.

First, it might be argued that value refers to "feeling," "desire," "satisfaction," "liking," etc., and that my attempt to "redefine" is a distortion of what is usually meant by value. C. I. Lewis expresses a widely held assumption when he defines intrinsic value in terms of immediate experience. But the transcendentalist has defined value as unrelated to human likes—and might raise the same objections to Lewis's "redefinition."

This raises an important problem: what type of statement is a value definition? Is it analytic, a terminological convention, synthetic, a meta-statement? If analytic, then the meaning of the definiens should be involved in the meaning of the definiendum. Philosophers who deny the definability of "good" would deny that "value" is "human nature." I agree: this is not an analytic statement, since the predicate is not deducible from the subject. Is this statement, then, a terminological convention or rule? In one sense, it is. The term "value" has no clear meaning in ordinary language, for this is notoriously obscure. In all the sciences common usage is rejected for more precise definition. Hence, it is possible to stipulate a meaning for value—to construct an artificial language. Once one does, an appeal to common usage is *non sequitur*. But if freedom of linguistic definition is possible, what are the criteria of such definition? One test is fruitfulness. A definition is useful in the empirical sciences if it enables us better to construct an explanation of a subject matter. But since explanations have reference to observable properties, this suggests that value is based upon fact, and that therefore a value definition is also a high-level synthetic proposition. But still further, the sciences of man may not require the term "value." If this should be the case, then value (like nature) is also a meta or philosophical category summarizing a theory of human nature. Thus there is some freedom in value definition. The test of a value definition is this: that definition of value is best which most effectively accounts for the way human beings behave; or, in philosophy, summarizes such an account.

Does liking or immediate satisfaction afford an effective account of human behavior? I think not. Liking is usually considered to be conscious. But it is very difficult to distinguish between conscious and other organic processes and activities. Where does one begin and the other end? Man is frequently impelled by somatic and unconscious drives without any immediate liking or anticipation of such in mind. It is not conscious feeling, unattended by organic states or the socio-cultural field which is alone responsible for action. Insofar as organisms attempt to avoid anxiety and achieve homeostasis, then the quest for immediate liking or satisfaction is not the basic law of motivation or end of life. Naturalism intends the first part of its theory as descriptively correct; but liking is an abstraction from the total context and affords only a partial explanation of behavior.

The widest possible explanation must be in terms of those basic life processes which are central to the continued functioning of life. Hence, the definition of value in terms of liking fails on this account and the one that I have put forth may be more adequate.

Second, it has been argued that all definitions of value are persuasive definitions. But must this necessarily follow? Let us assume for purposes of discussion that we have a choice between two definitions of value; one to the effect that value is "immediate liking," the other that it is "human nature"; the valu*able* being either the like*able* or the realiz*able*. What is the meaning of the suffix *able*? To say that value is the immediate likable or realizable may mean that it *can* be liked or realized in the future; that it *should* be liked or realized in the future (if normal conditions are present); or that it *ought* to be so liked or realized. If we were to allow the last mentioned signification of *able*, then the question of persuasive definition may possibly be raised. One may ask why ought *I* to like immediate liking or why ought *I* to realize human nature? But to deny the truth of either definition because you personally dislike liking or do not wish to realize human nature implies another definition of value in terms of *individual approval* and psychological motivation. You presuppose one definition of value to reject another. But, I am not willing to allow that value definitions are persuasive definitions, since I hold that the function of definition here may be descriptive not prescriptive. Hence, the only senses of *able* that need be admitted are *can* and *should*.

Another form of this objection is the open question argument: Why ought I to live? Why is life good or valuable? (After all, do not some people prefer nirvana or suicide?) My answer to this is that the question of individual obligation is irrelevant to value. The same open question may be raised against any true fact. Here, too, the question of private belief is irrelevant to that of truth. Both are practical psychological questions which cannot be resolved by cognitive answers (although I agree with Peirce that there is a connection between the method of fixing belief and truth). You can no more be sure of demonstrating the value of life than you can your own existence; yet both life and existence are necessary postulates of any significant question of value or fact. Life and nature are not intuitively certain or demonstrably provable. Thus there is no guarantee that the "bindingness" of obligation will be felt by every man.[10]

Would an objective observer agree that life and its expansion (in biological or socio-cultural dimensions) is good, such that if life were to disappear, value would disappear? There is no ultimate answer to this question. Whether this is the best of all possible worlds is beside the point: it is the world we find. In the last analysis nature and life must be accepted as the empirical given.

Third, it may be objected that life in *all* of its senses is natural (and good). Santayana claims that everything that is, is "natural," including death, disease, psychosis, anomie, and the "unnatural." Nature, says Santayana, may operate by law, but she has no preferences. If life is good, then the drama of life includes war, cruelty, torture, tragedy.

But because fact and value are related does not mean that whatever is, is natural. Certain aspects of life are more normal or natural than others—much the same as certain theories are truer than others. To argue that life in all of its senses is good (I would agree that it is in any sense better than the absence of life) would also imply that truth may be applied to everything. Whatever is, exists in some context; hence, error, misconception, and delusion "are true." But we do use truth in a more restricted sense as applicable to the warranted. Hence nature and value as applicable to life may also be defined in a selective way. It is simply a matter of the use of the term "natural." Everything in nature is natural in one sense; but those things which accord with the laws of its kind and the homeostatic fulfillment of life are more so.

But how are we to determine specifically the natural and the good? Some defenders of "natural law" have been inconsistent. Pope Pius XII wears glasses and false teeth, yet is opposed to the use of contraceptives; pain may be avoided through drugs, yet natural birth may not. The difficulty here has been that most attempts to define the "normal" have not been based upon scientific ground, but upon myth, dogma, or the status quo. Further, most definitions of man have been *pre*-socio-cultural, and have ignored the fact that reason and civilization, discovery and invention, are part of the nature of man. Thus what man does in the socio-cultural context is also human. Most natural law theorists have sought either an overall standard applicable to all cases, or structures essential for the nature of man. But what is normal is not deducible from an absolute criterion, but is an empirical discovery; and the search for necessary functions must supplement the search for necessary structures.

Whatever contributes to the maintenance and expansion of life is valuable; whatever inhibits it is dis-valuable—the normal refers to those functions which are necessary for life. Normality is not a statistical average; nor is it the usual; it may be the exceptional. But it may be asked, may not the psychotic or abnormal individual (or culture, economy, etc.) also achieve a level of adjustment or type of homeostasis in his (or its) own terms? Achieving some sort of integration is absolutely essential for the maintenance of living systems. But the survival value of "psychotic adjustments" are at a minimum. They either do not satisfy the basic needs of the system or do not allow for further growth and development.

Fourth, does this theory of value imply that mere biological reproduction and survival of life in the species at large are the highest values? True, the widest distribution of life among many things is a marvel. Yet man is not simply a biological being—he is also creatively expanding along other lines. He builds cities and adorns them with art. These, too, are important human activities; they tend to direct men's efforts from sexual reproduction to the pursuance of other goods. But which is better? Man's biological or socio-cultural self? Surely reproduction is an essential condition for the maintenance of the species—but that it is in itself sufficient betrays the very ground of human life. Culture indicates that some restriction of life at some point may be essential for life (as populations get too large). Culture is distinctive to man; that he should cultivate it cannot be proven. It is like the digestive system; why pursue culture is like asking the question why eat? It is the very fabric of life and a basic system for its development.

Further, because life is the basic good does not mean that each individual's life is to be sacrificed to the life of the species (or to society or culture as a whole). In one sense, each man is insignificant in the sea of life; but in another sense, respect and compassion for the individual leads in the long run to the greatest possible consequences. On occasion society will sacrifice individuals (as in wartime) for the good of the whole. Yet, as we have learned, the greater good in most situations is best served by respecting the individual good. Moreover, because life can continue only when conditions of homeostasis are present, does not imply a static conception as the ideal. Mere survival or maintenance of the *status quo* is not the inference; growing and dynamic homeostasis is.

In conclusion, I might add that this theory does not tell us what to do in particular situations. This is the task of a theory of valuation or decision. At most, it may say—maximize life, achieve homeostasis and growth. Why? Because men and women do so. Beyond that nothing may be said by way of imperative—a different level of discourse. But what will achieve these things depends upon knowledge of each situation.

The theory of value herein suggested as a hypothesis rests upon the scientific definition and explanation of human nature. Science (reason in the community) is the ultimate source of our knowledge of value. Science is a natural human affair; it is part and parcel of life. It discovers and creates ideal systems which contribute to the homeostatic expansion of life. Therefore, the extension of science is perhaps the chief practical good for humankind to achieve: this may only be accomplished by socio-cultural education and reconstruction. However, scientific and philosophical theories by themselves cannot be expected to provide "sure fire" imperatives to action. They can only suggest in each age a comprehensive theory of human nature and value and the possibilities inherent in such a theory. It is this cognitive function—the understanding of man— I submit, which is the first business of value theory to resolve.

# NOTES

1. Jean Paul Sartre, *Existentialism* (New York: Philosophical Library, 1947), pp. 18, 19.

2. Ibid., p. 28.

3. T. S. Eliot, "The Hollow Men" in *Collected Poems* (New York: Harcourt, Brace and Company, 1952).

4. There have, of course, been other significations of "nature." It has been used to denote the totality of existence, the whole universe as a system of processes. "Nature" has been used synonymously with the "objective" as contrasted with the "subjective"; or the "natural" in contrast with the "conventional," "human," or "social," etc. I am not concerned with these meanings of "nature."

5. A useful definition and explanation of coal (usually classed with minerals) might run as follows: Coal (an organic compound) varies from peat, to lignite, bituminous and anthracite. It contains varying degrees of fixed carbon (C; atomic weight 12.010; atomic number: 6) from 35 percent (in peat) to 90 percent (in anthracite), ash, moisture, and volatile matter, which will ignite under special conditions (of temperature, oxygen, etc.).

6. W. B. Cannon, "The Body Physiologic and The Body Politic," *The Scientific Monthly* 79, No. 1 (July 1954): 20–21. See also W. B. Cannon, *The Wisdom of the Body* (New York: W. W. Norton and Co., Inc., 1932). Also Ludwig von Bertalanffy, *Problems of Life: An Evaluation of Modern Biological Thought* (New York: John Wiley & Sons, Inc., 1952).

7. "Society" here refers to more basic structured activities (institutions); whereas "culture" refers to the ideological, religious, esthetic, philosophical, civilized expression of the group.

8. See Harry Stack Sullivan, *The Interpersonal Theory of Psychiatry* (New York: W. W. Norton & Company, Inc., 1953).

9. See Weston Le Barre, *The Human Animal* (Chicago: The University of Chicago Press, 1954).

10. I suspect that the problem of obligation is resolvable only in this sense—that insofar as we continue to live, we are already accepting the expansive power of life (the person who does not is probably abnormal). Fields of life are not simply individual but concern the species, the society, the culture; hence, obligation is applicable to these areas as well. But *why* should any field of life continue? An individual may refuse (so he thinks) to participate in interpersonal relationships or in culture. At least he cannot refuse to participate in his biological fields without death. Insofar as he does participate he has, perhaps unconsciously, accepted the value of life. The problem here is to show the individual that society and culture express his life on still higher levels of complexity and that he cannot dispense with them. You may not be able to convince him rationally, however. The question of obligation rarely arises for most of the other complex fields of life, such as the species, society, or culture, which rarely, if ever, accept self-extinction: it is the very principle of their being to continue.

# 8.
# Does Ethics Have
# Any Metaphysical Presuppositions?

## I.

Does *ethics* have any need for metaphysics? Or is it possible to investigate all ethical problems independently of a metaphysical commitment? The conception of metaphysics that I wish to focus on here is a highly limited one. And my purpose merely is to show that the criticisms of this form of metaphysical ethics have gone too far and that there is *some* connection between metaphysics as so defined and ethics.

The sense of metaphysics that I will elaborate is that which is pursued by most philosophers no matter what their labels or affiliations. In sophisticated philosophical company this is sometimes called the "philosophy of science,"[1] or more recently "conceptual analysis."

Metaphysics as I conceive it, at the very minimum, is concerned

From *Philosophical Quarterly* 9, No. 34 (January 1959): 5-12. Copyright © 1959 by Basil Blackwell. Reprinted by permission of the publisher.

with *uncovering and analyzing basic presuppositions*; it is an inquiry into *fundamental concepts and categories.* I maintain that any given subject matter, or any human activity or investigation presupposes certain *root* categories. A metaphysical analysis is an inquiry into the meaning and/or adequacy of such presuppositions and categories. But what is a "presupposition"? Its meaning is not easily definable, since it has been used synonymously with "supposition," "preconception," "presumption," "assumption," "supposal," "foundation," "ground," "postulate," etc.; and there are subtle differences between many of these terms. In general, however, a "presupposition" may be said to be a fundamental concept or category in regard to a specific system of sentences or beliefs. What is a "category"? Here, too, there may be many synonyms: "class," "classification," "division," "grouping range," "kind," "sort," "taxonomic," etc. A "category" is usually a large area generalization which isolates and distinguishes a set of entities, or events, or beliefs about them, and as such is of a distinct logical type. (In using the term "category" in ethics I am not dealing with the broader questions of "the generic traits of nature" as based upon the sciences of nature.)

A "presupposition" is that which is antecedently assumed, usually without question, as basic to a system of propositions or beliefs. It may be explicitly recognized, but is usually only implicitly present. To say that *p* presupposes *q* means that the holder of *p* (a word, sentence, theory, or belief) assumes an even more fundamental sentence *q*. To clarify the presupposition of a word would be to make clear the assumed rules of use.[2] To clarify a proposition would be to make clear the initial assumed rules and empirical generalizations held by the user. A presupposition does not necessarily refer to a necessary condition, or to a premise; or is it an *a priori* truth. Rather *q* here may refer to various types of sentences having different functions. These may be empirical generalizations, rules of procedure, decisions or values, that the commitment to *p* involves. In other words, every conceptual system itself is based on other propositions as foundational to that system. A metaphysical analysis examines the basic reasons for the choice of one system rather than another. It is not within a system so much as about it. Metaphysics is an attempt to interpret, reorder, and reorganize the sets of ideas with which we think about the world. It is a plotting of the main relief and contours of our conceptual map, particularly in an effort to find out the common features of our many branches of knowledge.

The view of metaphysics here advocated is not dissimilar to Kant's. A good case also can be made for interpreting Aristotle's *Metaphysics* essentially in these terms. The best defense of this conception, however, is made by Collingwood.[3] It may be, for instance, the natural sciences and their guiding conceptions of the universe. A metaphysical inquiry of this sort would entail a critical investigation of the foundations of the sciences at any one historical period (such as E. A. Burtt's study of Newtonian science). Or a metaphysical conceptual analysis might also be concerned with the grounds of the social sciences and their prevailing view of humankind. This would be a metaphysics of human nature. Metaphysics as here construed is related to empirical scientific inquiry. But how is metaphysical analysis to be distinguished from what the average scientist or specialist does? By its generality? Surely the physicist does not normally concern himself with his implicit framework (except at times of great change and intellectual ferment, or when he encounters obstacles in explanation); similarly the biological or social scientist is largely unconcerned with a broader perspective of his subject genus. But the philosopher is so concerned. He asks, "What is 'space,' 'time,' 'cause'?"; or "What is 'mind,' 'will,' 'behavior'?" These are questions of the highest metaphysical significance. The metaphysical analysis of categories and presuppositions is not carried on in isolation. The metaphysician, to be effective, must be a literate being. The metaphysician uses both his own experience and the public knowledge of his age. He expects to learn from science, art, religion, morality. He seeks analogies, unities, and similarities between various fields and subject matters. He strives to connect, relate, generalize, and broaden frames of reference. He tries to discover the various implications which different fields of inquiry have for one another. Yet his main interest is: What do they refer to? Are they warranted? Whitehead has called this "the critique of abstractions."

Some thinkers have considered epistemology to be part of the broader domain of metaphysics. Its key questions are, of course, thoroughly philosophical in character: What is "truth," "evidence," "validity"? What are the key methods and criteria employed in empirical inquiry and reasoning? The answers to these questions are meta-generalizations derived from the careful scrutiny of the many intellectual activities of humankind. It is the task of the epistemologist to render explicit and to criticize what other humans implicitly assume in the way of knowledge. But many have argued that ontological questions continually are intruding on the epistemologist—"What are sense data about?" "What is real?" etc.—and that epistemoloogy is dependent upon metaphysics for their solution. Now contemporary ethics largely has been concerned with epistemological and semantic problems. If we followed this kind of reasoning, then we might infer that ethics, too, is dependent upon metaphysics for the resolution of some of its problems. But I will not adopt this as the main line of argument. The relationship between epistemology and metaphysics is far more complex than the space we can give to it here will allow; and I wish to avoid the charge that I have solved our problem merely by definition. I do wish to argue, however, that the constant aim of a metaphysics which is critical, yet creative, is to make clear what is only vaguely understood and half-recognized by others. I submit that metaphysics, at the very least, is a *discovery, clarification, and criticism of the basic presuppositions and categories of any given subject matter.* This type of metaphysics is within the domain of conscious awareness; it is orientation toward our most fundamental assumptions. And it is the relationship of this type of metaphysics to ethics that I am especially concerned with elaborating.

## II

But what is ethics? It is first necessary to make a distinction between "morals" and "ethics." This usage is fairly well established today. "Morals" refers to the customs, mores, and ideals that a society cherishes and lives by, to the relations between people within it, and to the goals and ideals of an individual that control his conduct and character. "Ethics" (or "the philosophy of morals"), on the contrary, is *about* such customs, relations, conduct, and character. It is a critical investigation of customary and individual morality. Actually "ethics" is everything that philosophers have decided that it should be; for ethics is a human invention, a field of directed inquiry, grounded in the proposal that philosophers investigate a specific range of problems in a certain way.

There are a variety of problems and issues that have concerned ethical philosophers. In order to define the subject matter of ethics,

I will isolate only some of its main problems. They may be listed under three headings: First, *theoretical ethics*: This is the most fundamental type of inquiry. It deals with the nature of "good," "bad," "right," "wrong," "justice," "virtue," "obligation" and other basic concepts. It seeks to define them and to ascertain their nature, function, and analytic interrelations. In its broader sense, this inquiry may be called the metaphysics of morals: What is the ontological status of "good" and "right"? What is the axiological basis of morality, or the relationship of value to nature and to human nature? In its narrow sense this inquiry becomes meta-linguistic analysis. Here the main problem is the problem of the logic of language and meaning: What is the meaning of moral terms and concepts? May we define them? How are they used? Theoretical ethics is a cognitive enterprise which is primarily concerned with *knowledge* and understanding and only incidentally interested in recommending overt action or evincing moral persuasion.

Second, *practical ethics*: A great deal has been made of the contentions by some analytic philosophers[4] that ethics should be concerned first and foremost with action and conduct. This was one of the cardinal features of an earlier American pragmatism, although the initial lead for it had been given by Aristotle with his emphasis on *praxis*. The main problems of this type of ethical inquiry are usually epistemological: What is moral knowledge? What constitutes moral evidence? How do people reach decisions? Is there a logic of practice? Is there an ideal method, standard, norm, or guide to be discovered? Although the philosopher in this regard may not be directly concerned with offering advice or exhorting "noble" behavior, it is held that his inquiry is more intimately related to the processes of actual deliberation. To discover what are "good reasons" for one action rather than another allegedly is closer to the concrete situations of decision than to ascertain the nature of "good" or "right."

Third, *moral criticism*: Here we enter the actual area of moral recommendation. The philosopher who participates seeks to tell what he thinks is good, bad, right, wrong. He tries to offer solutions to moral problems. He may indeed try to arouse sentiment for one way of life rather than another—as, for example, in the devotion to the "life of reason" of Aristotle and Spinoza. He may try to persuade, motivate, educate, or inculcate a sense of obligation in his readers. In this capacity the philosopher is like the minister or social worker. He differs from them only in that he attempts consciously to formulate and rationally to defend his recommendations.

The dividing line between theoretical ethics, practical ethics, and morals cannot always be simply drawn. Each activity differs in degree and emphasis. All human activities involve proposals and choices. All express our value-preferences. There are, however, different levels of persuasive activity. The theoretical philosopher is dedicated to truth, meaning, or linguistic clarification. His therapy is usually limited to a small band of intellectual toilers. At most, his goal is to redirect the *beliefs about morals* of his fellow specialists and not to redirect their overt moral behavior. The philosopher of practical decision is perhaps more closely related to life. He may formulate a logic of practice, i.e., methods and rules of decision-making. This is based on both an inspection of how people *do* argue and a critical *normative* estimation of the types of reasoning considered to be the most adequate or valid. Inductive and deductive logic are likewise normative, since both set down and delimit the boundries of confirmability and validity. Yet the delimitation of the rules of logic in various domains may not necessarily lead to overt action. Commitment to the canons of scientific method or logic does involve value-preferences, at least implicitly. However, the commitment usually is not as direct or forceful as say the type of commitment found in activities related to moral criticism; for with moral criticism, sentiment and feeling are more closely related to action and belief, and the philosopher is not so much interested in understanding, viewing, or observing, as he is in participating and acting. In all three types of inquiries we have action, but in the last the action is directive, applied, and moral, whereas in the first and second it is comparatively more dispassionate, intellectual, and ethical.

In brief, then, ethics is the study of the basic concepts of moral behavior and the elaboration of the logical processes of decision; whereas morals is concerned more intimately with the actual direction and motivation of conduct and obligation along lines considered to be "good," "bad," "right," "wrong."

# III

But what is the relationship between metaphysics and ethics? The prevailing view is to deny any connection and to assert an absolute autonomy and independence for the latter. But I submit that there is an important relationship. Some of the questions of ethics *are* dependent upon metaphysics, and some *not*. I will now seek to define this independence more precisely.

There is at least a threefold relationship: (1) Ethical philosophy presupposes metaphysical assumptions and categories explicitly or implicitly. (2) Some of the conclusions of metaphysics have significance for ethics in clarifying its presuppositions. This is particularly true of the metaphysics of human nature, but it is also true of the metaphysics of nature. (3) Both ethics and moral practice reflect human experience. As such, they are capable of throwing some light on the problem of metaphysics and providing some test for the adequacy and inclusiveness of many metaphysical hypotheses. Metaphysics itself is rooted in a moral choice and value preference. Thus, as Kant showed, it is necessary for metaphysics to pay heed to the findings of moral experience. However, it is the first and second senses only and not the third sense that I will be concerned with investigating.

Every branch of knowledge assumes certain fundamental conceptions. Moral philosophy as conceived in the West has its own presuppositions: (*a*) It assumes that human beings are free and autonomous, capable of some choice. (*b*) It assumes that action can proceed from deliberation and a state of character. (*c*) Traditional practical ethics also holds that knowledge of moral principles has a role to play in life and that human beings may freely acquire and select standards, rules, or precepts in making such choices. (*d*) And finally, it presupposes that individuals (and groups) are responsible for their decisions and actions (in its Kantian formulation, that "ought" implies "can").

All this in essence involves a metaphysics, i.e., a theory of human nature. This metaphysics of human nature, having a classical, Greek and Christian basis, was formulated in pre-Darwinian and pre-social science terms. It takes the individual rather than the institution as central. It presupposes what are now familiar basic concepts: "freedom," "will," "motive," "consciousness," "mind," "choice," "deliberation," "responsibility," etc. This view of humankind is so pervasive in our culture that even the most recent and sophisticated studies of ethics for the most part accept them.[5] Yet the validity and adequacy of this picture of human nature has been seriously questioned by many tendencies within the contemporary sciences of human nature behaviorism, Freudianism, and cultural anthropology, to mention only a few. Behaviorism breaks down the dualism between mind and body; Freudianism points out the many unconscious sources of motivation; and cultural anthropology reveals the limits put on human choice by sociocultural forces. Is the classic picture of humankind ultimately correct, to be accepted as unquestioned? To argue in these terms is to behave ostrich-like in view of the great expansion in the twentieth century of our knowledge of humanity. It is fair, we believe, to argue that, if ethical inquiry is to progress, it is necessary to clarify the implicit assumptions of Western ethics concerning human nature.

As we have seen, *theoretical ethics* is an inquiry into basic ethical concepts. Both naturalistic and idealistic philosophers in the classic and contemporary tradition have been concerned with defining ethical or value concepts by relating them to human nature. Thus Plato, Aristotle, Spinoza, T. H. Green, Mill, Dewey, and Ralph Barton Perry, among others, relate good to their conceptions of human nature— self-realizationism, conativism, hedonism, cognitivism, or behaviorism. For those who accept this approach a necessary prolegomenon to any ethical investigation is a determination of the nature of humankind. Good (or value) is generally interpreted to refer to those processes which human beings maintain, strive for, bring into being, fulfill, realize, cherish, hold dear, like, desire, or prefer. In the human context "value" is said to involve conscious awareness and selection by the individual or social group. "Moral value" is only one species of value, that which is related to individual choice and to the obligations of individuals to each other. Those philosophers who have knowingly pursued this investigation of human nature have usually had either axiology, metaphysics, or *theoria* of value in mind. The question that may be asked, however, is whether *any and all* ethical (and value) investigations ultimately depend upon a metaphysical view of humanity?

Many ethical philosophers have devoted themselves to the meaning question independently of the ontological question. But can a complete theory of language be divorced from a theory of humankind or a theory of nature? Even those who have eschewed metaphysics have done so in terms of their own hidden metaphysical categories and criteria. For Moore, "good" like "yellow" canot be defined because it is a "simple quality." But what in the world is meant by a "simple quality"? Moore's analysis allegedly was in opposition to Hegelian metaphysical system-building; yet the injection of "nonnatural qualities" into nature is as much a metaphysical thesis as any metaphysical definition of good.

It is widely held today that moral value terms cannot be defined by reference to descriptive predicates. To say that "X has value" or "is good," according to Moore, is to attribute an objective ontological property to X. But most recent post-Mooreans have denied Moore's objectivist metaphysical foundations. The emotivists, for example, have interpreted value terms as emotive expressions and imperatives. And the school of ordinary language has argued that we cannot discover any simple referential meaning for value terms, but that the meaning of terms depends upon their uses.

Is this attack on descriptive ethics correct? Granted that the *term* "good" has no meaning independently of the language uses people adopt, but what about the *concept* good? Is there any objective entity to which it refers? People seem to use the concept in many different ways. The emotivists go far beyond the ordinary uses of moral predicates by offering a model for interpreting "value" as: "I like X, you do so as well." By their own criteria they fail because men and women do not always employ such predicates in the way that Ayer or Stevenson claim. The most important difficulty with the emotive theory is that it is based upon a dualistic theory of human nature: belief and attitude, intellect and feeling, cognition and emotion. Its theory of meaning thus presupposes a theory of man. The difference between classical ethics and emotive ethics is that the former recognizes this fact and turns to it directly; whereas the latter does not, yet depends upon it indirectly.

Is the view that the meaning of a sentence is to be discovered in its use devoid of metaphysics? If Ryle's *Concept of Mind* is any indication, then it, too, has its own metaphysics of human nature. This approach to ethical concepts is alleged to be a mild one devoid of any nasty philosophical commitments. Ordinary language is supposed to help us to discover the logic of language. Whose language? Not the English or Indo-European alone, we are assured, but all languages. But there are many uses; are we supposed to inspect them all? No, we are told, the problem is not that of descriptive linguistics, but of discovering the "typical" or "normal" uses of terms and concepts. But what is a "typical" or "normal" use? Surely, some language stocks are capable of expressing concepts which others cannot. What was typical three hundred years ago, or will be typical one hundred years from now may not be typical today. What special magic does "typical" possess anyway? Although we may learn what people think they mean by terms and concepts when they use them, are some uses truer or more acceptable than others? This, of course, brings us to the kind of questions which confronted Plato in the *Cratylus* about the ontological status of terms and concepts. And what else is the recent discussion of the functions of language, if not a metaphysical discussion of conventionalism versus realism? A rose is a rose by whatever name you call it, and metaphysics is metaphysics whether you choose to call it "logical analysis" or "metaphysics."

Thus theoretical ethics seems to involve some metaphysics; at the very least, it involves a metaphysics of man and a metaphysics of language. That ethics requires a full-blown metaphysics of nature or a *Weltanschauung* as well I am not prepared to argue. It is true that people who hold overall metaphysical views do find that these influence their ethical concepts and attitudes. For example, a person who believes that God is the supreme reality is more likely to define good in a way different from the agnostic. But since in this discussion I am interested in examining only a minimal conception of metaphysics, I will not pursue this question further.

Is there a connection between *practical ethics* and metaphysics? The relation here is much less evident than between theoretical ethics and metaphysics. Many recent ethical inquirers tell us that they are not concerned with theoretical ethics, axiology, or the definition of basic concepts. Nor are they concerned with moral criticism. They are, they say, interested only in discovering the logic of choice, the modes of moral reasoning, the nature of good reasons for an action. Aristotle's *Nicomachean Ethics* is taken as the model for this rather fashionable view.[6] But it must be remembered that the *Nichomachean Ethics* is one phase of a broader metaphysics of nature and that metaphysical assumptions permeate it. There is a theory of good and of human nature. For Aristotle deliberation and practical wisdom follow from his psychology. Thus practical ethics in the last analysis cannot be abstracted from theoretical wisdom or scientific knowledge. True, Aristotle tells us that ethics is not merely concerned with knowing good, but with making men good.[7] Yet becoming good depends upon a knowledge of what the chief good is for man, and this in turn depends upon a teleological view of the human species.

It is undoubtedly the case that we can discuss the methods of decision making without being overtly involved with metaphysics, much the same as we can investigate many of the rules of deductive or inductive logic free of entangling metaphysical alliances. But to develop a logic of practical choice involves some conception of what is good, bad, right, wrong, as standards of choice. And if so, we are sooner or later brought back to theoretical ethics. While there is some autonomy in developing the principles of logic, one is especially liable to encounter difficulties in normative logic since the rules of choice are not as well-established as in other fields. People are apt to ask all sorts of embarrassing questions: What is a rule? Why follow one rule rather than another? Why abide by such logical criteria? These questions inevitably lead us to the very grounds of decision making and rule making within human nature and to the metaphysics of man. Hence practical ethics sooner or later leads to theoretical ethics and metaphysics.

It is in regard to the third area of *moral criticism,* however, that the greatest freedom from metaphysics may be possible. I submit that many moral choices may be made without benefit of a philosophical clergy. One may follow the moral principles of any given society without always raising profound questions. One may be a moral being or manifest practical wisdom in regard to his choices. Thus there is more autonomy in moral choice. Similarly one may develop good physics without need of metaphysics. But it is when one's established principles and rules conflict, break down, or are questioned that ethical inquiry of a fundamental sort may enter. And at this point metaphysics may have some *influence* on action, and the philosopher may engage in moral criticism.

But let us be clear. One cannot merely deduce a moral prescription from a metaphysical assertion; there is no guarantee that a metaphysical belief will arouse motivation to action. Nor can a law of physics be deduced from metaphysics. Metaphysical systems such as those of Christianity and Marxism do have their own presuppositions and these may have implicit imperatives for action. But that a convinced Christian or Marxist, let alone a dissenter, will feel impelled to take moral action as a result is not so obvious. If nothing else, we have at least learned from the emotive theory of ethics that the relationship between a cognitive theory and a moral action is in part psychological and emotive.

But, of course, this also applies to emotivism, which claims no moral recommendations. If theoretical and practical ethics involve no necessary direct influence on moral action, neither does linguistic ethics. And first-order moral behavior may proceed to some degree without the benefit of meta-linguistics. This in no way denies our earlier contention (in contradistinction to the emotive theory) that *every* action, including linguistic clarification, involves some moral choice.

The chief claim of this chapter is simply *that ethics (theoretical and practical) presupposes basic categories (about the nature of the human being and the nature of language) and that ethical inquiry might be advanced by some metaphysical clarification of these categories.* If this is the case, *then the alleged divorce between metaphysics and ethics has been overcome.*

## NOTES

1. It seems as though Arthur Pap's analysis of metaphysical presuppositions is frequently in opposition to the term "metaphysics," and not "presupposition." (See "Does Science Have Metaphysical Presuppositions?" in *Readings in the Philosophy of Science,* ed. by H. Feigl, and M. Brodbeck, [New York: Appleton, 1953]). Unfortunately, the emotive repugnance to the term "metaphysics" is so strong that this frequently raises a false smoke-screen. Pap himself expresses the hope that the issue between metaphysicians and nonmetaphysicians is not merely a linguistic one about the use of a term. Sadly, this all too often has been the case in the past. I trust that the following account may be evaluated on its own merits independently of mere terminological prejudices.

2. See Max Black, "Definitions and Presuppositions" in *Problems of Analysis* (Ithaca, N.Y.: Cornell University Press, 1954), particularly for his analysis of the presuppositions of words.

3. R. G. Collingwood, *An Essay on Metaphysics* (Oxford: Clarendon Press, 1940).

4. See P. H. Nowell-Smith, *Ethics* (London: Penguin Books, Ltd., 1954); R. M. Hare, *The Language of Morals* (Oxford: Clarendon Press,

1952); S. E. Toulmin, *An Examination of the Place of Reason in Ethics* (Cambridge: University Press, 1950); S. Hampshire, "Fallacies in Moral Philosophy," *Mind* 58 (1949): 466–82.

5. See especially S. Toulmin, "The Logical Status of Psychoanalysis," *Analysis* 9, No. 2 (1948); A. Flew, "Psychoanalytic Explanation," *Analysis* 10, No. 1 (1949).

6. See especially S. Hampshire, "Fallacies in Moral Philosophy," *op. cit.*; A. Flew, "Philosophy and Language," *Philosophical Quarterly* 5, No. 18 (January 1955).

7. ". . . to those who desire and act in accordance with a rational principle knowledge about such matters will be of great benefit" (*Nicomachean Ethics,* Ross translation, 1095a, 10–11).

# 9.
# Rule-Making

From *The Journal of Philosophy* 54, No. 8, April 11, 1957): 208 17. Reprinted by permission of the publisher.

I

One of the great paradoxes of life, particularly of human life, is that it can continue only where both order and freedom prevail. A delicate homeostatic balance must be maintained in all living processes. Through long-term evolution, physico-chemical and biological structures emerge to provide order. For simple animals, instincts pattern behavior. For more complex forms of life, including human life, habits and conditioned responses contribute to stability in the field of interaction. On still more complex levels of behavior social institutions and cultural mores perform roles in many ways similar to those of structures and organs on the biological level.

These complex, systematic modes of behavior at first are largely unconsciously created. They emerge simply and gradually, with little knowledge by the participants of their overall significance or function. As culture develops, however, man becomes more conscious of himself and his activities. He begins to intervene in the processes of habit and attitude and to construct new modes of action. Consciousness both binds life and frees it. On the one hand, it strives to create and maintain order, pattern, homeostasis; and on the other, it contributes to the delight, enjoyment, and enhanced sensibility of life.

The fundamental task of intelligent awareness in man is to guide behavior. Human beings learn that old habits (especially psychological and socio-cultural) may be reorganized (within limits) and that new rules of conduct may be created. If we are to live, and live well, we must break from the hold of blind, unmastered forces, consciously create our own future, and open new possibilities.

Indeed, the "moral" or valuational problem originates at this point. Herein lies the problem of *decision:* Man, confronted with alternatives, must select a course of action. But which shall he choose and why?

By the time man becomes aware of his freedom of choice, he has already been conditioned biologically and socially to determinate modes of behavior. Thus (contrary to existentialism) the "present moment" of decision is not in an empty subjective vacuum, but is intimately connected to his previous likes, desires, habits, to his future expectations, and to the factual situation. What should be done presupposes a context of previous commitments. What is done will be consistent or inconsistent with what he has been accustomed to doing in the past. Man may either reinforce his habits, break them, or create new ones. When he learns consciously to control his habits, mores, and institutions, they take on the status of rules in the sense that he may modify them if he so desires. Thus the decision-problem is part of the broader functioning of life. It is two-fold. Man first asks for good reasons for his actions in concrete situations. But he learns that deciding what to do is in part resolvable if he can discover and apply a rule that governs the case. One of the great aids to decision is the invention or application of rules of behavior that have been found satisfactory. Indeed, it is through the construction of rules by means of science, technocracy, intelligence, and their preservation through memory and culture that man is increasingly able to deal with particular problems of decision.

A few references to rules in various fields will illustrate the point. Application of the rule "Brush your teeth twice a day" may do much to lessen individual problems of tooth decay. The "rules of marriage" in any particular society delimit for that society the conceivable modes of arrangements between the sexes and thus aid the decision problem; i.e., once a man and woman are attracted to one another, their subsequent conduct is defined by custom and law. Or still again, if one is to be properly understood in the English language, then "Each sentence should contain a subject and a predicate." This rule of grammar is formulated after the fact, but recognition of it will contribute to problems of communication.

Thus the decision problem in part is solvable by discovering and applying the right rule to the right situation. But one may ask: "How do we discover or create such rules?" and "Once we have them, how do we apply them?" It is with the former question that I want to be concerned. The latter problem is, of course, important, but it is so thoroughly tied up with concrete empirical facts that it is more difficult to find rules for applying rules than for making them. Is there a methodology of rule-making? What constitutes evidence for one rule rather than for another? The following is only an outline of some important factors applicable largely to rules of practice.

## II

There are, of course, many kinds of rules covering language, grammar, logic, mathematics, games, blueprints, experiments, medicine, engineering, art, law, etc. There are many synonyms for "rule": "regulation," "directive," "law," "principle," "proverb," "formula," "plan," "procedure," "policy," "code," etc. Although there are different types of rules and different techniques for constructing them, there are nonetheless certain characteristics which pertain to rules in general.

The statement "The goldfish is spotted" is an indicative descriptive statement. "$A < B < C \therefore A < C$" is a complex analytic statement. But the statement "All i's are to be dotted and all t's crossed" is a rule governing written language. The statement "No smoking permitted, except in lobby" is a regulation governing our behavior in a theater. And the proverb "Honesty is the best policy" is a moral rule. Thus a rule, strictly speaking, is neither descriptive nor analytic.

A *rule* may be defined as "any guide for conduct, action, or usage." A rule is a *prescription* of something to be done. This usually involves *future action* of some sort (physical, social, linguistic, etc.).

A rule is a type of *generalization,* in the sense that it sets down a general rule of procedure. Rules are *means* or instruments designed to fulfill particular *purposes,* goals, or ends thought important and worthwhile.

To have concrete uses rules must be connected to additional rules of application. This *may* further require persuasive, incitive, or imperative force. Many such rules employ *sanctions* to see that they are performed. If enforced by external sanction, a rule is a law or regulation. Legal rules use force and penalty; social or institutional rules, more subtle methods. If internalized, a rule is frequently considered a principle of "conscience." If unenforced by external or internal sanction, it is a principle of prudence; but here it is usually performed or not performed because of negative or positive consequences. Hence we may say that all rules to some extent are enforceable within their respective contexts by external, internal, prudential, or consequential methods.

Rules, as distinct from blind habits, must in some sense be *consciously understood.* Although the ultimate function of a rule may not be consciously understood, its intended function or meaning must be so understood by those who construct or follow it.

Rules may be arranged in terms of levels of importance. Some rules are basic, others subordinate, because in comparison the activities they prescribe are basic or subordinate. Basic rules have greater priority or generality, or they may be more essential than others. A set of fundamental rules may be called "by-laws," "charter," "constitution," "code," etc.

If human beings are to create good rules, there are certain canons that should be adhered to. Rule-makers should have clearly in mind the initial ends desired in the relevant area being considered. The value, need, and historical significance of the underlying goals should be understood. These, of course, may be modified in the process of inquiry. Rule-makers should be objective and unbiased. They should be interested in constructing as far as possible the best rules of conduct in the light of the available evidence. It is helpful if rule-makers have skill, training, and experience in the particular field at hand. Who the rule-makers shall be will vary from context to context and is an important practical problem. In medicine and engineering, for instance, they are usually highly trained experts—as they should be. In other fields, however, rule-makers are selected frequently on the basis of a variety of irrelevant factors, not the least of which are considerations of wealth, prestige, and power. In business and politics, it is the people who are in control that make the rules. In a democracy, rules are dependent upon a consensus of public opinion. In everyday life, rules are left to chance. As far as possible, however, rule-making should be done by those who possess the necessary qualifications.

There are three main factual tests of a "good" rule: (F1) a rule must fulfill its intended purposes or ends and be consistent with existing long-range desires. Granted certain assumed ends thought to be desired or worthwhile in any particular context, a rule is good if it achieves them. A rule that does so, is serviceable; one that does not, is not. (F2) A good rule is one which is framed in the light of the available and feasible means. It is based upon strategic probability calculations, estimates of expenditures, and considerations of efficiency. (F3) To be effective a rule should be grounded in the laws of nature and consistent with the demands of logic. If a rule is to work, it must conform to limiting conditions: physico-chemical, biological, psychological, and sociocultural. To the degree to which we expand our knowledge of nature and human nature, we add to our ability to construct adequate rules.

It is the combination of these three factors that provides criteria for constructing effective rules: the desired (existing satisfactions, habits, mores), the useful (means, resourses), and the probable (causal conditions and limiting laws). In other terms, it is through an appeal to precedence (common law), utility (pragmatic law), and nature (natural law) that we are able to evaluate a rule of behavior.

The connection between the above factual conditions (F1, 2, 3) and a prescribed rule ($R_a$) has provoked a storm of controversy, since it is held that one cannot derive a prescription from a descriptive statement. Yet there is an intimate connection between F1, 2, 3 and $R_a$. For *if* one is to have an effective rule $R_a$, then it must be framed in the light of F1, 2, 3. The relationship between F1, 2, 3 and $R_a$ is not analytic, since the former does not imply the latter; nor is there a simple empirical or synthetic relationship. Yet there is a type of hypothetical connection in reverse, in the sense that $R_a$ (for its effectiveness) *depends* upon F1, 2, 3. If one is to have a rule of conduct $R_a$ that is a good rule, then one must frame it in terms of knowledge of factual conditions F1, 2, 3. If $R_a$ is to be serviceable, then it must be based upon F2 (available means) and F3 (causal laws); and if it is to be acceptable to the people to whom it applies, it must have relation to F1 (that which is desired). Thus, if consequent $R_a$, then antecedent F1, 2, 3. The connection here is hypothetical, factual, probabilistic, and pragmatic.

# III

But it may be said that this still leaves open the so-called basic moral question. After all, one may talk about rules and test them by their effectiveness as means. But are there basic self-evident moral rules which need no further justification, as the deontological intuitionists argue? Or are these moral rules only means to some final end (happiness, pleasure, interest, etc.), as the teleologists argue?

Moral philosophers usually concern themselves with only one type of rule and mark these off as "distinctively moral." There have been many significations of the term "moral." It has been applied to both the good and the right, to the individual and society. Actually any practical problem is potentially moral. But any problem of practice potentially may also have a technological or practical solution. But what then is a "moral" rule? As a first approximation, I would say that moral rules emerge where there are no other clearly defined patterns of activity, where the usual rules of living break down, and where individuals and societies are left on their own to choose freely the actions deemed proper. But one must also bear in mind that with the advance of knowledge, rules are made to replace activities previously considered moral and that problems of decision are being resolved continually for whole societies by the construction of technical rules of behavior.

For instance, one of the most profound "moral" problems has concerned the care of the aged. In every society, as elderly people become unproductive and dependent, the question is raised as to who should bear the final responsibility for their care. Should anyone related most closely by blood or marriage be the one called upon to look out for them, at the sacrifice of his interests and those of his immediate family? Different societies have developed different rules for dealing with such problems of practice. In some Eskimo and Indian cultures, it was not infrequent that the elderly voluntarily committed suicide. In contemporary American society, the aged are frequently exiled to a senior citizen center in Florida. Only recently have progressive social plans been developed (annuity, retirement, social security, Medicare, etc.). What was once a moral problem is now given a socioeconomic solution. Another profound "moral" problem has been that of the poor. What rules shall we adopt in relation to a starving person? What obligations are involved toward him? In simple moral terms the answer frequently was to give him a good sermon on "moral responsibility" or to share one's bread with him. Yet society has been able to increase productivity and to develop rules of charity, welfare, governmental care, etc., in order to deal with what was previously a "moral dilemma." A child is stricken with poliomyelitis—this raises serious interpersonal problems. Obviously preventative medical rules can now handle what at one time was a "moral" problem.

Thus moral rules may in part be distinguished from other rules in the following way: A problem of decision emerges wherever there is a choice to be made between alternative courses of action. Given the problem, man attempts to discover or construct rules to guide behavior. Man is an interactive being. His activities may only succeed where there is some degree of order as provided by rules. Technical rules successfully structure large controllable areas of life. Some areas of human conduct are at any one time less amenable to technical rules of guidance. Hence the special role of morality is in those areas which are unchartered by law or technology. These moral rules may become well-established traditional habits in static societies. In dynamic societies where knowledge is expanding they may undergo rapid change.

Morality, however, is also said to apply to some of the "basic" rules governing human behavior. Rules governing the simple relations of individuals to one another (promise-keeping, truthfulness, etc.) are especially held to be moral rules. Because of similar factors in human behavior these rules are pervasive phenomena. They are considered so important that, wherever possible, legal sanctions (laws of contract, perjury, etc.) are imposed to prevent their infraction. The moral basis of these rules is especially emphasized in those cases where it is not possible to detect or punish transgression of them. Why are rules such as these "moral" as distinct from legal or technical? In one sense they have been taken as "moral" because they are thought to refer to the basic ends and ideals of an individual or his obligations, which govern "conscience and sin." In another more important and less subjective sense—one that I would stress—rules are called "moral" because it is recognized that each man's life is bound up with another's. "No man is an island unto himself." A necessary condition of life (as we know it) is its socio-cultural side. If this is so, then it would seem that moral rules deal with the general conditions governing the relations between people—in the sense (as Kant recognized, although for different reasons) that if their exceptions were universalized all human behavior in society would be virtually impossible.

But there are in certain societies other rules equally basic which have not always been called "moral." As Hobbes recognized, some measure of law and order is an essential ingredient of social life. The state is fundamental; without it anarchy would prevail. Traffic laws are usually said to be legal, not moral, laws. Yet without such traffic laws, the road would become a thing of terror; and it would be the task of morality, i.e., the "common courtesy" of the road to establish a system of order.

Thus legal rules frequently may be just as basic as moral rules. Nonetheless, there is a difference between them. Legal rules are enforced by physical sanctions and punishment, whereas moral rules are backed either by lesser sanctions of custom and conscience or by hardly any at all. Legal rules are usually based upon clearly developed common-law precedence or governmental legislation. Although it may be said that *some* laws fulfill moral rules and are even equivalent to them, still moral rules can be distinguished from particular systems of civil law. Rational ethical inquiry emerges when a legal system breaks down or needs revision. It provides an external criticism of a legal system. It does so by appealing to other better rules based upon more fundamental considerations. There are usually ideal standards or meta-principles which the ethical philosopher uses to criticize existing social and legal rules. Thus, in the long run, moral rules are appealed to in place of existing rules and customs.

But if these moral rules are not in themselves the only basic rules, are they instrumental to other more basic ends? Yes, there is a teleological aspect to moral rules: they do serve as necessary instruments to the furtherance of the ends of life. Still there is an unerring aspect of truth to the deontologists' point: moral rules are not merely instrumental but may be intrinsically pursued for their own sake. Why? I suspect that ends and means, the good and the right, goals and rules are identified because human life is so thoroughly sociocultural that moral rules become part and parcel of the ends of life. Moral rules are fundamental social rules exemplifying the demands of reciprocity. Without some guides life as we know it would be virtually impossible. Moral rules function as nonreducible qualities needing no further justification; they are in some sense final because they are the very substance and fabric of life in its social dimensions. That they are taken as intuitive is unfortunate, though understandable, since men have been conditioned to recognize their necessity in social organization.

Why "ought" we to observe a particular rule? To answer this question in normal life one usually refers to the relevant problem for which the rule has been framed, or to the broader context of interrelated rules to which any particular rule may be connected. We need not call the system of rules itself into question in order to reply. But a persistent questioner may not be satisfied with our answer and many question the whole context of rules. Thus, if a person wants to know why he "ought" to keep a promise, we can first reply to him by reference to the rule of promise-keeping. If he is still unsatisfied with the answer, we may defend promise-keeping in general by probing deeper. We may refer to the historical significance of promise-keeping as an ideal in various societies, to the broader code of a particular society wherein the rule is observed, or to the long-range satisfactions of desire which the people who observe the rule achieve. We proceed slowly, bearing in mind that there are different types of reasons relevant on different levels of discourse and that evidenee applicable on one level of rules may not be applicable on other higher or lower levels.

But this may still leave the question, Why have rules anyway? What evidence supports the whole body of human rules? This is a philosophical question which usually is unintelligible to one deeply involved in the business of living.[1] It is one that I nonetheless will try to answer. Looking at man in his purely natural capacities, we find that rules have a double function. There is the apparent function of a rule to fulfill the purposes or ends intended or desired by its creators in particular situations (F1). There is also the latent, more fundamental role of rules in human behavior, an underlying causal function (F3). Now it is possible for us to develop efficacious rules in terms of the first level of desired or intended goals in particular social systems. Here our rules grow out of the existing structure of habits and ideals. However, when our desired ends are not achieved, when they break down and conflict, then we may search for the basis of the whole process of rule-making itself. Here we see that the chief function and conditions, and needs of human beings. What these are can only be stated by the sciences of man. Heretofore, ethical theories have been based upon inadequate psychological theories of human nature—theories that have been largely speculative or subjectivistic. On the basis of existing social science, I would venture the hypothesis that there is at least one important controlling principle of behavior—that of homeostasis: all living systems and fields seem to be striving to maintain a type of growing and dynamic equilibrium. Hence, one of the ultimate functions of rules is to express and satisfy the strivings of life.

Knowledge of the necessary conditions and needs of human behavior (F3) (the normal, the valuable) does provide some aid in constructing rules. In their haste to disown the excesses of the theory of natural law, contemporary philosophers have gone to the opposite extreme in refusing to admit the importance of natural knowledge in valuation. Indeed, scientific knowledge of man, society, and nature, perhaps more than any other factors, enables us to construct good rules (witness, for example, the concept of health in medicine, dentistry, and psychiatry).

This appeal to nature for evidence, however (contrary to natural law theory), is not final in determining the best rules. For we must work with human experience as we find it. We begin with existing desires (F1); all that our knowledge of natural conditions can do is to *influence* our desires. As Dewey recognizes, one of our great problems is to get our intelligent appraisals (for him usually based upon means [F2]) to modify our prizings. Thus knowledge of the latent functions of rules, of the limits and possibilities of nature and human nature, is vital and necessary, although possibly not sufficient, in framing effective rules.

Nonetheless, rules need not be arbitrary or capricious. There are good reasons and relevant evidence for selecting particular rules. Rules are developed every day by doctors, engineers, navigators, psychiatrists, politicians. This indicates that it is *possible* in concrete contexts to construct rules (as prescriptive norms) in terms of selective criteria. The implicit logic employed by such practical techicians is not based on the elusive pie in the sky.

It is the task of philosophy to make explicit the methodology of rule-making and to analyze critically the methods employed. But this, after all, is the logic of practical wisdom held by Aristotle, the theory of valuation advocated by Dewey. The development of the methodology of rules is not, and need not be, restricted to "what conforms to common usage" or to "natural languages" as so many philosophers today argue—although undoubtedly this is an important problem. In a very real sense, rules have a factual basis, since if they are to be effective they must be grounded in knowledge of the desired, the useful, and the natural conditions of life. Philosophers may inquire into the above topics. Moreover, they can contribute to the construction of "artificial languages" in order to explain human behavior without committing the "naturalistic fallacy" and without themselves engaging in firsthand persuasive rhetoric or attempting to arouse personal motivation or obligation.

# NOTE

1. This question also makes no philosophical sense unless it is asked by a rational person. Whether or not an individual or group is sufficiently motivated to perform a rule or rules is not here at issue. It is undoubtedly true that rules are not made in a vacuum and that in constructing good rules we must know whether or not they will be performed. Hence, they must be sufficiently persuasive so that people will comply with them. But the open question "Why ought I to do this rule?" *ad infinitum* may be illegitimate, since the moral question becomes solely the one of obligation as motivation. One can never be sure that all people will feel motivated to accept rules. If an individual tells us that he doesn't want to satisfy his desires or ends (through rules), then I suppose that there is no answer to him, for he is really asking the same question "Why live?" That he should live we may not be able to convince him psychologically. Our only answer to him is that *if* we are to live, then we need rules.

# 10.
# Need Reduction and Normal Value

## I

Contemporary ethical discussion has failed to examine the full context of valuation and meaning. Value judgments are examined independently of their sources and referents; ordinary meanings are analyzed in abstraction from their function. Miss A., we are told, may like apricots, algae, athletics, the A.A.U.P., be altruistic, and use affected speech; Miss B. prefers berries, beef, basket weaving, the B.B.C., is bitter, and barely utters a word; but these are expressions of private attitudes. In some cases, so the tale runs, such attitudes are modifiable by an appeal to belief, but not always; ultimately only a persuasive appeal may resolve disagreements. Meanings are discovered only by examining common usage. And many allege that beyond this nothing more may be said.

But why must immediate attitudes or expressions in ordinary language be taken as the final locus of value or the ultimate subject matter of ethics? Emotivists, noncognitivists, and ordinary language

From *The Journal of Philosophy* 55, No. 13 (1958): 555–68. Reprinted by permission of the publisher.

philosophers apparently agree in their initial assumptions. They by-pass the data of the social sciences, feeling that one ought not to commit the naturalistic fallacy. But can the current impasse in value theory be overcome without raising descriptive questions concerning human behavior? For instance, if we were to follow this prevailing point of view, it would be a mistake to introduce notions of pathology, neurosis, normalcy, or health into value discussions. Yet people constantly refer to these normative concepts in everyday life and in the therapeutic sciences. Either the above philosophical analysts have ignored an important type of commonsense language, or else they cannot deal with such topics within the confines of their assumptions. In either case, most people assume that questions of normalcy are relevant to value (and moral) judgments. Are they completely in error, or is theirs a deeper insight into behavior?

I submit that there is a meaningful sense of "normal." But in order to indicate it the causal basis of value must be explored. Ethical analysis ultimately takes as its subject matter concrete human experiences. And such analysis sooner or later is found to imply a theory of motivation. But most of the prevailing discussions of human motivation are limited to surface questions: Is reason, desire, or emotion central in choice? Can cognition control behavior? What is the relationship between belief and attitude? Do ethical judgments have a descriptive or imperative function? Many writers refer to Hume's claim that reason by itself moves nothing without feeling or sentiment; others express their faith in reason and cognition.

Actually, the problem of motivation is only a part of the broader question: What are the *determinants* of human behavior? But, as the social sciences indicate, there are undoubtedly many causal factors. Most of the theories of motivation have been based on earlier limited psychologies: primitive hedonism and attitudinalism, speculative self-realizationism, or naive cognitivism. Does contemporary psychology shed any light on the problem of motivation? At least one type of motivation theory, need reduction, does provide an important advance. This theory is not without its difficulties. Yet it does provide us, I think, with a more encompassing theory than is usually encountered in philosophy; and this has considerable significance for value theory.

## II

There is a continual struggle on the part of living organisms to reduce tension and maintain homeostasis. Disturbances of essential constancy of inner tissue or psychological balance lead to tension or anxiety. Such disturbances are induced by internal or external stimuli. Internal stimuli are frequently constant forces found operative in all normal members of a species; as such, they are continually flowing sources of endosomatic stimulation. External stimuli are environmental entities (real or imagined) which confront the organism. The organism is motivated to overcome such stimuli disturbances, thereby reducing tension and maintaining a dynamic homeostatic tension balance.[1]

In the course of living a variety of differential needs develop which must be satisfied if life is to be maintained. Needs in general are states of tension-disequilibrium. These eventually lead the organism to restless drive activities in an effort to reduce the initiating stimulation and resulting imbalance. But the dichotomy between internal and external is only one of degree. Recurrent internal needs frequently have been called "instinctive" (although this term is inappropriate when applied to man). Such basic needs have developed in a species only after long processes of evolution. Definite structures emerge in all normal members of a species. These take on the specific function of restoring organic harmony. Moreover, pleasurable sensitivity appears to accompany and accentuate processes of restoration. Needs which are based on external conditioning also have as their function the maintenance of homeostasis.

Both internally and externally conditioned needs interact and influence one another. Indeed, it might be appropriate in general to conceive of a need as the tension-lack of a *field* of organic processes containing inner and outer events. The organism, strictly speaking, does not end at the cellular surface of its skin. There is a continuous internal and external environment, as in respiration, where both the lungs and external oxygen play a role, or in perception, where both sense organ and objects or qualities in the environment are necessary. Hence effective stimulation anywhere within the organic field may eventuate in organic activity in order to reduce disequilibrium or maintain a tension level.

Living organisms thus constantly seek to maintain themselves through homeostatic means. This is the root principle of life found in all normal members of a species. But there are also other life-functions tending toward fulfillment.

Reproductive structures and capacities are also found in living things. There is a tendency to transmit a discontinuous life of biological endowment through members of a species. This, too, is present in all normal members and is a basic principle of the species at large (although it may be absent in pathological cases).

In addition, living things have the capacities for growth, maturation, and functioning. At certain stages in life, general ontogenetic needs and properties are revealed in each normal member of a species. A person develops new capacities at different phases of life. Each stage generally follows a normal pattern of development: the ability to see, grasp, sit, crawl, stand, walk, speak, reproduce sexually, etc. Thus there is a steady increase in functions during the maturing process. But when is maturity reached? Empirical evidence tends to indicate the fact of continuing growth; at least, well into old age. Growth is not merely physical; it manifests itself in the increase of emotional, intellectual, esthetic, religious, economic, political, and other capacities and skills.

There also appears to be a vital tendency on the part of living organisms to release surplus energy. Given adequate levels of balance and growth, there are constant manifestations of expressive activities. A dog will romp; an infant kick its limbs; a child play; a man laugh or create a work of art. These vital activities are intimately connected to the whole dynamic organic process and must be accounted for in any general theory of human behavior.

## III

There seems to be a need on the part of human beings to satisfy the above life tendencies. Motivation is closely connected to such need-reductive activities. Needs are frequently expressed in everyday human life on the conscious level as wishes, desires, attitudes, wants, and likes. But they also remain deep-seated and partly hidden. There are somatic and "unconscious" sources of needs in the organism. These are brought to the surface occasionally in dreams, wishes, fantasies. They are discovered by the psychiatrist often only after the greatest effort.

Many recent psychological theorists tend to reduce all motivation to the primary biological needs of hunger, thirst, sex, etc. Secondary needs for them are learned needs and drives relative to the socio-cultural environment. Clark L. Hull related secondary drives to conditioning mechanisms.[2] Through associative and trial-and-error learning the organism discovers that certain objects will reduce one's primary needs and that others will not. Continued pleasurable reinforcement of stimuli-response patterns tends to increase the strength of the response.

But Hull and others continually have underestimated the innate character and role of internal stimulation. At least, in all normal members of a species there seems to be growth processes in which standard invariant stimuli come into play at various stages in the maturing process. Moreover, social psychology today seems to make it clear that man is a social being; hence, many of the so-called secondary or derived needs have to be considered as primary needs. But how can we speak of primary social needs in the face of the apparent relativity of socio-cultural behavior?

Human behavior and motivation is a function of the total field of interaction. The full act involves the following phases: There is a need. This leads to impulse and activity. Goal objects to satisfy the needs are sought; when achieved, homeostasis results; when not achieved, tension (or anxiety). Life activity accordingly presupposes at least two sets of conditions: *needs* and *objects*. Organic needs require objects or goals (actual or perceived) as a means for reducing them. Such goal objects may be natural and socio-cultural in character. Processes of behavior may be understood from the standpoint of both tension-lack (bio-chemical) and purposive striving (molar). In this chapter I am concerned with isolating the *invariant needs* of the organism as typical of the species. Any complete theory of behavior requires a delineation of all factors of the field. This entails an investigation of the socio-cultural objects of striving to determine the invariant conditions governing their organization. Durkheim and others have argued (correctly I think) that social phenomena cannot be reduced simply to psychic or biological determinants, and that a separate conceptual framework must be developed here. Accordingly, the invariant potentialities of human behavior are dependent upon both the individual organism and species *and* socio-cultural materials and events.

Now I submit that there are certain native needs which cannot be ignored without peril to the organism. This does not mean that there are not a *variety* of ways and many different objects capable of satisfying these basic needs. Humans require food for survival, but the kinds of food which will reduce this need depend upon alteratives presented by the environment. Apricots and algae may reduce Miss A's hunger at times. But B's needs may be satisfied by berries and beef. There are a multiplicity of objects capable of meeting this biological need. Needs are vague tensions until specific objects are discovered which will reduce them. As Joseph Butler long ago indicated, when people desire or like they have specific objects in mind. The continued satisfaction and pleasurable reward of berries and beef may soon reinforce these goal objects. An interest in the objects is sustained in its own right. Long after the initial motive has been forgotten the interest-goals may remain. These interest-goals become structured in the personality. A unique set of such interest-goals distinguishes one personality from another. Yet a person's preferences are often only end results or surface manifestations of deeper need-requirements. If ways of satisfying such psychological phenomena are regularly supplied, they become structured in the personality. Continued pleasurable stimulation emphasizes and reinforces interest in particular objects. Specific kinds of activities meeting these specific wants develop. Social rules and institutions also do much to regulate random wants into patterned modes of response. Thus a peculiar type of behavior finally may come to exert a dominant role in a way of life. A drug addict or alcoholic, for instance, emphasizes dope or alcohol all out of proportion to normal functioning; and a military society centers its interests on heroic virtues and passions.

Are these unique interests and wants to be interpreted in terms of need reduction? Is an individual who craves dope, alcohol, or military honor, for example, expressing a need? Surely a distinction must be made between the *general* function of needs on the one hand and the *specific* object-contents of needs on the other. The general function of a need is to reduce tension, maintaining homeostasis and the life and growth of the organism; but the *way* tension levels are maintained, the specific object or content of the need-goal as expressed in a desire, want attitude, or interest, is another matter. We are motivated to seek specific objects, but the ultimate function of a motive is to satisfy a general need. Any particular need is a complex function of both general needs and derived conditoning processes. This distinction is similar to that made earlier between primary and secondary needs. Primary needs refer to general functions; secondary needs are those which arise on the level of object-contents. Such derived needs are usually generated by external stimuli (although they have their internal correlates). That is why some societies over-emphasize one pattern of behavior (e.g., head hunting, money gathering, etc.) to the exclusion of others, and why some individuals will direct their lives along one line (e.g., dope addiction, or art, etc.) rather than others. These derived needs arise so structured in the personality that unless they, too, are satisfied tensions will result.

## IV

The basic philosophical question that may be raised, and one that has the highest significance for value theory, is: Are there basic general needs intrinsic to all men, and does this enable us to make a distinction between normal and pathological needs? My answer is in the affirmative. There are, I believe, basic general needs that are found in all normal human beings. What are they? This may only be determined empirically. On the basis of recent investigations in the life and social sciences, I wish to propose the following tentative list of trans-cultural needs:[3]

### Biogenic Needs

(1) There are certain fundamental *physico-chemical homeostatic* needs required for the maintenance of life: salt, sugar, calcium, protein, fat, acid content, water, and oxygen are among the most important. These physico-chemical needs are expressed in differential tensions, such as hunger and thirst, and are satisfied in different functions, such as eating and drinking. As far as I can discover there are few, if any, exceptions to the homeostatic principle on the physico-chemical level. It is important to recognize that homeostasis is never

a merely static state. Indeed, it is doubtful if it is ever fully attained. It is a dynamic metabolic affair of ongoing exchanging process.

(2) There also seems to be present in each normal member of the species the need to *grow*, mature, and develop. Inherent in man are evolutionary constructive forces which urge him to realize his given potentialities. But obviously this statement is too general, since it is necessary to interpret growth and realization in more specific terms. Empirical studies seem to indicate that each stage of life, from embryo to adult, reveals new capacities and needs and their continued functioning. Gesell, for example, has studied the early cycle of growth. But it is not clear whether his findings are entirely devoid of the unique influences of our cultural prejudices.[4] Lehman's remarkable study of creativity—from mathematicians and musicians to philosophers and poets—shows the uniform relationship between age and achievement.[5] Gerontological studies show other interesting results of the loss of functions in the aging process. A good deal of the basis of growth is biological in character. But this is not entirely so, since in all human functioning, objects are required, and these usually are socio-cultural in kind. Indeed, socio-cultural materials continually make possible the revealing of new potentialities of man.

Unless the above homeostatic and growth tendencies are fulfilled, the organism cannot be called healthy. Extended privation or hindered development leads to serious disease and malfunctioning. It is possible to give, within limits, a clinical interpretation of these biogenic needs. Indeed, a basic biogenic need may be defined as that which is necessary for the *continued maintenance and growth of the organism.*

## Sociogenic Needs

But there are other highly complex needs which also emerge and appear to play a decisive role in human life. These needs have a physio-chemical side; but they are largely emotional and socio-cultural in origin and quality. They are usually satisfied in relation to other people. They appear to come closest to what have been called the "self-realization" needs of man.

(3) There is the need for a type of psychological *security*. A

lack of security is not merely grounded in physical fear. The whole personality may be challenged in other subtle ways. There is the need to overcome threats to the structure of personality involvements. The normal organism is able to organize his world and his place in it, as far as possible, in order to avoid real dangers and to ignore unreal ones. Continued fear may be a source of mental disorder.

(4) That there is a need for reciprocal *love* is a widespread assumption of contemporary psychiatry. There seems to be a human necessity both to give and receive love. Some psychologists have related this to the need for satisfaction of the sexual libido. Thus Sullivan calls it the need for lustful satisfaction which is concerned with genital activity in pursuit of orgasm. Clearly, sexual needs are present in man and have a biogenic basis. But love is something more than this. There is, according to Sullivan, also the need for intimacy, i.e., for collaboration with at least one other person. Although love is difficult to define precisely, we may characterize it as any state of responsiveness with others as its goal. Whether this craving for love is innate or culturally determined, and whether it may best be satisfied by human love objects, is a difficult question, especially since our Western and Christian culture tends to overemphasize the role of love. However, there is considerable evidence which *seems* to indicate its root need in most living things. For example, rats and other mammals are known to develop severe gastro-intestinal and other troubles if deprived of the caressing, fondling, and licking care of the mother in the early days of life, thus indicating a need for cutaneous stimulation. Young children will cry bitterly when deprived of love; if continually frustrated along these lines, severe maladjustments will develop. The mothering care received during early childhood hence has its later effects upon adulthood. But, further, the dual character of sexual reproduction suggests the need for continued love, biogenic with psychical components, as does the interdependent basis of many human relationships.

(5) Man is so thoroughly a dependent being that there appears to be a continuing need for *belonging* to some community. Man's nourishment, his unfolding, indeed, his very language, art, religion— the symbols by which he dreams and thinks—are socio-cultural in character. Is there a need for man to identify himself with some community, some group, or cause? To be completely alone and unto oneself is to invite alienation, one of the fundamental sources of

neurosis. And, if carried far enough, it actually makes a person less than human (as we know him), since he will not possess the requisite objects, symbols, and rules that society and culture have discovered as full aids to growth and functioning.

(6) The need for *self-respect* and acceptance of the self is an essential requirement of the normal personality. Self-hate can be as destructive and consuming as physical hunger and disease. People frequently set up high ideals for fulfillment, and, being unable to reach them, seek to destroy themselves in condemnation, as Karen Horney has pointed out.[6] All persons (at least in our society) have a need or desire for a stable, firmly based high evaluation of themselves, for self-esteem and for the esteem of others. There is a desire for strength, achievement, competence, and confidence in the face of the world. There is the desire for recognition, prestige, appreciation, and respect from other people, as Alfred Adler has shown.[7] These needs may very well be exaggerated once again by our culture. A *minimal* statement, however, can be given: If there is excessive self-hate, or feelings of inadequacy, inferiority, and helplessness as a person, mental disorder and malfunctioning will undoubtedly develop. As is obvious, there is a close similarity between the above needs—security, love, belonging, and self-respect.

(7) Arising out of the expressive tendencies of man is probably the need for *creative expression.* Homeostatic and growth processes are basic to human life. Man is a problem-solving creature. Consciousness is one of the main instruments by which human beings may cope with their environment. In this sense, man is a productive working animal. But it is also necessary to leave room for expressive activities and needs. Expressive activities have a role in the growth and functioning of healthy organisms. The opportunities for self-expression and release must be present in all normal functioning. Play, art, poetry, song, and dance may draw their initial impetus from this underlying need.[8] Expressive needs are surely part of the human being's actualizing tendencies. Indeed, they frequently serve as a test of growth and development.

(8) We find in humans the unique *cognitive* tendency or need. This is made possible by man's involved nervous system (his capacities for consciousness, memory, anticipation, imagination, perception, and reflection) and his cultural endowment. This intellectual capacity enables him to rise above the limitations of his immediate

spatial-temporal context. Man seems to want to come to terms with nature, and to reach an understanding of himself and his place within it. The demands of everyday life initiate the use of thought. This may very well be the source of the scientific and philosophical enterprise. Dangers, tragedy, and death lead to awe and wonder. Perhaps this is the basis of mythological, religious, and metaphysical systems. Some question may be raised as to whether the cognitive constitutes a separate need. Much scientific and cognitive behavior appears to be a high-level instrument for problem solving; but a good deal of thought is expressive in function. Much religious and philosophical behavior may be subsumed under the demand for psychological security and stability. Further, cognition may at times lead to more anxieties than it resolves. In the last analysis, however, cognitive symbolic systems do seem to have a homeostatic function, one that appears only at the higher levels of growth. Inmates of mental institutions are out of cognitive touch with part of the real world. A minimal statement hence is in order: Some cognitive contact with one's own and external reality must be present to preserve mental health.

The fundamental characteristics of these sociogenic needs is that *they must be satisfied if the organism is to maintain adequate mental health and continue to develop along normal lines.* Failure to satisfy these needs leads to mental imbalance and inability to grow properly. Freud suggested a definition of neurosis in terms of the lack of homeostatic balance of psychic energy.[9] This usually leads to the upsetting of the physico-chemical balance of the body. The disturbed person attempts to overcome his anxieties by constructing unique pathological systems of behavior: escape and protective mechanisms, repressions, compensations, reaction formations, etc. The sick person is attempting "to re-establish a lost equilibrium."[10] In extreme cases only a complete withdrawal into psychotic unreality can prevent distressing anxiety. In abnormal behavior there is frequently a dissociation of the pleasure principle from natural needs; pleasure is extracted from its normal behavior and unduly emphasized. Only these compulsive reactions are believed to give the person some "peace"; though they frequently provoke anxiety. Presumably the relatively healthy, adjusted person can function on all levels, work, love, and is in cognitive touch with reality—the abnormal person, particularly the psychotic, is not.

There is also such a thing as pathological growth and development. Fromm claims that "mental health is achieved if man develops into full maturity, according to the characteristic laws of human nature. Mental illness consists in the failure of such development."[11] It is a regression or fixation to earlier stages of development and a disturbance in one's relations to oneself and to others. For Horney, the neurotic process is a special form of development and growth which hampers natural growth.[12] Favorable conditions are necessary for healthy growth. Society may either fulfill or frustrate the needs inherent in human nature. On this theory the "death wish" or destructive impulse in man arises only from the frustration and thwarting of such normal needs and may not be itself innate.

## V

What are the implications of the above list?

It is possible to use this tentative list of basic needs in philosophical analyses of human conduct. The list is a descriptive instrument for understanding man. It is predicated on the assumption that any conscious motive, attitude, wish, liking, desire, or want must be interpreted in its broader context, and that, if we are to understand choice and meaning, both the manifest and latent functions of conscious states must be dealt with. Unfortunately, many philosophers have taken the surface expressions of needs and motives as the core of value. But in view of what I have argued, to deal with such vital biases without tracing them to the conditions governing their occurrence is a partial approach (as Dewey recognized).

This theory presupposes that there are norms built into the framework of the human species. But what is the justification for using the term "norm"? It is a purely empirical one. The only reason for saying that something is normal is that all or most members of the species tend to behave in that way. In other words, human beings *do* strive to maintain life, to achieve equilibrium, to grow and express themselves. *Shoulds* are part of the very structure of human beings. Men tend to their own maintenance and growth. Value is connected to the biogenic and sociogenic basis of the striving process. Value is another term for the complex of need-desire-satisfaction. There are primary general values and secondary derived values, the latter being interpreted by whether or not they fulfill the former. Value is thus always related to the whole ongoing direction of vital activity.

But it must be recognized that to treat value in this way is to make a proposal. Normal value is here considered to be present under conditions of healthy functioning. That is, when specifiable objects or activities contribute to the general need-reductions and satisfaction of organisms without undue tension or anxiety, and when they contribute to homeostasis, survival, reproduction, growth, and expressive activities, then we may say that the organism is normal.

Actually, however, the above statement is intended as an empirical explanation of the way in which most members of the species tend to function under standard conditions. As such, it is a hypothetical statement summarizing a fundamental law of human behavior, and is either true or false on scientific grounds.

Why *ought* the organism to behave so? is a question that frequently has been raised. Indeed, the meaning of the term "ought" has been an important problem of linguistic analysis. But, as far as I can discover, there are no absolute logical justifications to be given about matters of fact. Causal connections are best interpreted as probability relations, not logical inferences. Thus the only answer to the above question is that human beings do behave in the way we have specified; and that they can, will, and probably should so behave. Any other meanings of "ought" are usually predicated on an implied theory of private motivation and individual freedom of the will. Nor is the naturalistic fallacy here at issue. If the above statements are true, then they are merely factual accounts of life, not persuasive definitions or private obligations.

Of course, there is the important problem of moral choice and decision. I think that we can investigate value phenomena and develop a theory of value without becoming involved in such questions at every point. This does not mean, however, that the above theory of value does not have important implications for the decision problem. For it is *possible* for men to appeal to normal values as partial evidence in reaching decisions. Such evidence may have some direct relevance to the solution of their practical problems. At least, both in ordinary life and the applied sciences, men and women constantly criticize other individuals, their decisions and practices, by referring to normalcy and health as standards. Particular attitudes thus may be interpreted, their meanings analyzed, evaluated, and criticized by their role in a personality system. The question may be asked, how far do such items satisfy the normal needs of human beings, or contribute to homeostatic maintenance, growth, etc.? Similarly, a socio-cultural system may be evaluated to a degree as normal or abnormal by whether it satisfies standard human needs.

But once again, I wish to emphasize that *a* fundamental problem for value theory independent of the problem of personal moral decision is to understand our real deep-seated needs. The significant problem that this line of approach raises is not the linguistic problem of analyzing abstracted meanings or feelings, but rather the question: are there universal needs of man? This is a thoroughly philosophical question presupposing no prior commitments to hypostatic meanings, ordinary usages, or covert theories of human motivation. It is a question which can only be answered by an understanding and synthesis of the empirical findings of the sciences of man. Accordingly, it is not germane to raise the same old objections, as recent philosophers are wont to do, against this type of naturalistic inquiry.

## NOTES

1. The best statement of biological homeostasis is by W. B. Cannon, *The Wisdom of the Body* (New York: W. W. Norton and Co., Inc., 1932). The best statement of psychological homeostasis is by R. Stagner, "Homeostasis as a Unifying Concept in Personality Theory," *Psychological Review* 58 (1951): 5–17. Other recent articles on homeostasis: P. Kurtz, "Human Nature, Homeostasis, and Value," *Philosophy and Phenomenological Research* 17 (September 1956): 36–55 [see chapter 7 of this volume]; L. C. Kubie, "Instinct and Homeostasis," *Psychosomatic Medicine* 10 (1948): 15–30; C. A. Mace, "Homeostasis, Needs, and Values," *British Journal of Psychology* 44 (1953): 200–210.

2. See: C. Hull, "Value, Valuation, and Natural Science Methodology," *Philosophy of Science* 11 (July 1944): No. 3; *A Behavior System,* (New Haven: Yale University Press, 1952).

3. Several writers have suggested other lists of normal needs. The above list is a convergence of the main features of these lists. Perhaps the most important work in this connection has been done by A. H. Maslow. He lists a hierarchy of basic needs: (1) physiological needs, (2) safety, (3)

belongingness and love, (4) esteem, (5) self-actualization. He also adds cognitive and aesthetic needs (*Motivation and Personality* [New York: Harper and Brothers, 1954], pp. 80–98). For Harry Stack Sullivan the basic needs of man are: (1) the need for personal security, or freedom from anxiety, (2) for intimacy, (3) for lustful satisfaction (*Interpersonal Theory of Psychiatry* [New York: W. W. Norton & Co., Inc., 1953], p. 140). Erich Fromm: (1) animal needs, (2) relatedness (love), (3) transcendence (creativeness), (4) rootedness (brotherliness), (5) sense of identity (individuality), (6) frame of orientation and devotion (reason) (*The Sane Society* [New York: Rinehart and Co., Inc., 1955], Ch. 3). Ralph Linton: (1) emotional response from other people, (2) security, (3) novelty of experience (*Cultural Background of Personality* [New York: Appleton-Century-Crofts, 1945], pp. 7–10). For Werner Wolff normalcy is defined in terms of (1) development, (2) integration, (3) co-ordination, (4) adjustment, (5) activity, (6) self-assertion, (7) productivity, (8) equilibrium. Distortions of function in abnormality are: (1) fixation, (2) isolation, (3) dissociation, (4) maladjustment, (5) passivity, (6) self-destruction, (7) sterility, (8) unbalance (*The Threshold of the Abnormal* [New York: Heritage House, 1950], p. 436). Carl R. Rogers describes all organic and psychological needs as partial aspects of one fundamental need: "The organism has one basic tendency and striving—to actualize, maintain, and enhance the experiencing organism" (*Client Centered Therapy* [Boston: Houghton Mifflin Co., 1951], p. 487). M. F. Ashley Montagu defines a *vital* basic need as any biological need necessary for the individual group to survive (he lists several). An *emotional* (nonvital) basic need is any biological need which is necessary for the organism to develop and maintain mental health. A *socially emergent* need arises out of the process of satisfying the above basic needs and may under certain conditions become necessary for the maintenance of mental health (*The Direction of Human Development* [New York: Harper and Brothers, 1955]: pp. 150–51).

4. Arnold L. Gesell, *Child Development* (New York: Harper and Brothers, 1949).

5. Harvey C. Lehman, *Age and Achievement* (Princeton: Princeton University Press, 1953).

6. *Neurosis and Human Growth* (New York: W. W. Norton & Co., Inc., 1950).

7. *The Practice and Theory of Individual Psychology* (New York: Harcourt, Brace, 1929).

8. There may also be a need for stimulation of the sense organs. But this need appears to be connected to the general tendency to live, grow, and function.

9. Nigel Walker claims that Freud recognized and used homeostasis in his theories a generation before Cannon or the cyberneticists ("Freud

and Homeostasis," *The British Journal for the Philosophy of Science* 8, No. 25 [May, 1956]: 4–13).

10. Werner Wolff, *The Threshold of the Abnormal,* p. 438.

11. Erich Fromm, *The Sane Society,* p. 14.

12. *Neurosis and Human Growth.*

# 11.

# Has Ethical Naturalism Been Refuted?

A view that is widely shared in the analytic literature of ethics is the view that ethical naturalism has been decisively refuted. Most writers in ethics claim that there is a basic logical muddleheadedness in naturalistic ethics; and they wish to disassociate themselves from such confusion. The roots of the familiar critique can be located in Hume, G. E. Moore, and the emotivists.

R. M. Hare, however, has provided the most extended recent analysis of the "naturalistic fallacy." In his book *The Language of Morals,* he says that naturalism in ethics will constantly reappear so long as there are people who have not understood the fallacy involved. The fallacy occurs whenever someone claims that he:

> . . . can deduce a moral or other evaluative judgment from a set of purely factual or descriptive premisses, relying on some definition to the effect that V (a value word) means the same as C (a conjunction of descriptive predicates).[1]

From *The Journal of Value Inquiry* 4, No. 3, (Fall 1970): 161–71. Copyright © 1970 by Martinus Nijhoff Publishers, Dordrecht, Holland. Reprinted by permission of Kluwer Academic Publishers.

In refuting the naturalist, Hare would have us first ask him to be careful that C contains no expression that is covertly evaluative. Most naturalistic definitions, he believes, will break down at this point; for most of them do contain a value judgment, however covertly. If the definition offered by chance is purely descriptive, then Hare would have us next ask "whether its advocate ever wishes to commend anything for being C." If the naturalist claims that he does, then we must point out, says Hare, that he cannot; for his descriptive definition precludes it. But he cannot say that he never wishes to commend anything for being C, for commending is the whole purpose of his ethical theory. In other words, the failure of the naturalist, it is alleged, is that he has overlooked or left out the essential function of value terms, which is the *commendatory junction.*

Hare again repeats his indictment of naturalism in his book *Freedom and Reason.* Here he claims that the mistake of the naturalist is to:

> . . . hold that the rules which determine to what we can apply value-words are simply descriptive meaning rules, and that these descriptive rules determine the meaning of these words completely, just as in the use of descriptive expressions.[2]

The fallacy of the naturalist is that he interprets a value word as "just one kind of descriptive expression."

Naturalism allegedly is also mistaken about its conception of the nature of value or moral judgments. The naturalist again incorrectly maintains that such "judgments are a kind of descriptive judgment, i.e., that their descriptive meaning exhausts their meaning." According to Hare, such a descriptive analysis of value judgments leaves out their essential characteristic, namely their *prescriptiveness.* In the last analysis, he again insists, there can be "no deduction of moral judgments from statements of fact."[3]

If we were to summarize the indictment against naturalistic ethics, we see that at least three main charges are being levelled:

First, that any attempt to identify moral or value terms with descriptive properties is fallacious;

Second, that moral and value judgments are not descriptive in meaning or function but are primarily commendatory, evaluative, or prescriptive; and

Third, that one cannot logically deduce moral or value judgments from statements of facts.

Is anything left of the naturalistic program given this critique; or has naturalism finally been vanquished?

As is often the case in philosophy, philosophical inquiry proceeds by refutation of what other philosophers say. But what is often the case also is that one's philosophical opponents, if not real, are invented. I sometimes wonder who the philosophical naturalists are who are accused of the above logical blunders. Are they actual writers or only straw men? It is not often that one can catch a philosopher in a logical howler; and if one can succeed, one indeed has a remarkable achievement. In other words, that naturalism has or must equate fact and value, either in its definition of terms, its conception of value judgments, or its attempt to support them, I think is a mistaken view of naturalism.

## VALUE TERMS

It is true that some naturalists have attempted to offer definitions of value and that these definitions have been primarily descriptive or designative in function.[4] Naturalists often have introduced meanings to value terms which were based upon scientific studies. Here they have emphasized descriptive or explanatory inquiry rather than linguistic analyses of the diverse uses of value terms. In these inquiries, they were concerned primarily with *understanding* "value phenomena" and the "data of value experience," not recommending. In some of these writings, some naturalists have no doubt committed "persuasive definitions." However, there is one curious feature in all naturalist-type definitions, and that is that the alleged natural properties to which they refer are implicitly evaluative in character; for they refer to qualities in experience—either interest, desire, or immediacy of enjoyment—which human beings find worthwhile. Most of the naturalistic definitions which had been offered are relational, and they refer not to some natural property independent of experience, but to some interest in relation to an object. R. B. Perry's definition of value is most instructive here, for he considers value as "any object of any interest"; and he defines "interest" as any "state, act, attitude, or disposition of favor or disfavor."[5] Most likely, this should be interpreted to mean that value refers to commendatory, prescriptive, and evaluative aspects of behavior.

There are few naturalists today who will dispute Hare's view that value words are not to be construed simply as descriptive but are commendatory. But they would be careful to point out that in Hare's writings these evaluative terms depend upon certain "good-making characteristics" (i.e., empirical assertions concerning properties), comparative judgments applicable to classes of objects similar in kind, as well as evaluative criteria. Thus terms such as "comfortable," "rude," or "sweet" do not denote simple descriptive properties. They are evaluative terms; though they are based in some important sense upon properties that the objects possess on the basis of which we apply the predicates.[6]

The central issue that I want to focus upon in this chapter is the question as to whether naturalism is committed to the doctrine that value judgments are *logically deducible* from factual premises. The answer that I would give is negative; first, because value judgments in their distinctively normative sense are not wholly or primarily descriptive in function, but prescriptive and evaluative; and second, because although the naturalists would insist that there is an important relationship between facts and values, the relationship is not one of deductive entailment, but of practical decision.

## VALUE JUDGMENTS

An assumption about naturalistic ethics which critics assert without proof is that naturalism is committed to the doctrine that value judgments are *in toto* descriptive, because naturalists have claimed that value judgments may be tested empirically. On the contrary, many naturalists have insisted that value judgments are primarily prescriptive and directive in function. The writings of John Dewey, a leading naturalist, bears out this interpretation. For Dewey considered value judgments to be at root *practical* and to concern means-ends in relation to action. Indeed, Dewey went so far as to maintain "that the *entire* use and function of ethical sentences is directive and practical."[7] "A judgment of value," he held, "is simply a case of a practical judgment." And a "practical judgment" he defined as "a judgment of what to do, or what is to be done." "Practical judgments," he said, "do not therefore primarily concern themselves with the value of objects, but the course of action demanded. . . . The question is of better or worse with respect to alternative courses of action, not with respect to various objects."[8] Thus value judgments are not primarily descriptive, as Hare charges, but "prescriptive," "directive," and "imperative," in that they function to recommend or advise a course of action as based upon evaluation and appraisal.

The key logical issue for naturalistic ethics is the relationship of evidence or reasons to judgments of value and decisions. It is important to point out that naturalistic inquiry has not focused exclusively upon ethics, but also has seen fit to deal with the theory of valuation, the logic of judgments of practice, and decision-making theory. Naturalists have thought it important to investigate the logic of practical judgments in general and not simply the logic of ethical judgments, because moral decisions are only part of the broader class of practical valuations and decisions. Most analytic philosophers have eschewed this kind of inquiry and have concentrated instead upon the logic of moral language; for they have not appreciated the necessity of investigating valuation theory and decision theory separate from classical moral philosophy. I must concede that many or most of the questions that naturalists have chosen to deal with under other headings do eventually emerge in one form or another in ethics; though I do think there is some merit in a division of labor. In any case, the whole point of naturalistic inquiry is that there is a continuity between the methods of practical decision-making in ordinary life and in the experimental sciences on the one hand, and the way we frame ethical decisions and judgments on the other. The naturalists claim, on the basis of their inquiry, that both practical judgments and ethical judgments, in principle at least, are amenable to some degree of objective determination. Thus the naturalist thinks that he has uncovered an implicit "logic of the judgments of practice," in which there are rational principles guiding choice, and that these principles also apply to ethical matters.

Insofar as this is the case, there has been an important reunion in ethics and valuation theory between recent analytic ethics and naturalism. Analytic philosophy has developed an appreciation for the "objectivity" and "reasonableness" of moral decision, based upon a detailed analysis of ordinary language and the ways we reason in morals; and naturalists have reached a similar conclusion based upon an examination of the judgments of practical behavior and the hypotheses in the applied sciences.

The significant contrast in meta-ethics today which still exists would be between either naturalists and subjectivists on the one hand or naturalists and absolutists on the other. In answer to the subjectivists, naturalists do not think that ethical judgments are meaningless or incapable of verification, nor do they depend in the last analysis upon taste and caprice. And in answer to the absolutists, they do not think that ethical judgments are absolute, necessary, or universal.

The present-day union between analytic philosophy and naturalism in ethics is shown by the fact that they have both returned to the Aristotelian tradition.[9] Both agree that there is a kind of practical wisdom in life. Even though we cannot be as precise in ethics as in the sciences or mathematics, nevertheless some degree of ethical objectivity is possible.

The essential point that the naturalist would still wish to maintain is that practical judgments may be *supported* by reference to evidence, though again I do not know that analytic philosophers need disagree. Perhaps it is only a matter of emphasis, the questions to be raised, however, are first, what kinds of evidence, and second, what is the relation between the range of evidence and the ethical (or practical) judgment?

In all processes of practical judgmental reasoning or decision making there is, I submit, an *evidential base,* in terms of which the judgment functions. A judgmental inquiry is related to decision or choice and this is connected to action. In a problem of decision we are faced with a number of alternatives, one or more of which we wish to select. Our choice is teleonomic, intentional, and purposive in the sense that there is some end in view, some goal or aim that we wish to achieve.

The judgment or decision is practical in that it is related to *praxis* or conduct. Only those decisions which are connected to action and which are voluntary are the subject of ethical inquiry. Some responses of human organisms are causally determined by physico-chemical or psychosomatic factors. Some responses, however, are conscious and rational and may be modified or influenced by reflection and deliberation.

Practical decisions (as distinct from theoretical decisions) spill out into the world of objects and events in the form of behavioral interactions. Practice decisions are relational; they are situational and contextual. Insofar as the problem of decision is to motivate the person to act, the decision involves passion, feeling, and desire, and has its roots within the conative and bio-chemical soma. Insofar as the decision involves social policy, its content and reference is social and cultural.

The question that especially concerns the ethical philosopher is the kinds of evidence that we appeal to in the deliberative process, and by means of which we may say that our decisions are "adequate," "correct," "wise," "judicious," or "prudent." Certain fairly basic kinds of evidence are immediately presented as relevant to the ordinary man, who reflects on how he makes choices in everyday life: To be meaningful, a decision must be related to (a) his practical action, hence it is by its very nature prescriptive and directive; (b) his decision must also have some reference to the context or situation in which it arises and in terms of which it applies and to the objects and events within it, hence it has a descriptive aspect. Thus his decision has both a prescriptive and descriptive element and it must take into account certain empirical factors as "givens" within the range of practical behavior.

Choices which are not capricious or irrational and have some basis in our intellectual judgment must have some reference to an evidential base. The appeal to an evidential base in ethical deliberation is analogous to the use of an evidential base in ordinary life and the experimental sciences when we are concerned with establishing certain descriptive hypotheses; it differs in *what* is contained within the base.

One part of the evidential base is relatively "value neutral," i.e., it includes knowledge on the part of the agent(s) within the situation of the particular facts that confront him, i.e., the objects and states of affairs immediately at hand, the circumstances and other agents involved. We may say, then, that a rational decision is possible only if one is fully aware of the relevant particulars.

213

The evidential base also includes, to some degree, knowledge of relevant causal conditions, regularities, and generalizations. If an agent is to act, his action is limited by causal conditions within the encountered situation. Knowledge that "if I do *a,* then *b* will most likely follow" is, according to C. I. Lewis, an elementary instance of a causal regularity which is essential to my kind of intelligent behavior.

That we must have knowledge of both particular facts and general conditions should be rather obvious to anyone who reflects upon the way we frame judgments in practical life. Frequently the commonplace is overlooked. Naturalism has claimed that full attention to the range of descriptive and explanatory knowledge is an essential condition for any kind of ethical knowledge. Naturalists have argued that our ability to frame practical judgments is functionally related to our factual knowledge, and that insofar as we are able to expand our knowledge of man and his world, we are better able to resolve the complex problems that arise. In the evidential base, I would include data from biology, psychology, and psychiatry about human needs and requirements—what I call "natural" or "normal needs."

However, in no sense does naturalism stop here; and it would be ludicrous to think that one's normative judgments may be derived or deduced in any way from a neutral descriptive account of the situation, the particular and general facts of our world (or the nature of man). What is essential to the evidential base in ethics, unlike science, is that it be extended to include what Abraham Edel has called a *valuational base;*[10] that is, among the important or crucial "evidence" to be considered in a decision procedure is the whole range of value experiences, value judgments, principles, norms, and ideals given with the situation. Indeed, far from claiming that what "ought" to be the case may be derived from what "is" the case in any antiseptically pure value-free sense of "facticity," the naturalist would insist that any normative conclusions drawn, can only be developed on the basis of those already intrinsic to the valuational base. The charge of Protagorean relativism no doubt applies; for the naturalist wishes to relate practical judgments to an existing set of *de facto* value prizings, principles, and rules. This is where decision begins, with an existing body of norms; though this is not where it need end or remain.

There are two sets of "factors" to be considered within the

evidential—valuational base. First, it refers to the interests, and felt needs of human beings, the things that they desire, prefer, or appreciate. That is, it applies to the value experiences and judgments of the things that are considered good and bad, as based upon previous inquiries. One's preferences, likes and dislikes, have been inherited, or imbibed, but they have also been modified in the light of experience. Second, it refers to the principles and ideals to which human beings are committed and to which they appeal in justifying their decisions and acts. These principles (whether legal, political, social, religious, or moral) are conditioned in individuals and become embedded in social habits and conventions. Thus, there is both an individual and a social basis for value judgments and normative principles.

I have used the term "evidence" here to describe value judgments and principles because I do not find them to be mysterious psychic or ontological entities. They are, in my view, natural modes of human experience within nature, having both psycho-biological roots and social-cultural dimensions.

The question of which decision should be adopted and acted upon in a given situation is always related to the set of antecedent value judgments and principles that are implicated within the situation. They are the "data" to be examined as to their adequacy. One cannot consider problems of judgment and decision without taking into account the existing valuation commitments.

Where decisions are practical, real, urgent, they always have a prospective orientation. To choose means that there is a course of action which is apt and that there are alternatives. This presupposes that there are instruments and tools at our disposal. In other words, action which strives to attain objectives involves means-ends considerations. Critical judgment is intrinsically related to the means that we are able to use. Decision is dependent upon the range of possibilities open to us. What we can do is always a function of the means. If our means are limited and impoverished, we are limited and impoverished. If our means are many, our opportunities are increased. The extent to which we can expand our technological resources as means enables us to expand the alternatives before us. Creative thinking in practical decision is not simply linear or additive, but novel and seminal. Choice depends upon invention, which is a form of creative imagination. The extent to which we can think up new instruments to implement and further our interests is the extent to which we are liberated from our limiting animal environment. Technnological imagination has a profoundly emancipating effect upon human life. Accordingly, naturalism emphasizes the need to develop the technical arts and policy sciences as important contributions to creative decision making. If we cannot solve a problem in traditional ways, we can experiment by going around or over it, by adventurously leap-frogging in new departures. As Sartre has pointed out, man is in a sense able to recreate himself; for his future life is pregnant with possibilities.

A central factor in practical methodology is the means-end continuum. It is not the end that justifies the means, rather our ends presuppose and are contingent upon the means at our disposal. Decisions are a result of weighing means on a comparative scale, strategically calculating costs and expenditures, as well as inventing and bringing new ones into being.

However, there is still another important criterion of choice. Inasmuch as decisions display themselves in action, we may observe and evaluate what we do in terms of the effects of our decisions upon our lives. We continually learn from experience. We discard old methods because they no longer serve us and adopt new ones because we think they will. Some judgments are well-tested in practice, are generalized and become social guides to conduct. Indeed, they may eventually become enshrined within tradition and are supported by religion and morality. A whole body of moral duties and responsibilities may develop to support them. Great efforts are made to stabilize and institutionalize social rules and to base them upon universal moral principles. We eventually discover that all rules and principles have exceptions and that they must be modified in the light of new conditions. Thus rules and principles, introduced to assist individuals within society in making decisions, are themselves fallible, tentative, hypothetical. They are continually being evaluated by reference to their observable *consequences,* by how well they serve our desires and our needs.

In the above, I have only touched on *some* of the factors that I think go into the evidential-valuational base, as materials for consideration in any judgmental decision process; particular facts, general conditions (including statements about human nature), *de facto* value judgments, principles, means, consequences. There are no doubt others.

What is the relation of a judgment or decision to the evidential-valuational base? It is, I submit, practical, teleonomic, functional. A decision is considered fitting, appropriate or adequate to the present situation. The decision cannot be deduced from "the facts," it is not entailed by them. It does relate to them; but it is drawn by reflecting upon them in a creative decision procedure. The decision drawn is not a mere summary generalization; it is not tested inductively. Its relationship to the evidential-valuational base is not necessary as is the case with formal inference; it is not probabilistic, as in the relationship between a scientific hypothesis and the data to be explained. I have elsewhere described the relationship as "act-ductive" to indicate that it involves a special kind of practical logic.[11]

I am not denying that inferential procedures enter at some point into practical reasoning, but this does not provide either a decisive or complete account of the deliberative process. The deductive aspect enters when we are concerned with general rather than particular cases; though even here whether to use a specific principle in a situation cannot be determined solely by *a priori* deductive rules of inference. Inductive procedures also enter into a decision process, as factual claims are made and tested in the process of investigation. But in the last analysis the logic of judgments of practice has its own kind of autonomy and rationale. Objectivity and the logic of deliberative thinking in ethics and life is practical, not formal or inductive.

One should be clear that in any decision process we start in the *middle,* not at the beginning. This means that we do not have in most cases to justify our decisions by reference to "first principles." If called upon to defend any one principle of the many that we hold, we may do so at the appropriate level of discourse. Though here we have a new situation of inquiry in which we appeal to a new evidential-valuational base. We deal piecemeal and contextually with our principles and value judgments, and we do not need to demonstrate deductively their "truth" *a priori*; nor can we. Indeed, we assume a body of principles as given. Justification emerges only when a particular principle or judgment is criticized or attacked and thus requires special justifying reasons. It is a mistake in meta-ethics to look for one or more basic principles (for example, the greatest happiness principle or the categorical imperatives) on the basis of which all others are deduced. As a matter of fact there are any number of principles and rules, value judgments and commitments, and I might add, responsibilities, obligations, duties which we hold and which may have to be considered in any decision procedure.

The above model of decision making is based upon an analysis of how we reason about our choices in practical life, and how we refer to an evidential-valuational base in supporting our decisions. It does not claim that all problems of decision may be resolved. One's decisions may be such that there seem to be nothing but *un*desirable consequences available (the Vietnam war, for example). There is both an optimistic and pessimistic appraisal of decision making. Some optimism is warranted, because given a commitment to the rational methods of practical judgment, at least many or most of our decision-problems may be resolved. Yet there is a tragic aspect to decision, for we are limited by the materials with which we work and the range of actualities before us, and in some human situations there seem to be no available solutions.

The above model also does not presuppose that all objective and impartial inquirers will necessarily agree as to what is good, right, or wise within a given situation. They are likely to agree only if they operate from the same evidential-valuational framework. If the evidential-valuational base from which two or more individuals or groups operate differs, then the decisions drawn may differ. Although the fact that there are common human problems and needs, and that men and women of different backgrounds share many similar interests and principles, suggests that in many situations we may be able to reach common conclusions. We live in the same world, a world in which traditional barriers are breaking down, and in which an individual may be influenced by normative principles from several traditions at the same time. We can argue and disagree, inquire and dispute, and out of the process we may hope that some consensus on common principles may emerge. But we have no guarantee.

One basis for disagreement no doubt is the fact that some moral systems presuppose mistaken facts or theories about nature or man— thus evidence and valuational principles in the base are closely related. Given a detailed factual inquiry we may be able to modify those principles which are incorrectly related to mistaken facts. In a dispute with a racist, for example, if his beliefs about blacks are based upon his view that they are "inferior" in talent and ability, then we can show that he is mistaken, and hope that his judgment may be modified. In a dispute between a Thomist and a humanist, we may empirically investigate whether a fetus may be said to have a "human personality" as preliminary to our judgment about whether or not it should be aborted. In arguing with a Marxist we can examine his claim that there are dialectical laws of history, since this influences his judgment about social policies. A dispute about birth control is dependent in some sense upon empirical data about trends in world population growth. The principles of men, whether racists, Thomists, humanists, or Marxists, I take to be human commitments; and accordingly they are available to careful scrutiny and critical analysis. Such analyses hopefully may assist us in modifying elements within our given evidential-valuation base. The naturalists believe that the more we are able to learn about man and nature by means of continuing inquiry into the facts, and the more we can critically examine our inherited principles, the better able we are to build common bridges. However, no one can guarantee that we will succeed. And the emotivists may be correct; for there may be basic disagreements in both beliefs and attitudes which it is hard to resolve or to change. Still one has no other alternative than that of reliance upon reason as the best guide in the practical and ethical life.

The above is a statement of a naturalistic theory. It is a theory in meta-ethics, which argues for one key point: namely, that although normative conclusions may *not* be deduced from factual premises, judgments of practice (including ethical judgment) are amenable to some objective treatment, by reference to the operative evidential-valuation base. Does the above meta-theory itself presuppose any normative principles? The answer is a qualified yes. I do not think that one can do pure meta-ethics without some normative commitment: and it is self-deception to think that this is possible. What I have done in this chapter is to try to analyze and uncover the logic of practical reasoning that I think is embedded in ordinary life when we deliberate about our decisions; I would go further and recommend that we use this logic as a guide. Deductive and inductive logic are also normative. If one wants to be consistent, then he must abide by the rules of formal inference; and if one wants explanatory and predictive hypotheses, then he must abide by the criteria of scientific methodology and inductive logic. Similarly, if one wants wise judgments of practice (following Aristotle), then there is a model for practical judgment which he may use. The analytic philosopher who seeks to uncover the rules of use of value language, or wishes clarity and the avoidance of confusion also presupposes certain normative principles. The very commitment to philosophy itself is normative. Therefore, I think that meta-ethics cannot be sharply distinguished from normative ethics; for there are at least minimal normative standards implicit in any act of philosophical analysis—though there is surely some difference between a dispassionate philosophical analysis on an intellectual level and the actual recommendation of a course of action in concrete moral situations.

In this latter regard, I think that it is a fundamental mistake for philosophers to withdraw from the area of normative ethics to a linguistic meta-sanctuary. Philosophy has had many missions besides analytic clarification, and among the most significant is the Socratic mission which not only attempts to define what we mean by certain key moral concepts, but also recommends the adoption of a set of moral principles and a way of life.

I have not tried in this chapter to move beyond the analysis of certain meta-issues in ethics to my own substantive normative principles, though perhaps at times they were implied, if only minimally, in what I have said. If I were to lay bare my own normative position, the valuational base from which I operate, I would label it "humanistic ethics" rather than simply "naturalistic ethics." What I would try to show is that although most Anglo-American philosophers may dispute on the meta-level concerning their theories of meaning and truth, they nevertheless share in their own lives certain common normative principles, principles which are perhaps naturalistic in their metaphysical foundations, but are humanistic in their application to man.

# NOTES

1. R. M. Hare, *The Language of Morals* (Oxford, England: Oxford University Press, 1952), p. 92.
2. R. M. Hare, *Freedom and Reason* (Oxford, England: Oxford University Press, 1963), p. 16.
3. Ibid., p. 2.
4. See especially, C. I. Lewis, R. B. Perry, Stephen Pepper.
5. Ralph Barton Perry, *General Theory of Value* (New York: Longmans, Green & Co., 1926), Section 49.

6. For an extended discussion of my views here see my *Decision and the Condition of Man* (Seattle: University of Washington Press, 1965), chs. 12, 13.

7. John Dewey, *Theory of Valuation* (Chicago: University of Chicago Press, 1939).

8. John Dewey, "The Logic of Judgments of Practice," *The Journal of Philosophy, Psychology and Scientific Methods* 12, No. 19 (September 1916): 505-23.

9. See especially P. H. Nowell Smith, *Ethics* (Harmondsworth, England: Penguin Books, 1956).

10. Abraham Edel, *Ethical Judgment, The Use of Science in Ethics* (Glencoe, Ill.: The Free Press, 1955).

11. Kurtz, *Decision and the Condition of Man*, chs. 14, 15.

# 12.
# Moral Faith and Ethical Skepticism Reconsidered

There are two contrasting approaches to the moral life. The first I shall call "moral faith," and the second, "ethical skepticism." Moral faith has been the deepest and most pervasive force in human culture; and the proponents of this approach to the moral life have had the predominant influence. Ethical skepticism has been relatively rare in human history and has been espoused by only a small number of intellectuals. It has been considered by Establishments to be an extremely dangerous position. Its earliest known proponent was Socrates, at least insofar as he questioned the reigning orthodoxy of his age; though his own position later became enshrined as part of a new faith.

Now there are other possible postures that we may adopt in respect to morality. One can, for example, be largely indifferent to the demands of morality and not take it seriously. One may be a

From *The Journal of Value Inqiury* 19 (1985): 55-65. Copyright © 1985. Martinus Nijhoff Publishers, Dordrecht, Holland. Reprinted by permission of Kluwer Academic Publishers.

cynic about it, or even assume the role of the nihilist and reject it entirely. These positions, though interesting, I will not attempt to deal with here; though perhaps some verge on ethical skepticism. Rather, I shall focus on the above two alternative views of morality. I myself will attempt to explicate and also defend one variety of ethical skepticism, though there are many different forms that skepticism may assume.

# I. MORAL FAITH

Now the term "faith" is usually employed in reference to transcendent beliefs, that is, beliefs that describe, designate, or point to some existent reality that we cannot demonstrate exists. To say that one has *faith* usually means that one accepts beliefs in a state or reality for which there is insufficient evidence; though there is the conviction that this reality exists in some form. Faith is that portion of one's psychological belief-state that transcends the evidence offered for the belief. A moral belief on the contrary is normative or prescriptive. It does not simply allege that something is the case, but that it ought to be; and it recommends bringing into being a state of affairs that is considered to be "good," "just," "valuable," "right," or has some other commendable properties. Those who express a moral faith hold it to be *true* in some sense of the term true; that is, they believe that moral values or principles have some reality independent of the person who espouses them, and that therefore we have an obligation to fulfill or obey them. Now those who espouse a moral faith usually also express some deep-seated commitment to that faith. Indeed, the term faith implies some fidelity or loyalty on the part of a person to instate or defend his moral commitment. It implies that there are deep roots within the individual personality or the social institutions that espouse the faith. It is not simply an intellectual commitment on the level of cognition, but involves passion and feeling. It is both *imperative,* in the sense that those who hold the faith believe that what it recommends ought to exist if it does not as yet, and it is *expressive* in that it evokes an emotional response. But it is not merely emotive, and it is not simply a matter of taste or caprice, for it gives vent to our *deepest* attitudes and longings. Thus a moral faith is generally grounded in one's first principles.

To talk about a person's faith in the area of morality is analogous to talking about a person's faith in religion. When we probe a person's moral roots, we know that we have touched rock-bottom when we are able to elicit a blush or a stammer. Faith is at the core of a person's value structure. Once challenged, it often provokes an intense defensive reaction.

There are at least two fundamental ingredients to a person's moral faith: (1) basic values, and (2) moral principles. Though we may distingiush them in kind, values and principles overlap and are intertwined within a personal or social framework. (1) The *values* of a person or a society refer to the things that are found to be good and worthwhile, that are cherished and held dear. In behavioristic terms, values refer to preferential, selective, or teleonomic behavior, the attitudinal-cognitive-conative motives that impel us to achieve goals and purposes. A person has a great number of values, from immediately liking a glass of vodka, a chocolate ice cream sundae, a melody, or an embrace to approval of an intellectual position or the long-range quest for happiness. In philosophical language, teleological theories have focused on the ends and goals that are considered to be most enduring and worthwhile. Now there has been a wide range of experiences that have been cherished and diverse ends that have been pursued. One's basic value commitments, whether to love, piety, science, or the general happiness, express one's deepest values and the kind of a world that one wishes to bring about. For some this refers to ideal ends to be achieved.

A second component of the moral life is moral principles. I use the term "principle" here to refer to a rule of conduct, a standard or norm governing action. A principle is usually taken to be universal or general in that it lays down policy guides for future conduct, or it limits or proscribes other forms of human action. It is clearly prescriptive or prohibitive, recommending, advising, or commending us how to live or behave. Generally, the philosophical schools that have emphasized this are called "deontological." They emphasize our obligations and responsibilities to obey or fulfill the principles which serve as moral guides. They underscore the demands of justice and fairness. There are any number of moral principles that have been expressed, such as the biblical proverbs: "Love thy neighbor as thyself." "An eye for an eye, tooth for tooth, hand for hand, foot for foot; burning for burning, wound for wound, stripe for stripe." "Do unto others as ye would have them do unto you." But there are many other moral principles that we recognize in conduct: To tell the truth; not cheat, steal, kill, or injure another; to keep your promises and be sincere. Moral principles are often revised and new ones introduced. Two recently enunciated moral principles have aroused intense debate and commitment in democratic societies. There is, for example, the libertarian principle: "An individual should be permitted to do whatever he wishes, so long as he or she does not interfere with the rights of others." And there is the egalitarian principle: "All individuals are equal in dignity and worth and entitled to equality of opportunity, ethical consideration, or equal desserts." Still other moral principles have emerged today involving the recognition of human rights.

There are a great variety of moral values and principles that have prevailed in history, and there are alternative moral codes: the Samurai warrior, Christian priest, bourgeois entrepreneur, Bohemian poet, scientific investigator, or Marxist revolutionary express different values and principles. Thus there is the familiar problem of cultural relativity. Each social group seeks to inculcate its cherished values and principles. It provides sanctions for those who flout them; and it rewards those who conform and are considered to be the paragons of virtue.

Moral systems that are rooted in faith generally take their basic values and central moral principles as universal; these are held to express deep truths about the universe of man. Values and principles are not taken as subjective or considered merely to be a matter of taste or caprice; they are allegedly grounded in the nature of things. Thus there are efforts to derive them from religious, metaphysical, ideological, or scientific doctrines. Moral values and principles are not without cognitive support, they are conceputalized and defined, and attempts are made to justify them by an appeal to reason, and to defend them against their critics. All of these codes, however, have religious or semi-religious qualities and elements of faith attached to them.

There are no doubt differences in the degrees of faith with which moral systems are held. On the one extreme is moral absolutism. Here moral principles are considered to be absolute commandments, and they are enforced by the threat of punishment, whether from Jehovah or the state. There is apprehension about flouting them.

Moral phobias develop. Principles become inviolable. Orthodox religious moralities have absolute prohibitions against divorce, adultery, or homosexuality. Such systems can be highly repressive, even tyrannical.

A strongly held faith more often than not involves some self-righteousnesss. There is a fear of heretics, disbelievers, or aliens, who are taken as "immoral," or "wicked," and are condemned as the corrupters of the true morality. And there is a sense that one has a duty to further the moral faith and to oppose or even destroy offending adversaries. There may be a heightened sense of a cosmic struggle between the forces of good and evil and a conviction that one's side needs all the support it can get in its holy crusade against those benighted souls who reject its moral point of view or choose to live differently. While these attitudes apply to religious believers—whether orthodox defenders of the holy faith or the disciples of a newer cult—they also may characterize entirely secular movements, which may likewise be engulfed by ardor and the need to sacrifice for the cause.

One's moral faith may be considered to be far more important than one's religious belief; for often it is not what you believe in that counts, but what you do, how you bring up your children, and how your women are treated. These matters touch at the very core of one's sense of propriety; and they can arouse intense hatred if they offend it. Public approbation or disapprobation may not be sufficient to support the moral code. If so, other institutions emerge to enforce compliance. A priestly class employs the symbols of God's power and the threat of excommunication or damnation. Or it is the state which becomes the ultimate guardian of morality for it can enact and enforce the laws. Although it is the state that may legislate morality, all of the institutions of society may be charged with inculcating and reinforcing moral conduct: the family, the schools, economic institutions, even voluntary associations.

Appeals to the fatherhood of God are a familiar psychological device for sanctifying one's moral principles, but there are secular equivalents of divinity. The twentieth century is all too familiar with secular ideologies, which involve ethical-political doctrines and principles that are held to be implicit within the womb of nature. Instead of God, Marxists appeal to the dialectical laws of history in which higher forms of social relations struggle to emerge, and in which one's highest duty is said to be to assist the oppressed or to achieve a classless society. Following Darwinism, Herbert Spencer and others sought to defend free enterprise and the struggle of the fittest for survival. Others defended the data of inevitable human progress. Gobineau and Chamberlain later provided the basis for Nazi racist policies, but these were based upon the mistaken notions of biologically superior and inferior races. No doubt one can indict such simplistic approaches—we ought not to commit science to a dogmatic moral faith. Perhaps the above theories were not verified, but were forms of pseudoscience. The above illustrates, however, that scientific theories can be translated into ethical prescriptions and be used as justifications for repression. There are many other illustrations of the uses of science in moral persuasions: the debate about I.Q. and race, sociobiology and the instinct for aggression, etc. Is science relevant to ethics? Can it function, not as a faith, but in another way?

One fault in the above systems, I submit, is that they present a hierarchical structure of values and principles; that is, they take one value or principle and seek to make it all-controlling. This is a common approach in any system of faith. But one should guard against the tyranny of principles, i.e., using a principle as an absolute and not admitting any exception to it. To illustrate: those who argue that it is wrong to take an innocent human life—the fetus is held to be a human person and innocent—maintain that any form of abortion is always wrong under any circumstance, even when the fetus is grossly retarded, or the pregnancy is due to rape or incest. Conversely, the libertarian defends the principle that an individual should be permitted to do whatever he wants, so long as he doesn't harm others. Thus Thomas Szasz comes out against any involuntary commitment to mental hospitals, even if a patient is seriously disturbed or schizophrenic. He denies any evidence for the latter. To be consistent, we are told, the principle means that heroin and all other addictive drugs should be legalized—even if this would mean the death or debilitation of a large sector of the population. Thus for dedicated moral faith root values and first principles cannot be held in contradiction. Consistency is the ultimate test as to whether one is true to his principles. A deeply held moral faith can, if pursued to its ultimate conclusion, become ludicrous if it is applied without distinction.

Now in the above cases, one's faith is often the product of one's unexamined assumptions. We imbibe our moral faith at our mother's knee and it persists without reflection. It is nourished and fed in the socio-cultural context in which we grow and function. It is pre-rational and affective-conative in character. Some justification for our moral faith-state is sought when it is challenged by others. At that point, appeals may be made to one's higher religious faith, or our moral faith may be derived from an elaborate ideological system. Or we may seek to justify our faith by reference to science, and to use that to support it by reference to its research findings. Should we equate a moral faith based upon religion or ideology with one based upon science? Is that not stretching it too far? Are there not important differences? I think that there are. Yet I fear that some degree of self-deception lurks under the mantle of science. In its most extreme form there is worship of the faith that "science will save us." The scientific intellectual is not unlike the religious intellectual waiting in expectation of Godot, who never arrives. For the scientific believer, we are waiting for our own Godot, the salvation promised by science.

We should not deceive ourselves into believing that scientific intellectuals are any more fair-minded or impartial than others when it comes to their own cherished values and moral principles. These often reflect their own deepest prejudices. This can be seen vividly in the area of political belief. For many intellectuals, politics often functions religiously. I am often struck by the deep partisan bias—in most cases to a liberal-left orientation—and the intense animosities displayed towards individuals or parties that oppose it. Intellectuals are not unique in this regard. Their emotive bias is similar to those who hold a conservative right-wing faith, especially business or corporate executives. Alas, all too few intellectuals recognize their political faith for what it is. There is some need for political skepticism about all strongly held partisan positions, whether of the left or the right.

I do not mean to suggest that all moral faiths are intransigent or non-self-critical. There are periods of conversion in history when there are radical paradigm shifts and when new values and principles emerge. Some moral faiths are unyielding; others are receptive to modification in the light of intellectual criticism. And that, as I view it, is the essential role that ethical skepticism can play in reforming and liberalizing pre-existing systems and making them responsive to alternative conceptions of the good life or the just society.

## II. ETHICAL SKEPTICISM

Now I do not wish to deny that science is relevant to ethics. But it is important that we be clear about what scientific inquiry can and can not do. It can never, in my judgment, free us entirely from ethical indeterminacy. Some skepticism is essential to the life blood of the scientific enterprise itself.

What is ethical skepticism? Let me describe it as it developed in the field of twentieth-century meta-ethics. Interestingly, it has been used most directly against naturalistic and scientific ethics, i.e., the confident expectations of philosophers and scientists that we might develop a science of ethics and value.

Now there are three parts of the skeptical critique:

(1) there are inherent logical difficulties in defining our basic ethical terms and concepts;
(2) there are epistemological difficulties in testing ethical principles and judgments or deriving "ought" statements from "is" statements, values from facts;
(3) there are existential difficulties in justifying first principles and root values.

G. E. Moore was among the first to raise some serious questions about the meaning of ethical terms and concepts. In particular, he argued that the "good" was indefinable, and that all previous ethical theories that had attempted to provide a definition or theory of the good had committed a logical fallacy, which he labeled as the "naturalistic fallacy." This fallacy applied to any effort to derive the good or other normative concepts from nonnormative equivalents. Moore leveled his attack upon the utilitarians (especially John Stuart Mill), who were influential at the turn of the century. The utilitarians had attempted to create a science of ethics. They sought to derive normative ethics (the good was defined as pleasure or happiness) from a descriptive theory of motivation (psychological hedonism, i.e., that all humans seek to maximize pleasure and avoid pain). It was a mistake, said Moore, to try to find a nonnormative substitute for "good." He offered his famous "open question argument": for any definition proposed, one could ask, but *is* it good and *why* should I accept your definition? "Good" is "good," said Moore, a "simple nonnatural quality." It is "indefinable," like yellow, though we can know what it is directly and intuitively. Moore's objection applied not only to scientific naturalism, but to any and all efforts at definition. It applied equally to metaphysical or theological definitions: to those in which the good is identified with "God's will," "human progress," the "general happiness," or anything else.

As I argued in chapter 6, I think Moore was mistaken about much of this. His reasons for rejecting normative definitions were questionable. He thought that the property "good" was a floating, "nonnatural," Platonic essence; that is why it was indefinable. We can raise the open question argument against Moore himself: why accept his epistemological definitions of "good"? If Moore is correct, then a definist's fallacy might apply to *all* scientific efforts at descriptive definition. One could not provide rigorous operational definitions in the sciences for anything. A thing is what it is and not something else.

Other neo-Kantian intuitionists in twentieth-century ethics (Sidgwick, Prichard, Ross, etc.) did not focus on teleological terms, such as "good" or "value," which they thought were derivative and definable, but upon deontological terms such as "right," "wrong," or "justice." These they found nonreductive and indefinable. Although such ethical predicates are knowable, they argued these are not translatable into nonethical terminology. Neither Moore nor the deontological intuitionists were skeptics or subjectivists. They believed that ethical knowledge was meaningful and possible and that there was such a thing as ethical truth.

Of special interest to scientific naturalists are the further perplexing questions that they raised: What is the proof of axioms, postulates, and first principles? Mill thought that he could not prove his first principles. For him, the basic point of utilitarianism was that all moral rules are to be tested by their consequences, by whether or not they contribute to the greatest happiness. Mill committed a logical blunder: the only proof that we could give that something is visible is that it can be seen, or audible is that it can be heard, and therefore the only proof that something is desirable is that it can be desired. The fallacy here is figure of speech, for in the conclusion the suffix "able" implies that it *ought* to be desired—not that it can—and this has *normative* force. Thus, Mill's attempted proof of the basic premise of utilitarianism was formally invalid. Whether Mill, one of the leading logicians of the day, had his tongue in cheek when he wrote that is open to debate. The key conclusion that the critics of scientific naturalism drew was that normative judgments could not be derived from descriptive premises. No less an authority than David Hume, the leading skeptic of modern philosophy, is responsible for recognizing the fallacy in attempting to derive an imperative statement from a descriptive one.

There are two key issues here. First, can we define ethical terms and concepts? Second, how can we test ethical judgments? Two additional schools in twentieth-century philosophy—logical positivism and existentialism—had further assaulted the foundations of classical philosophy, undermined our confidence in reason and the conviction that we could create a science of ethics or values based on science. The logical positivists agreed with Moore and the intuitionists that we could not define ethical terms and concepts. The reasons for this, they argued, are different from Moore's: Normative terms were nondescriptive and nondesignative. Ethical language had other functions. It was expressive or emotive in character and imperative in function. The reasons why we could not define ethical terms was because they had no identifiable empirical referents in the world, no sense data to which they referred. Being evocative, they gave vent to our feelings and attitudes and sought to arouse similar responses in others. Any effort to provide objective definitions were thus bound to fail and were in the last analysis "persuasive."

The emotivists in ethics drew a threefold distinction between: (1) descriptive, (2) analytic, and (3) emotive sentences. The first could be tested by some empirical verification, at least in principle. The second were tautological and formally valid in terms of the rules that governed their use. The third had no identifiable means by which we might confirm them. There were no criteria by which we could determine their truth values. Thus value judgments and ethical sentences had no intersubjective methods of confirmation. They were often prey to indeterminable disputes. This question became pivotal: how could we resolve normative disagreements?

C. L. Stevenson provided us with a modified emotive theory.

Many disagreements, he said, were rooted in beliefs. These could be resolved, at least in principle, where factual matters are at issue. Presumably disagreements in the descriptive sciences could be overcome by reference to empirical confirmation or disconfirmation, indirectly if not directly. Ethical disputes, where they are grounded in cognitive beliefs, could be resolved by pointing out the mistakes about factual conditions or the consequences of proposed policies. But ethical disagreements that are rooted in attitudes may be difficult or impossible to resolve. It all depends upon whether or not we share similar attitudes. A science of value thus might reach a hopeless impasse; for whether or not we can solve a moral dispute depends upon whether we share the same moral faith. And when we hit rock bottom, we may not hold the same ethical convictions.

On this last point existentialism is especially pertinent. For it has maintained that there is a kind of absurdity concerning first principles, and that how we choose to live in the last analysis may depend upon a leap of faith. At crucial turning points in life we may be confronted with a kind of radical freedom—to choose or not to choose—and there are no ultimate guidelines. Our first principles are beyond proof. They grow out of and are validated in the process of living; and there is no deductive proof that can be given for one style of life rather than another.

Now there has been a lot of water over the dam since the emotive theory and existentialism burst upon the scene. And there is an extensive critical literature that has examined their claims and shown them to be excessive. First, although we may not define ethical terms arbitrarily, their meanings are embedded in our language, and they have a wide variety of uses, which are not simply emotive. Although normative terms are not primarily descriptive, factual considerations are relevant to their definition and uses, and it is by reference to descriptive properties that we apply value terms to objects. For example, if we say that, "this chair is comfortable," we may attribute the term "comfortable" because the chair as a matter of fact is "soft" or "supportive" and has other descriptive properties.

Second, although value judgments cannot be deduced from descriptive sentences, descriptive sentences are relevant to their verification. There is a logic of judgments of practice. For example, we employ these in the applied sciences, such as medicine, engineering, psychiatry, or pedagogy. Value disgreements are not primarily a question of feeling or caprice: there are objective considerations that are relevant to the context under analysis and the decision-making procedures.

Third, in an ethical dilemma we usually do not have to trace ourselves back to first principles, but we resolve our moral problems by dealing with the values and principles that are relevant. The situation provides some guidelines and parameters for our choice. A return to first principles only occurs in special crisis situations. Normally we deal with principles of the middle range. Thus there is a kind of practical wisdom that we discover in experience, a kind of objective relativism. What we do is relative to the situation in which we have to make a choice, and these are amenable to some intelligent criticism. Thus there are objective considerations and standards in the field of ethical judgment.

Yet in spite of the above, *some* degree of ethical skepticism still remains, and I do not see how we can transcend it entirely. There are, however, two kinds of ethical skepticism. First, there are those who maintain that ethics is entirely capricious and emotive and that no knowledge is relevant to choice. This kind of nihilistic and negative skepticism is self-contradictory and belied by life itself. Some intelligent basis for criticism is necessary, if we are to live and function. Second, there is a kind of modified ethical skepticism, which uses knowledge and data, but is never entirely able to prove its first principles or find a decisive verification for its values or principles, for those who do not already accept them. Although it rejects moral faith as self-deceptive, it recognizes that the ultimate act of choosing a way of life and the form of being already embedded in a context of values and principles—as the de facto given—are beyond decisive confirmation. We can at best vindicate our basic principles and values and make them seem reasonable to other humans; it is difficult to prove or verify them in any conclusive way.

# III. A MODIFIED FORM OF ETHICAL NATURALISM

In what follows I wish to outline a modified form of ethical naturalism. Let me indicate, however, what it can and cannot do: (1) It cannot hope to derive or deduce from our scientific study of nature, society, or human nature a complete set of moral values or principles that everywhere applies. (2) It cannot hope to derive universal values or principles that are objectively verified in the same way as descriptive hypotheses and theories are. What I wish to suggest is a weaker form of ethical naturalism. Simply stated it is as follows: *scientific knowledge is relevant to our choices and values and should be part of the evidential and valuational base from which we can formulate ethical judgments.*

Now my underlying premise, which no doubt some will question, is that man is a free, autonomous, and creative agent: at least in the sense that he faces problems and is capable of choosing between alternatives. As a decision maker, knowledge can assist an individual or a community to make wiser or more effective choices.

The basic questions that we face are, How shall we choose? and What values and principles should guide us? I would suggest the following range of relevant facts:

(1) We first have to consider the *factual knowledge* that we have, as drawn from everyday life and the sciences. This refers to:
    a) the particular facts of the case and the specific circumstances in which we are involved.
    b) the *causal conditions* which are operative, the social conditions that have led to the present state, the invariant casual regularities;
    c) the *means* at our disposal, the techniques that are available;
    d) the likely *consequences* that might ensue, the results or effects of various courses of action;
    e) the *common normal needs* of human beings, as preconditions of survival, health, and functioning.

The above are value-neutral.

(2) We also need knowledge of pre-existing *values* (teleological ethics):
    a) comparative knowledge of values that other humans have had, whether in the past or in the present;
    b) those which we are now committed to or find controlling in our lives.

(3) We need knowledge of *moral principles* (deontological ethics):
    a) comparative knowledge of the rules, norms, and common moral decencies that have governed mankind, empirically based data, about the rules of the game;

    b) the moral principles that are now relevant to the individual and/or the society in which he lives.

What we ought to do is a function of the above three conditions: knowledge of (1) facts, (2) values, and (3) principles. The second and third considerations suggest a kind of *de facto* involvement. These are in one sense contingent and relative to our particular existential situations in history. What we ought to do, how we ought to live is conditioned by our past. But it is also a function of creative inquiry in the present and it entails a balancing of facts, values, and principles in the concrete contexts of choice. I believe that there is a role for objectivity: but it is neither universal nor a priori, but contingent and existential. There is no ultimate justification for the framework in which we happen to exist, or our basic socio-cultural perspective. These are semi-arbitrary givens. They may be revised or reconstructed, but we are limited by the range of possibilities. Hence my skepticism about universalistic ethical systems that ignore actual phenomenological contexts in the life world. There is a kind of irreducible pluralism about human reality and the human condition. Ethics is thus relational to the frames of reference in which we find ourselves. Knowledge is relevant to human choices, but our choices are not simply deducible from propositions or principles. Life precedes thought. Cognition is only one phase of our conative-affective or socio-cultural existence.

The universe of man is thus open and uncharted. It is changing, not fixed or final. Life is full of striving and endeavor. It is in part precarious, uncertain, and indeterminate. Knowledge can serve us in the ongoing process of living. It is not a substitute for life. Science is a tool, no doubt the most important that we have, but it is not always infallible or reliable. Our existence precedes our essence. Accordingly, some faith is always present in the act of living—animal faith if you will. Hence, we need some skepticism about even the reaches of science or the possibilities it provides for reforming our moral life, let alone the pitfalls of religion or ontology or ideology.

Critical scientific inquiry nevertheless, I submit, has high value as a human enterprise. Comparatively it still provides the greatest promise for solving our problems. In particular, it should provide us with a powerful critique of the methodologies and orthodoxies that reign in every age, the chauvinistic delusions, the systems of narrow moral faith that lord over human behavior or suppress freedom.

Ethical skepticism is not only an epistemological position. It no doubt presupposes a number of moral values. It prefers clarity to confusion, truth to illusion. Skepticism also can contribute to a sense of humility and an awareness of the fallible and problematic character of all human efforts. It enables us to appreciate other points of view. It cultivates a willingness to negotiate differences and to reach compromises. Ethical skepticism tends to liberate us from vain pretensions. It enables us to moderate and humanize intolerant doctrines. It says no to those who would sacrifice us to their excessive moral faiths. There is nothing as unprincipled as men of principles. Get out of their way, since they are all too prone to consume others in the name of their moral dogmas. Their most intense hatred often is directed against heretics, dissenters, or skeptics. Indeed, all sides seem to loathe the skeptics the most, for they see through their shame and pretensions and do not take their shallow intensity seriously. Hopefully, some skepticism can chasten moral impatience somewhat. Perhaps it can reduce the level of moral hysteria and protect us from the worst excesses of moral faiths, whether they are proclaimed in the name of religion or ideology or science.

The sad truth is that no person can live without some moral faith, not even the skeptic. The difference is that the skeptic is aware of the limits and pitfalls of his own cherished principles and values. The paradox for the skeptic is that he, too, needs some motivation and enthusiasm for his values and principles, else life would be empty and devoid of zest: hence the role of faith. Skepticism is vital, however, for it gives us pause; it restrains our zeal; it moderates our passions; it civilizes our follies. It is both the beginning and the end of wisdom. It calls us back. It is a corrective, an antidote to the morally intoxicated of every age.

# Part III

# Naturalism
# vs.
# Phenomenology
# and Existentialism

# 13.
# Phenomenology and Naturalism*

Philosophical schools often engage in warfare, but they also tend to converge; the mark of the contemporary scene is the intense dialogue of warfare and convergence between the philosophical schools. Witness, for example, the efforts that have been made at conciliation between analytic philosophy and phenomenology, or existentialism and Marxism, however shaky and feeble these may be.

Marvin Farber has been attempting in a series of books to bring together naturalism (the native American and also materialistic brand) and phenomenology. This development is of considerable historical significance, especially in view of Husserl's frontal attack in the earlier part of his century upon naturalism as a form of psychologism, and of Farber's central role in the phenomenological movement. Farber is clearly the key figure in phenomenology in the United States, for he more than anyone else is responsible for bringing it to these shores

Originally published in the *Journal of the History of Philosophy* 7 (1969): 74–78. Reprinted by permission of the publisher.

*This is a review article of Marvin Farber's *Phenomenology and Existence: Toward a Philosophy Within Nature* (New York: Harper Torchbooks, 1967), and *The Aims of Phenomenology: The Motives, Methods, and Impact of Husserl's Thought* (New York: Harper Torchbooks, 1966).

241

and for seeing that it received a fair hearing. Farber doubts much that goes under the name of phenomenology, particularly of recent existential and phenomenological psychology. He recognizes not only the genuine contributions of Husserl but also his serious limitations. Phenomenology is incomplete by itself, says Farber, for it may become subjectivistic and irresponsible, and it may serve as a mask for obscurantism. It needs to be completed by being related to naturalistic and objective foundations.

Farber attempted to marry naturalism and phenomenology in an earlier work, *Naturalism and Subjectivism* (1959); the marriage is consummated in his two later works, *Phenomenology and Existence* and *The Aims of Phenomenology*. This union must not be construed as a reluctant effort to accommodate features here and there of phenomenology with naturalism; rather, it is a fundamental and wholesale revision of phenomenology and its incorporation into naturalism. *The Aims of Phenomenology* is an introduction to and a critical review of the history of phenomenology and of recent developments. *Phenomenology and Existence* is the more significant of Farber's two works, for in it he states his own mature convictions. Yet, in reading Farber one question that continually arises is whether he is still a phenomenologist, and in what sense?

Farber's basic premise is naturalistic: *science is fundamental to our understanding, and any philosophy that is unrelated to the sciences is subjective and speculative.* Farber has no use for nonnaturalistic transcendental entities or anything which claims to be outside of nature or independent of its causal grounds, and he is critical of many of the tendencies in phenomenology that lead in this direction. His main thrust is thus to put a phenomenological philosophy back into nature.

Although it is true that Husserl conceived of philosophy as a rigorous science, Farber is fearful that phenomenology, particularly in the later Husserl, tends toward a form of anti-scientific subjectivism. Husserl considered naturalism and the "natural attitude" to be "naive" and "dogmatic"; he wishes to "suspend" all judgments of existence and validity by means of a phenomenological reduction. This reduction utilized a "pure," "radical," and "transcendental" reflection which focuses on the experiences themselves without any metaphysical commitments. Husserl restricted philosophical inquiry to the reflective description of experience in order to uncover essential meanings and structures. But Farber maintains in criticism that phenomenology has as a result developed "the most conspicuous form of pure subjectivism" in the twentieth century and became in the later Husserl "the historical successor of philosophical idealism."

The real difficulty, according to Farber, is the mistaken attempt to disengage the thinker and his experience from the world of nature and the social setting. Thus the "pure subjectivity" of phenomenology, which is at most an abstract methodological device, cannot be converted, as it is in Husserl, into a metaphysics of idealism. Farber insists that although phenomenology is useful, within clearly circumscribed limits, as a phenomenological instrument, it cannot be used to defend a nonnaturalistic and nonmaterialistic metaphysics. Indeed, he claims that for phenomenology to make any sense at all it must be based upon a solid foundation of the natural and social sciences.

It is the problem of the existence of the world which, according to Farber, is crucial and cannot be suspended. Farber thus clearly stands with the realist in claiming that external objects exist independently of the knower or his consciousness. Much of Farber's critique is raised against the possibility of a pure reduction or a presuppositionless phenomenology.

The ideal of emancipation from all presuppositions has had some historical significance, for it has freed philosophy from undue political, social, or religious influences. However, a completely presuppositionless philosophy is impossible, says Farber, and to demand it only leads to an extreme subjective solipsism of the present moment. The ideal of freedom from presuppositions is only a preparatory stage for inquiry, but in exaggerated form it may replace the very absolutes it has overthrown. One cannot leave the natural world when questioning it; existence prior to the knower is a fact that can never be suspended. And existence is spatial, temporal, and historical; in human terms it includes the social context, historical causes, institutions, and culture (something Husserl left out).

In his argument, Farber agrees with naturalists, materialists, positivists, and analysts who have accepted the commonsense view of the world—though he disagrees with those philosophical analysts, who, like Husserl, wish to divorce philosophy from science. According to Farber, although philosophy is autonomous, it is not and cannot be divorced entirely from the sciences, but is an extension of them.

In dealing with questions that are philosophical, one must refer to empirical matters. To claim that philosophy is founded or dependent upon the sciences does not in any way undermine its legitimacy or use. On the contrary, the cardinal error of philosophy is to ignore the sciences, thus paving the way for subjectivism.

Farber's attack on subjectivistic phenomenology applies not only to Husserl but also to its more recent existentialist views. He believes that the latter-day union of phenomenology and existentialism does not rectify the subjective development but accentuates it. Indeed, he believes that the existentialism of Heidegger and others only distorts what might be useful in phenomenology. He considers abortive Heidegger's turning to the world of Being, since this ignores the sciences for poetry and philology. To begin with Dasein in an effort to probe Sein is also a mistake, for man, like nature, is open to the method of scientific inquiry. This means that the development of a philosophical anthropology by Husserl, Scheler, and the existentialists, independent of scientific anthropology or social science, is predicated on a mistaken premise. The very words "philosophical anthropology" involve a two-world theory and a dualism between mind and body or man and nature. To talk about "man's essence" or "what lies innermost" in man is sheer nonsense. And much of what passes for philosophical anthropology is merely generic and not based upon painstaking factual inquiry.

This same critique applies to the "Lebenswelt" which some find so novel in the later Husserl. Farber's attack upon Merleau-Ponty in this regard is highly instructive. One cannot solve the problem of the life-world phenomenologically and subjectively in terms of analyses of the pre-given core of "pure experience." Such analyses may be useful up to a point, but they say nothing about natural events which cannot be eidetically imprisoned, for man's world of lived experience is thoroughly entangled with the world of nature. It is a mistake to believe that the immediacy of the life-world is pre-scientific, or that scientific evidence removes us from the immediacy of evidence. Those who plumb the depths of the life-world look for its essential structure—but no one knows or experiences a life-world in abstraction; as such it is always lived in a specific historical context.

"Essences" are themselves open to change and mortality. The essences that are read out of natural events become frozen, non-temporal, and idealized, but they must be referred to the events of the natural world. For, says Farber, the realm of physical events comes first, not only for us but in nature itself, and "ideal existence" has no basis in fact.

According to Farber's naturalistic point of view, "in order to be said to exist events must be located spatially and temporally in nature, and they must have physical properties" (*Phenomenology and Existence*, p. 162). Thus the view that the world of lived experience eludes the ordinary objective methods of inquiry and that existence is a region not accessible to science is a fundamental error. Indeed, Farber denies that there is a special core world of inner experience; hence all sense of mystery about it must be abandoned by the subjective phenomenologist. The starting point for analysis is the world, not the life-world or Dasein independent and apart.

Farber's view implies that the concept of "transcendence" which one finds in the phenomenological literature is vague and ambiguous. Husserl was well aware of Kant's noumenal realm of insoluble problems; thus he talked about the "riddle of transcendence." If one defines pure consciousness by the suspension of belief and by bracketing, i.e., if the *epoché* is here considered not simply as a methodological device but as a metaphysical claim, then, says Farber, the problem of transcendence becomes crucial. If, on the other hand, one does not attempt to suspend or reduce consciousness and does not thus make an ontological distinction between the subjective and objective aspects of experience but considers them both available to scientific inquiry, then the problem of transcendence does not arise.

Not only can there be no experience without a world, there also can be no experience without an experiencing being. The egocentric predicament upon which metaphysical idealism is based is fallacious, since there is an objective foundation for the knower and the known which is independent of the act of experiencing or knowing. Farber draws upon Marxist premises to demonstrate that one should neither begin with the isolated, solitary thinker as a basis of the phenomenological reduction nor ignore the objective world of social realities. One must fit one's experience into a social network of relationships and dependencies: familial, economic, cultural, political, etc. Thus the full ontological view of a person reveals that he is enmeshed in social relations which cannot be suspended, and that cannot "transcend" the natural conditions of experience, whether physical or social.

Efforts have been made to transcend the natural attitude by means of an ethical transcendence and by postulating a transnatural realm of values. The phenomenology of values begins with feelings, desires, and insights as manifested in experience by persons, only viewed abstractly and "essentially." Yet a structural study of various modes of moral experiences and reasons must not ignore the fact that desires, feelings, and moral insights are conditions and develop within a natural and social context, and that for any inquiry to be complete these roots of moral experience must be taken into account. Thus any reference to the phenomenology of moral experience which is independent of a causal or factual basis is in error. Farber rightly insists that ethics and value are within nature, and that ethical experience and reasons make no sense unless they refer to social and natural facts. Farber thus opts for a naturalistic and situational ethics in which facts and reasons are relevant to moral decisions. Farber's views in ethics and value only illustrate anew the central theme of his thought—a fundamental rejection of subjectivism.

Philosophers of other persuasions will no doubt welcome Farber's careful analysis of the limitations of phenomenology, particularly the covert metaphysics that may be involved. Yet one question remains to be answered: what is left of phenomenology after this rather thoroughgoing reinterpretation and critique? Farber makes it clear that although phenomenology has its defects, it also has its merits. It has value if it is taken solely as a descriptive method. It has virtue, because in focusing on the subjective it contributes to our understanding of experience in all its forms. Its merit lies in the fact that it lays down a challenge to other forms of inquiry that "all statements be tested in the light of direct experience under the conditions of pure intentional analysis" (*Phenomenology and Existence,* p. 233). Descriptive phenomenology involves analyses of meaning, clarification of the structures of experience, and a recognition of the creative aspects of thinking. In this sense, i.e., as a descriptive inquiry, it is entirely consonant, according to Farber, with the philosophies of experience which have flourished in America—the philosophies of Peirce, James, Dewey, Lewis, and Ducasse. And Husserl must be acknowledged as one of the foremost contributors to the philosophies of experience.

Farber has made a real contribution by emphasizing this aspect of phenomenology. What is not clear, however, is precisely how the phenomenological method works, what it would accomplish, and how it would warrant its findings. Phenomenology often is programmatic when is should be concrete. When one studies phenomenology one looks for actual results that one cannot get elsewhere. In a sense the proof of the utility of phenomenology is in its results. Surely one must take into account the data and structures of "raw feels," the whole range of "inner" moral, aesthetic, perceptual, and cognitive experience, as Farber so correctly points out. Many other philosophical schools now recognize the importance of this demand. But *how* the phenomenologist would deal with "raw experience" in a way that other philosophical methods could not—and in what sense—is not always clearly specified or defined to the satisfaction of other philosophical schools. Does one describe what it means to live, enjoy, suffer, think, perceive, or does one grasp the "essential structures" within such experience? And how does one know when one has them—by subjective intuition, by the use of linguistic analysis, or by cooperation by means of empirical evidence?

Farber is, or course, aware of all of these criticisms of the phenomenological method. And he insists that description of the subjective is never sufficient but is one type of descriptive inquiry among others. The complete account of experience is an ideal which requires the analysis not only of the individual knower's experience but also of his place in reality and the social world. Inasmuch as consciousness is never outside of the world but is a complex of behavior and communication, there can never be an exclusive, private, or subjective methodology. Hence phenomenology must be modified by objective modes of scientific inquiry. The phenomenological method is an explanatory device; it is to be appraised by its usefulness to science, philosophy, and ordinary experience. With all of this one would gladly agree.

According to Farber there are some advantages to subjectivism, but only if it is well-defined and logically controlled. Subjectivism is a specialized mode of inquiry which must be subordinated to the requirements of a general methodology. Moreover, to be useful it must be purged of its misleading terms: "transcendental," "pure," "constitutive," "a priori," "eidetic intuition," etc.

What Farber does is attempt to deflate some of the claims made in the name of the phenomenological method. Phenomenology is not the only defensible approach to philosophy or the only radical beginning, as many of its zealous advocates maintain; both naturalism and materialism have shown the excessiveness of these claims.

The core of Farber's argument is that we need to employ a plurality of methods in philosophy in order to meet the great diversity of problems. I agree that descriptive phenomenology within strict limits has its uses but would add that these uses must be spelled out in greater detail. However, Farber insists phenomenology must be supplemented by other methods. The various methods of inquiry should be used cooperatively, not in opposition. No one philosophical school, says Farber, has the right to legislate for all others the proper function of philosophy. And it is this advice that those philosophical schools which insist upon an exclusive method would do well to heed; otherwise a ludicrous situation might develop in which philosophical schools may outlaw each other. Farber believes that phenomenology can take its place along with the other methods as part of the total organization of scholarship, but only if it does not disparage naturalistic methods and if it recognizes the need for a plurality of approaches. The key point to bear in mind is that naturalism relates philosophy to the sciences and does not believe that we can develop any kind of special knowledge independent of them; insofar as phenomenologists attempt to do so they deviate from that central methodological criterion.

# 14.

# Existentialism, Kierkegaard, and Naturalism

"Existentialism" has enjoyed widespread popularity. Some have heralded it as *the* true philosophy for our time, presenting the proper image of man; others have deplored it as a philosophy of despair, cynicism, and irrationalism. How does it contrast with philosophical naturalism?

The writings of the Existentialists divide roughly into two classes: on the one side there is the religiously oriented form of theistic Existentialism, of which the nineteenth-century Danish writer, Søren Kierkegaard, is the first and foremost influence (and which includes the theologians Tillich, Berdyaev, Marcel, and Buber). But on the other side stand the atheistic or naturalistic Existentialists (especially Heidegger and Sartre) who, although influenced by Kierkegaard, nonetheless go back to Nietszche's warning that "God is dead!" and his admonition to men to face up to the fact that they are responsible for what they are and that they must forge their own destinies by free choice. The question that we shall pose in this chapter is whether Kierkegaard's brand of Existentialism provides an appropriate philosophical basis for the present age.

It is paradoxical that Søren Kierkegaard, a solitary individual largely unknown to his century, should be rediscovered in ours and provide the inspiration for present-day Existentialism. Why was Kierkegaard virtually forgotten until the twentieth century? Some have suggested that had Kierkegaard published in German or another influential European language besides Danish, his thought might have had an earlier impact upon Europe. But his obscurity perhaps was also due to the fact that he stood outside of and against the intellectual and social life of the Europe of the first half of the nineteenth century, and he had rebelled against everything that his countrymen held dear. Kierkegaard's main point of view as an author was *how to become a Christian,* how an individual might develop *inwardness of faith;* and he thought that Speculative Reason had lost the true meaning of Christianity. But he also stood against Christendom as it existed in the Europe of his age, and he attacked the established Danish church for sham and hypocrisy. Kierkegaard was a bitter foe of conformist institutionalized religion and mass society for obliterating the individual. And so he lived a lonely and solitary life. He had to bear throughout most of his adult life the cruel ridicule of his fellow Danes; his name became associated with vain philosophical pretension. Unappreciated in his own day, today, however, he has become the fountainhead for the departure into Existentialist philosophy. Is it because the present age is a crisis age that the present climate of opinion is more receptive to the Kierkegaardian mood?

The central concept of Kierkegaard's philosophical outlook is the individual and his choice. In *Either/Or,*[1] Kierkegaard poses a dilemma. There are two stages of life: The first type is the *aesthetic.* The main trait of this kind of life is the search for pleasure and delight, such as that pursued by the epicurean and voluptuary. Don Juan is the ideal prototype. The aesthetic person flits from experience to experience, lives for the present moment of enjoyment, and revels in its subjective immediacy and sensuousness. But the perspective of this style of life is limited, the outlook narrow. Being interested in objects for possession and enjoyment, he is dominated by external circumstances. Instead of developing serious inner qualities, he is at the beck and call of the objects that he seeks. As a rule, the hedonist soon finds that external goods are fleeting and ephemeral. The most devastating enemy of the aesthetic life is boredom and *ennui,* and though one may appear gay to others, one is really masking a deep melancholy. For one can never be satisifed with his perennial quest after elusive objects. (As Plato observed, in the *Philebus,* the life of pleasure is like a leaking pitcher, it can never be filled.) Indeed, the aesthetic individual frequently becomes skeptical about pleasures; and he may even become a cynic and abandon the search for thrill altogether. But there is a second type of life, the *ethical.* This represents a dynamic effort and unending quest. The ethical individual holds external objects and goals transitory and illusory, and he prefers to concentrate on self-development. The morally dedicated person seeks happiness in the moral virtues; and he settles down and performs his obligations and duties in society: in marriage, business, and a career. This person is motivated by practical rather than theoretical reason. He is a realist, not a romantic. He strives to be kind, considerate, charitable. But he is often simply bourgeois, and his life is ultimately incomplete, for there is a kind of teleological suspension.

In *Either/Or,* Kierkegaard dramatizes the aesthetic and ethical stages of life, but he selects neither, leaving it for the reader to make his own choice. Yet for Kierkegaard there is still a third kind of life, a higher stage. Indeed, Kierkegaard himself rejected the first and second stages and devoted himself to the *religious life.* All of his later books, his aesthetic productions, philosophical works, and "edifying" religious sermons work toward this ideal.

For Kierkegaard, both the aesthetic and ethical lives are full of gnawing despair and dread. They are limited in their perspectives and empty of ultimate meaning. Indeed, he wrote:

> . . . there lives not one single man who after all is not to some extent in despair, in whose inmost parts there does not dwell a disquietude, a perturbation, a discord, an anxious dread of an unknown something, or of a something he does not even dare to make acquaintance with . . ."[2]

There is a "sickness of spirit," and though we do not always face it, it grows in the remotest depths of our inner souls. For our life is one of finitude, and as such involves hopelessness. There is a suffering and pain that eats at our roots. As Heidegger later emphasized, each man faces nonbeing and his own death; and though he may put it out of his mind and fly from it, it must meet each of us directly one day. We think that death happens to other persons, or that it applies only to the old; yet we are each focused on the inevitable.

This brings us directly to the crux of Kierkegaard's Existentialism; that is, the *individual's existence,* and his *subjective consciousness.* Kierkegaard's religion is sustained by the pulse of the individual— by it alone is it quickened or does it languish. The essence of Christianity is the individual and the dilemmas he faces and human choice always is of a concrete human personality. Thus religion, Kierkegaard was convinced, if it is to have any vitality, must be related to the individual, and it is tested by what it does for him.

Now there are two main points that I wish to examine here, and they lie close to Kierkegaard's Existentialism. First, I wish to deal with Kierkegaard's attempt to defend Christianity by his famous doctrine that "subjectivity is truth," his attack on Speculative Reason and the divorce of philosophy from life, and his defense of passion. And second, I wish to discuss his emphasis on the category of the individual, the depths of human psychology, and his discovery of human freedom. And this is precisely where "Existentialism" derives its name: for "Existentialism" refers to the concrete existing individual who is the primary starting point of all knowledge and being.

Let me deal with Kierkegaard's theory of truth first. The problem for Kierkegaard, as I have already indicated, concerns the third stage of life, the religious life. But *why* ought one to choose this way of life, and *why* in particular ought one to become a Christian? Kierkegaard observed that most of his fellow Danes were nominal Christians, having been baptized and taking part in the external paraphernalia of religious life. Yet none of them had ever really taken their Christianity seriously enough to live it; they had not really appropriated it into their inner lives.

Philosophers have always asked for the justification of religious doctrine, and theistic and Christian theologians, especially since the time of St. Thomas Aquinas in the thirteenth century, have tried to give a rational proof for belief in the existence of God. But these proofs had come under severe critical attacks by modern philosophers. Kant had shown the impossibility of proving by logical argument the existence of God: one could "demonstrate" both the existence and nonexistence of a necessary being by the use of pure reason; but all such deductions failed, for they were devoid of perceptual observation. And arguments for the divinity of Jesus, as the Son of God, which were based on alleged historical evidence of miraculous occurrences, were also seriously questioned by the empirical philosophers in the Age of the Enlightenment. Christianity was held to be mere superstition, too mythological a tale for rational persons or skeptics to swallow. David Hume has said with tongue-in-cheek that Christianity *indeed* was based on a miracle, but the only miracle was that people were willing to believe its incredible truth by subverting all evidence and reason of the understanding!

But it was Hegel who especially troubled Kierkegaard. For Hegel was the leading metaphysical philosopher of the day and he had an enormous reputation and influence in the universities. Hegel replaced biblical Christianity with rational religion. For Hegel, the Absolute or Divine Reason was universal and was becoming aware of itself through history. Christ was only one incident in the march of consciousness through time. Religion expressed itself in general institutions, but these, too, were only part of the deeper development of Historical Reason.

Now Kierkegaard reacted strongly against the reduction of religion to reason, whether for or against religion. In his major philosophical work, *Concluding Unscientific Postscript,*[3] he asserts that *religious faith or belief* is not the same as reason and that it need not be given a rational proof. Faith is a persuasion resulting from conviction, which is not capable of deductive demonstration. He protested against the view that the only justification of religion that is possible is the sort that the speculative philosopher can give. It is fantastic, he thought, that the religious man must await the philosopher's decision before he can believe. Abstract concepts, he claimed, have very little to do with concrete experience. Hegel's system is like a ballet of bloodless categories. It substitutes empty and universal concepts for real life. Life is an intense and personal thing, so is religious belief. Reason is not the whole of life, nor can it ever replace it. In terms of analytic philosophy, religious language is not solely cognitive or descriptive but has other functions. Passion digs deep into our bowels, and religious faith has its roots in our passionate nature, our inwardness. The speculative philosopher talks about objective reason. He wishes to give a systematic account of Reality. But Kierkegaard maintains that as a result he usually loses the subject, the person, the concrete and existing individual. The existential process is not static and independent, but it is temporal and involves movement. Rational philosophy is divorced from life, and rational religion from religious experience. Philosophers all too often want to discourse on what Christianity is, its objective side, its cognitive aspect—yet without knowing what it means to be a Christian. Socrates, at least, whom Kierkegaard admired above all other philosophers and considered to be an "Existential" philosopher (as a matter of fact, many contemporary philosophers from different schools claim Socrates as their own), never lost sight of the significance of philosophy to life; but where philosophers follow abstract reason they betray the legacy of Socrates and are untrue to life. To know what it means to be a Christian, *one must live the faith;* and if any be needed, this is its sole vindication.

Here Kierkegaard is claiming that *subjectivity is truth.* In other words, knowledge is private, inner, intuitive, and subjective. It is only the truth that *edifies* that truth for me. It is something that I only learn about by living, doing, and being a person, and not by discursive or dialectical analysis. This is a central theme of contemporary Existentialism, its key starting point. The individual begins with his own existence first, not *"cogito"* nor *"ergo,"* but *"sum,"* not the "I think," or "therefore," but the *"I am," "je suis," "Ich bin."* Within this and in relation to this he builds his world, the world of the conscious self *first,* not the world of external objects out there and unrelated to me. The only reality for an existing individual is his own ethical reality. The real act for him is not the eternal act but the *internal decision.*

But what of Christianity? Is it true? Does God exist? Was there a Christ? Christianity appears ludicrous and paradoxical. It rests on contradictions between the eternal truth of an eternal happiness and a subjective self, and between an eternal divine truth and a God who takes on flesh, becoming man in history. These paradoxes for Kierkegaard are irreconcilable. There are no logical or scientific proofs available for Christinaity. Yet with Tertullian, the early Father of the Church, and Hamann, his near contemporary, Kierkegaard says: I believe, though it is absurd. Why? Because of the meaning of faith in my life. Within my deepest psychological self there is the premonition of dread, a vague and unidentifiable anxiety about life and the human condition. In such a psychological state I am unsatisfied, my self is inauthentic, I am only partly existing. There is a "fear and trembling," a "sickness of the spirit unto death" that will devour me—unless, that is, Christ truly is the mediator and Son of God, the light, the way, the truth for all men, but especially for me. I experience guilt, I have inwardness of sin, and here I am the furthest distance from the truth. But my finitude can be transcended and I can be made whole only by my faith which provides a bridge to God: an inwardness of conviction that is not rational at core, but passionate and captures my whole existing being. To commit oneself to Christ is to make a choice, it is to make a leap of affirmation beyond reason. "How may I participate in the happiness promised by Christianity?"—*that* is the question which my passionate nature demands. When one falls in love with another person it is the subjective feeling that is central, and argument and reason are peripheral in justifying the passion; similarly when one loves God. To express love for God in the face of objective uncertainty about the validity of Christian doctrine is the highest act that a man can perform. And it is significantly true for *me* only because it is so keenly felt and vitally appropriated into my being. Grasped in the anguish of pain of sin, facing the risk of objective insecurity, faith is a subjective truth and commitment. And it is justified because it transforms and emancipates and makes me whole. Objectivity can destroy Christianity, only subjectivity can sustain it.

Kierkegaard's equation of subjectivity with truth is essential to Existentialism. Although Kierkegaard uses this epistemological principle to defend Christianity, others, including atheistic Existentialists, also adopt it as their starting point. This is how one may read the use of the phenomenological method which Sartre and Heidegger inherited with modification from Husserl. They begin with the given in the field of subjective awareness and seek to analyze its structure. (Husserl thought his method objectively scientific. And Heidegger is not merely concerned with private subjectivity, but with the ontological structure of existence. But Heidegger, in *Sein und Zeit,* concentrates upon the analysis of Dasein, or human being: dread, grief, suffering, nonbeing, death—and here the impact of Kierkegaard is unmistakable. He denied that he was an "Existentialist" in Kierkegaard's sense, for it is not the subjective self alone that he was concerned with, but only the structure of subjectivity insofar as it reflected the metaphysical nature and structure of Being. Heidegger does, however, agree that subjectivity is truth, as his essay on "Hölderlin and the

Essence of Poetry" indicates,[4] though he is apparently more willing than Kierkegaard to use dialectical reason.)

Now what is distinctive in the repeated statements of Kierkegaard and other Existentialists that "subjectivity is truth" is the constrast of this with the main line of development within Western philosophy and science. For the Western mind, as distinct from the Asian and the Oriental, let us say, has been conceptual, abstract, and deductive. Perhaps the most characteristic aspect of Western civilization is the development of logic (from Aristotelian to symbolic logic) and scientific method (of which our technological civilization is the most immediate result). In the East, the immediate and intuitive are pervasive. One thing that is apparent when one studies the philosophies of both Europe and Asia is that a contrast, though difficult, *can* be found. In the West, we have emphasized deductive logic and science, but in the East, feeling, passion, immediacy, and inwardness. Now it is notable that Kierkegaard and the Existentialists' doctrine that "subjectivity is truth" is similar to the reliance on affective inwardness in the Orient. Although there have been other subjectivists historically in the West (and indeed conceptualists in the East), the special emphasis of Kierkegaard in the West *is* unique: he is not primarily a romantic, and he is not a mystic in the ordinary sense. Yet he emphasizes inwardness. It is one thing to think, but it is another to exist in what has been thought, and Kierkegaard is emphasizing this latter.

Although I have refrained from any criticism of Kierkegaard's thesis thus far, I must express serious misgivings about the epistemological doctrine that "subjectivity is truth." I fear that there is great danger that *any* belief may be justified in the same way. If all standards of evidence and consistency are abandoned, as I fear Kierkegaard does, then the door is left open to an irrationalism of the most dangerous sort. If Alice in Wonderland encounters a Humpty Dumpty who can make "up" appear "down" and "down" "up," then the world of fact becomes topsy-turvy and chaos reigns. Zen Buddhism, like Kierkegaardianism, introduces paradox. D. T. Suzuki tells us that a master would frequently dramatize the truth by remaining silent, for the truth is inexpressible, or perhaps reply to a question of a disciple by a blow on the head!

But this leaves all but the initiated exasperated. *When* is a proposition false? Is it consistent? May it be verified? Canons of objectivity have been developed by slow, hard, and sober work. And we may argue that they are the most effective rules that we have for warranting belief. For the naturalistic philosopher who differs with Existentialism, the methods of logic and science are open and public, one may repeat the steps required to arrive at warranted assertions. The hypotheses derived are tentative, piecemeal, problematic. They are tested by their internal consistency and their relation to factual observation and verification. To claim that "subjectivity is truth" is to throw caution to the winds, and this can only perplex the careful analytically minded person—for it may lead to irresponsibility in belief. Using Kierkegaard's method, Mohammedanism, Buddhism, Nazism, or any other doctrine may be made true if inwardly appropriated by some individual. I do not see where Kierkegaard's standard of truth places Christianity in a special position or saves its doctrinal truth from the attacks of critical philosophy. It is paradoxical that while Asia is discarding its intuitive religious tradition and adopting Western philosophical attitudes in science, logic, technology, and political thought for a great leap forward, Western thinkers who advocate Existentialism are lapsing into a kind of Asian neo-intuitionism.

Now one must surely not substitute the abstract for the concrete, and this is a valid point of Kierkegaard. Other philosophers have made a similar point, especially empiricists and pragmatists. But Hegel and German idealism are not the only alternatives in philosophy to Kierkegaard. Moreover, in science the controlled use of objective methods has been employed with great success. Surely concrete facts are not ignored here, but are essential in explanation. Since Kierkegaard's time, the psychological and social sciences have made immense strides in an effort to explain subjectively human processes. Rather than gloss in subjectivity, contemporary science seeks to understand it. If there are limitations to reason, the alternative is not to lapse into subjectivity. Kierkegaard's own criticisms of Hegel proceeded from a highly involved and subtle use of dialectical reason. Indeed, he recognizes this when he says in his work *The Point of View for my Work as an Author* ". . . I am reflection from first to last."[5] Thus pure subjectivity itself is not possible as an approach, for it would mean the end of all linguistic and symbolic communication. Many in the West would claim that the only alternative to confusion is the objective method. The problem of our time, perhaps, is not that reason, logic, and science have failed us, but that they have not been extended far enough into the area of human values.

There is an important aspect to Kierkegaard's work that should not be minimized, however. And this I take it is a second major point that present-day Existentialism emphasizes—the individual as a fundamental category of existence.

Kierkegaard was a careful observer of human experience, a kind of introspective psychologist who probed into the depths of our being. To classical Greek philosophy, man was a rational animal, a featherless biped who could deliberate before choosing. And for the liberal or the enlightened view, a person (even if a self-interested hedonist) could guide his destiny rationally. Thus the dominant Western philosophical view was rather optimstic concerning human potentialities: all men seek the good life, and happiness was possible within a just society. But this to Kierkegaard was not true to human experience as it is actually lived. For there is suffering and anguish, fear and torment, boredom and death. Some have labeled Kierkegaard a "dismal Dane" because he dwelt on the morbid. But Kierkegaard maintained that this is a side of life that we all know about deep down and that we must never forget. Thus he helped to expand the domain of awareness of ourselves. "Know thyself," he said, following Socrates and emphasizing self-knowledge and self-realization. And later Dostoyevski, in describing the underground of man's soul, also found terrifying aspects. Freud went deeper into the roots of the unconscious, especially as expressed in neurotic personality, to discover infantile eroticism, the domain of the sexual libido, and other hidden motivations. And contemporary Existentialists, especially Heidegger and Sartre, go still further into Existential psychoanalysis of depths of the psyche. And what do they find? Man, the individual, a single, solitary being, is all alone in his private consciousness. Man is the only being who is aware that he is going to die and who can comprehend his historicity and finitude. Man stares into the abyss of nothingness: *le néant*. And in this light his loneliness takes on full meaning. His feelings of dread and anxiety express a generalized fear, not toward this, that, or any other object, but about the human condition itself. Philosophy and science, which postulate a universal human nature or which construct systems of general law to explain the human being, frequently end up by leaving out altogether the existing individual and his concrete experiencing. This is what Kierkegaard maintained and this is what the Existentialists today insist upon: clarity about the roots of our inner being. Although the individual seems to be vanquished by pessimism in much Existentialist literature, it must be remembered that Kierkegaard's despair had an ultimate optimism; for in the end the individual might be saved from his debasement by the redeeming grace of religious experience. The answer to my death will help me to transform my life and to live existentially. Man stands between being and nothingness, the finite and infinite, the temporal and eternal. And faith is the leap over to the positive state of existing.

Thus there is a moral aspect to the emphasis on the individual. The individual stands alone and against the crowd. Kierkegaard (like Marx) thought that modern industrial society had endangered the dignity of human personality. Men are oppressed, thwarted, and reduced by social pressures. Men are estranged and alienated from their true selves. They have forfeited their lives to the "they" of social consensus. Each self at root is free. One's freedom has its source in self-consciousness and is radical and ultimate. Yet the demands of social pressure and external authority compel many to forfeit their individual freedom and self-determination. Many forget what it means to be individuals. Their existence becomes "inauthentic." Individuals need to reawaken the possibilities for self-control. What is needed are uncommon men who will take the first steps toward a renaissance of personal integrity. Marx, a student of Hegelian thought, like Kierkegaard, also reacted against Hegel's Speculative Reason, though he accepted Hegel's collective interpretation of the individual; for Marx the solution to individual alienation was rationally to reconstruct a society in which the means of production will be raised to satisfy the real needs of the community. Both Kierkegaard and Marx shared fears that modern industrial society was destroying the individual. But their remedies were far apart: for if Marx turned outward to remake the material or economic conditions of life, Kierkegaard turned inward to the heart: each individual must awaken the possibilities of self-determination that slumber within and thus remake himself.

For recent Existentialism, the whole point of Kierkegaard's emphasis on the individual is that the individual has the choice to be himself. "Man," according to Sartre, "is condemned at every moment to make man." Man has no determinate essence, unlike the stone or the dog. As a consciously existing being, he is free to decide his own future and to create his own destiny. For Kierkegaard the stakes are great, but the option for the individual, of course, is the kind of life offered by Christianity, as it is for other religious Existentialists. This is the answer to the problem of human existence. But while Sartre accepts the human problem roughly as defined by Kierkegaard, he rejects Kierkegaard's solution; for the religious ideal is dead and offers no real promise to man. Rather, man (individually and socially) must build a secular and naturalistic world, and is responsible solely for himself. There are no values independent of man. Yet both Kierkegaard's and Sartre's alternatives are connected to individual existence and human freedom. For Existentialism, the highest opportunity for an individual is to become whatever he wants, to recognize that he is his own master. Only insofar as he can recognize his own potentialities and fulfill the projects he sets for himself can he begin to achieve the highest level of his authentic being. Only then can he become fully existential. We must, says Heidegger, heed "the call of Being," in this sense Dasein or our individual being. And since every choice we make emanates from our existential selves, it is fraught with danger, for it verges on the brink of disaster: to make or destroy ourselves. If every act of choice is an expression of radical freedom, then every act skirts the fine line between basic success or achievement on the one side, and failure or destruction on the other.

Now a good deal of this account of human freedom is no doubt true. Many will say that it is time that men face the fact that our values are not given to us *a priori,* but that they are relative to each person and that each is responsible for his ultimate existence. Many will approve on moral grounds of the protection of individuality against the inroads of conformity and collectivization. But the old question of freedom versus determinism rears its head again. Although human beings make decisions which affect their subsequent behavior, still it is difficult to deny that our decisions and actions are determined to some extent; at least, there appear to be causal conditions present in every situation of choice. Undoubtedly, man is an existing individual, but one may also argue that every thing that exists, exists in some sense as a particular existent. And individuals may be classified, interpreted, and explained by means of the concepts and hypotheses of the sciences. Man has a determinate nature in the sense that the species may be distinguished from other things by means of general properties. We must surely guard against the fallacy of glibly attributing an absolute or universal human nature to man, and there is always the danger of reading into it our own social or psychological traits; yet the social and bio-psychological sciences presuppose that there is some order in human conduct as the basis of scientific prediction and explanation. Although we are purposeful beings who make choices, these are always within the limits of our natures: whether physical-chemical, biological, psychological, or social. To claim that man has no nature but only an "existence" is to make inexplicable the facts of science that we already know about him, and these are considerable. And to admit that he has a biological nature and not a psychological nature is to erect a false dualism between body and mind. Subjective "consciousness" is dispensable as a category of explanation within the sciences. And the facts of awareness are explanable to some degree at least by experimental methods. I would ask that the Existentialists study our sciences of man: instead of a "philosophical anthropology" which they claim to give us, I would ask for a "scientific anthropology." Thus the Existentialists, and especially Kierkegaard, are deficient in their accounts of man because they leave out science.

But Existentialism is a *normative* philosophy of practical import as well as a "metaphysics of human being." The Existentialists no doubt are saying something important when they point to the fact of human decision and to the "ultimate" character of *some* human decisions: for our choices to some extent *are* existential; and they *may* involve the whole being of a person. But the Existentialists do not sufficiently appreciate that most of our choices are particularized and connected to actual concrete *contexts.* Our choices are *not* purely subjective; nor need they be capricious or arbitrary; and external facts and social norms within the context are intimately related to our value choices. Thus we find already present in every situation structures which help to provide some basis for choice. And we need not, except in the most extreme cases, call into question the whole framework of the situation or of our being. There are important norms available, such as those which practical reason and the applied sciences and arts have discovered, and we constantly use these in reaching wise decisions.

There is a close parallel on one point at least between present-day Existentialism and the logical positivism of the 1930s: both try to reduce ethical choice to emotive subjectivism. For the positivists, ethical judgments were expressive and imperative, and not based upon factual belief. Today within philosophy there is widespread criticism of the emotive theory: for in ordinary life we do argue about our ethical choices, we think that there are some standards of reasonableness, and we recognize that there are "good reasons" and "bad reasons" for decision. Moreover, our scientific knowledge about nature and man may help us to make more effective and better informed choices. Both Existentialism and the emotive theory are correct when they claim that knowledge of facts by itself does not tell us what to do. We cannot deduce an "ought" sentence from an "is" sentence. Yet knowledge may still be relevant to decision and action, and the degree to which we expand our understanding we expand our ability to make decisions. If absolutism cannot be defended in value theory, the alternative is not complete subjectivism, but perhaps a kind of middle ground, objective relativism.

Another difficulty with the Existentialist theory is this: we are social beings to a greater extent than it will allow. Most of our projects and plans, hopes and expectations, passions and affections involve other persons. The "self" is not merely an "inwardly" existing being but is to be defined by interactions in a natural *and* social-cultural world. The "I" is individuated and given meaning by the "we," and the "we" need not necessarily destroy the individual but, indeed, is required for his very preservation and fulfillment. The intellectual, aesthetic, scientific, religious, and philosophical developments of culture are essential for the nourishment of the individual in any of these dimensions. Without them, man would be a helpless beast. Only with them can he achieve the highest reaches of "individuality."

But, of course, Existentialism seeks to emphasize the "ultimate human condition"—for despair and nonbeing are said to await every individual. For, it is said, we may call into question at any time the whole project of our life or the entire structure of our moral or social code. Here the metaphysics of human being comes to the fore. The Existentialists claim that though our particular choices may be made in terms of the particular rules, values, and facts present in contexts of choice (and may provide some basis for "reasonable" action) we may nonetheless call into question our *basic* commitments. And one may always ask, as does Heidegger, "Why does anything exist at all?" or with Camus, "Why live?" It is this latter question that is said to be of crucial relevance to normative choice. Man may always inquire into the "meaning" of life.

But if we reject Kierkegaard's defense of the Christian explanation of man—as I think we must because of a total lack of evidence and because inwardness is *not* the criteria of truth—then according to atheistic Existentialism, at least, one is led to inevitable despair. Atheistic Existentialism begins at the same points as Kierkegaard—the human condition; but it never really succeeds in overcoming man's basic moral dilemma. For atheistic Existentialism, one can give *no reason* for my being, other than I am. And one may, as Camus, find it ultimately "absurd" that I exist or indeed that anything exists. The bitter dread and foreboding implicit in nonbeing, we are told, are thus ominously present, lurking, ever waiting to be called forth.

Undoubtedly the mature individual should be aware of the "human condition" and put things in their proper focus; he should strive for free and authentic existence. But is it not a question of to what degree and to what extent such "ultimate" awareness should absorb one's attention? One English philosopher quipped: "We all have to die one day; why do they keep reminding us of it?" Unfortunately, the Existentialist mood may become excessive in its metaphysical anguish. And this can accentuate and create the very mood that it claims is ominously present. While Existentialist awareness is important in its proper place, it thus can be distorted. Excessive concern with the roots of my personal being (or the lack of them) may even dampen my natural enthusiasm and gusto for life. In contexts of crisis, an attitude of despair may become prominent, as in the death of a loved one, the loss of a career, hopeless frustration, racial violence, or war. And here one may well inquire into the basis of his ultimate values and commitments.

But actually basic existential questions are rarely posed by ordinary people, except in times of crisis, even though they may be raised theoretically by philosophers.

Our time is a time of indecision and drift, and many people look hopefully to Existentialism as an appropriate philosophy. Marxism presented a philosophy of growth and expressed an optimism reminiscent of the Enlightment, basing upon Marxist ideology and technological science the messianic hope of mankind. The Existentialists claim that this lacks a sense of the "tragic" and that it has lost the individual. Yet aspects of a philosophy of growth have had a wide appeal to the underdeveloped countries of the world which look ahead to a better life. But many in the West have become frustrated—by our relative loss of power and prestige in the world, by nuclear terror, and so on. And for some, there has been a real "failure of nerve" and a loss of faith in the capacity of reason or science to develop the good life, with the result that many individuals have turned from confidence in science or progress to individual pathos. But one must, I submit, have profound reservations about a lapse into the Existentialist mood. Surely we must pay heed to our existential situations, yet I do not believe that excessive attention to it is necessary or desirable, nor that it is the whole of philosophy of life. Existentialists would no doubt retort that I here express too much of the "naive" frontier spirit to really appreciate the subtler pathos of human existence. And I readily admit the charge; but I would defend the posture. Life carries within itself its own seeds for development; whether one is to live a robust and expansive life or to retreat in the face of our precarious animal existence depends upon the attitude that is adopted. Existentialists might deny that they have overemphasized the element of despair or that their philosophy is a philosophy of inaction. Yet the tendency, I believe, is still there; and as a result, Existentialism fails to provide the challenging impetus for a good life of high motivation; and it does not measure up to the highest needs of man, whether of the contemporary or of any other age. In particular, the regression to a doctrine that "subjectivity is truth," if taken seriously, may have fearful consequences; and it can undermine one of the central factors that has contributed to the greatness of modern civilization, especially in the Western world, and that is the development of objective knowledge. The ideals of reason and science have not been effectively refuted, yet they are in constant danger of being undermined by an Existentialist type of reaction.

# NOTES

1. Søren Kierkegaard, *Either/Or,* translated by David F. Swenson and Lillian M. Swenson (Princeton, N.J.: Princeton University Press, 1944).

2. Søren Kierkegaard, *The Sickness Unto Death,* translated with an Introduction by Walter Lowrie (Princeton, N.J.: Princeton University Press, 1941), p. 32.

3. Søren Kierkegaard, *Concluding Unscientific Postscript,* translated by David F. Swenson and Walter Lowrie (Princeton, N.J.: Princeton University Press, 1941).

4. Reprinted in Martin Heidegger, *Existence and Being* (Chicago, Ill.: Henry Regnery Co., 1949).

5. Søren Kierkegaard, *The Point of View for my Work as an Author,* translated by Walter Lowrie (New York: Oxford University Press, 1939), p. 81.